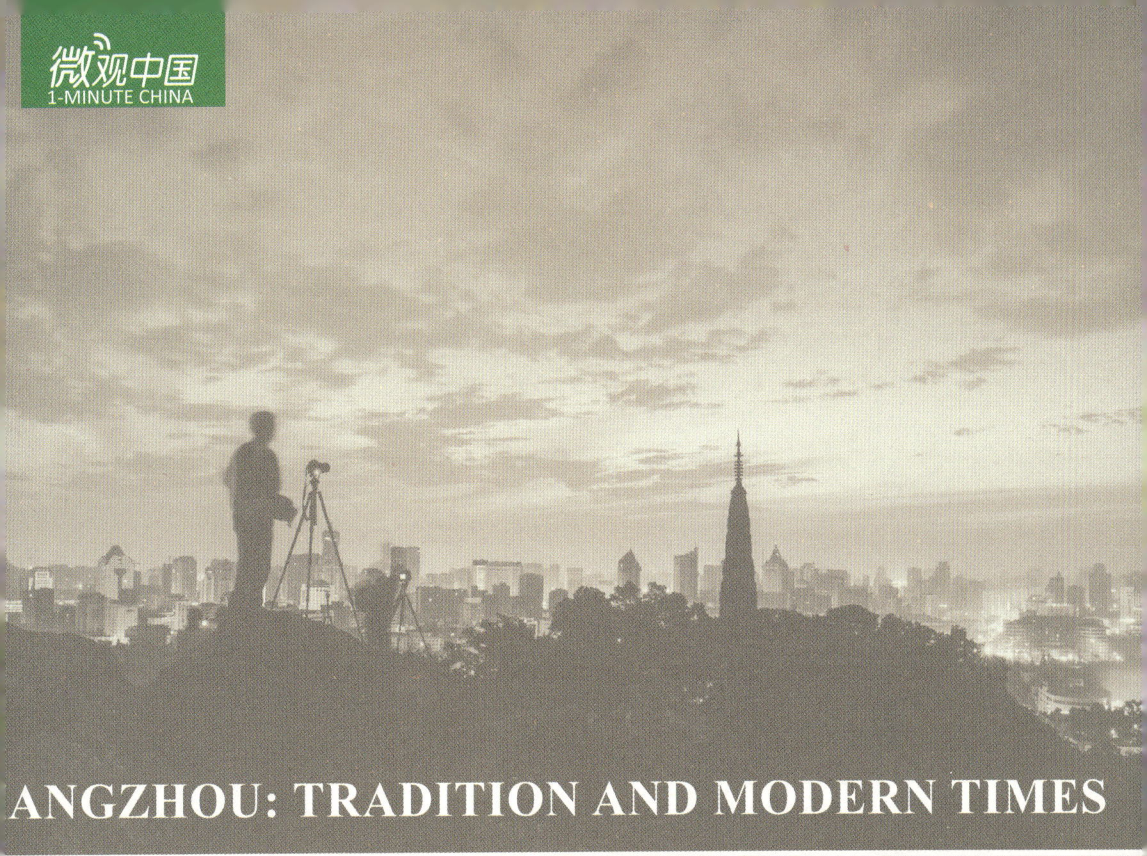

ANGZHOU: TRADITION AND MODERN TIMES

   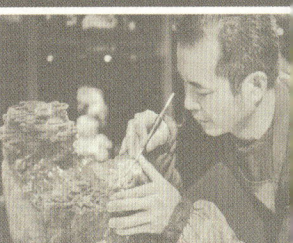

微观杭州

（汉英版）

王建华 主编

2016年·北京

丛书策划　周洪波　聂晓阳

主　编　王建华
副主编　俞燕君
撰　写　（按音序排列）
陈海芳　陈　杰　程永艳　崔赛凤　樊　华
冯　芹　傅佳玲　葛瑾萍　顾永芳　韩晓芬
侯晓岚　胡云晚　季　洁　江　坤　李雨霖
刘天捷　刘兴宇　陆　磊　陆　洋　马思敏
潘益青　茹彦龙　沈贻伟　施麟麒　孙宏茂
王晨露　王　贵　王杰于　王　津　王　嫱
王庆铃　夏利亚　谢　媚　徐征难　杨慧丽
杨　瑞　杨同用　杨新红　余优留　俞燕君
俞　洋　张　娜　赵翠阳　赵海涛　周　珊
周　毅　朱玉芬

英文翻译　梅　皓（美）
英文审订　赵海涛　严慧仙
英文编辑　张显奎

责任编辑　刘玥妍
装帧设计　东方美迪

Chief Producer	Zhou Hongbo Nie Xiaoyang
Chief Compiler	Wang Jianhua
Deputy Compiler	Yu Yanjun
Compilers	Chen Haifang Chen Jie Cheng Yongyan Cui Saifeng Fan Hua Feng Qin Fu Jialing Ge Jinping Gu Yongfang Han Xiaofen Hou Xiaolan Hu Yunwan Ji Jie Jiang Kun Li Yulin Liu Tianjie Liu Xingyu Lu Lei Lu Yang Ma Simin Pan Yiqing Ru Yanlong Shen Yiwei Shi Linqi Sun Hongmao Wang Chenlu Wang Gui Wang Jieyu Wang Jin Wang Qiang Wang Qingling Xia Liya Xie Mei Xu Zhengnan Yang Huili Yang Rui Yang Tongyong Yang Xinhong Yu Youliu Yu Yanjun Yu Yang Zhang Na Zhao Cuiyang Zhao Haitao Zhou Shan Zhou Yi Zhu Yufen
English Translator	Mei Hao (USA)
English Reviewers	Zhao Haitao Yan Huixian
English Editor	Zhang Xiankui
Executive Editor	Liu Yueyan
Art Design	EmDesign

序

世界上最华贵的天城

2016年9月,杭州要成为中国政府的外交主场——"二十国集团首脑峰会"(G20峰会)将在这里召开。杭州,这个历史上早就闻名于世的城市,迎来一个新的机遇。该如何向来自全球各地的朋友展示自己?是当下杭州面临的一件迫切而重要的事情。

描述杭州,既有"上有天堂,下有苏杭"这句耳熟能详的老话,又有白居易"忆江南,最忆是杭州"和苏东坡"欲把西湖比西子,淡妆浓抹总相宜"这样的千古名句。她是南宋故都、文化名城,孕育了良渚文化、吴越文明,最是温柔富贵。她是浙江首府,现代都市,美丽、时髦、新潮,具有包融气质。她是江南的代名词,一直被视为"最适宜居住的城市"。她又是国际名城,数百年前就被马可·波罗称为"世界上最华贵的天城"。

改革开放三十多年来,杭州有了更多的发展变化。她获得过一系列荣誉:国家森林城市、国家环保模范城市、国际花园城市、联合国最佳人居奖,西湖和大运河还联袂成为世界文化遗产。而在中国政府未来规划中,杭州城市的新定位是:历史文化名城、创新活力之城、东方品质之城、美丽中国样本、国际旅游胜地、创新创业新天堂、一流国际大都市……很少有一座城市像杭州这样汇聚了如此多不同的身份。

要全方位认识新的杭州,是不容易的,要向中外朋友全面介绍新的杭州,更是相当的困难。需要从多个角度,采用不同的表达方式,概括地说,"世界上最华贵的天城"是精到的评价。具体又可以从"精致、和谐、大气、开放"四个角度来展开。

——杭州精致。西湖"淡妆浓抹总相宜",钟灵毓秀,是柔美山川的杰作。近年来,西湖西进,杨公堤成为与苏堤平行的又一跨湖卧波彩带。西溪湿地开发,原生态的水乡景致秀丽多彩。小河直街青瓦黛顶,层层叠叠,绵延不断,人家尽枕河。三台山的茶楼近水依山,幽中藏雅,飞檐翘角,亭阁宛然。被桂花汁浸得丹红的米藕,咬一口,软软粘连,满口清香。杭州的女孩与生而来带着一股仙气,清水出芙蓉，天然去雕饰。西泠桥边枫树林，秋来霜红雾紫，鲜艳夺目。太子湾的潮湿阳光，从肩头流过，落下一地芬芳。一首诗，一阕词，一座桥，一尊塔，一匹绸，一叶茶，都是那样的精美、雅致，展现着当代中国城市的高端品质。

——杭州和谐。杭州"三面云山一面城"，山、水、城、人最为协调相配。引入了钱塘江活水的西湖，更为清澈，周围的山，可远观亦可近昵，在西湖水的滋养下，灵秀无比。一个拥有洲级规模高铁站、地铁与高铁齐飞的城市，竟还保留着一条绿皮火车线路，为职工和居民通勤。杭州的居民和农民的收入之比为全国最低，生动诠释着城乡协调和谐发展的真谛。虎跑寺的弘一法师了断俗念，青灯古佛，与凡尘就此别过，耶稣弄的司徒雷登本是美国人，却生于此，葬于此，魂归杭州。众多百年老店坚守着濒临灭绝的手工技艺，代代相传，而梦想小镇和"西溪创意产业园"的创业机会，带给年轻人无限的希望。随处可见的免费自行车租借点，是杭州新的风景线。斑马线前车让人，已成为公众的习惯，也谱写出城市和谐文明的新篇章。

——杭州大气。"天下西湖三十六，就中最美是杭州"，在外地众多名胜纷纷涨价的时候，西湖沿岸的各类一线景观多年前就免费向游客开放，被誉为"回眸西湖最大气"。钱江新城建设，让杭州的发展由小家碧玉式的西湖时代走向磅礴的钱塘江时代，滨江区、大江东、阿里、网易、三星、西门子、ABB等高新科技新兴产业气吞如虎。杭州大剧院60元的惠民票，让普通民众轻松地欣赏着话剧、舞剧、演奏会这些高雅艺术。钱江新城里，设备高端的杭州图书馆竟允许流浪汉入馆读书，旅游景点的流动书柜，给每一位休憩的游客以惊喜。如此尊重个人权利，温暖温馨，让人直呼了不起。

——杭州开放。"K155"路公交因编码酷似"KISS"，激发无数人的浪漫遐想，保住了这条本要调整的线路，并赢得"杭州最浪漫公交车"称号。原为大妈专属的广场舞，居然有打扮挺潮的小伙子加入，步伐轻快，律动和谐，跳出了时尚。每年的毅行活动，新老杭州人和国际友人用脚步和毅力丈量美丽的杭州。浙江大学，一所承载着国人"世界一流大学梦"的高等学府，正在渐渐走向理想的目标。设计师王澍，2012年国际建筑界普利兹克奖得主，用一砖一瓦实践着他的设计理念和个性。"i-hangzhou"信号覆盖全城，杭州成为全国首个免费开放WiFi的城市。"西湖发布"矩阵服务全面，大到政务、金融、医疗、教育等，小到商场智能停车、公交站牌实时路况，智慧城市充满生机。创新创业已成为杭州的新风尚，未来科技城、城西科创走廊交相呼应,"阿里系"企业位列全球行业前5强。以支付宝为代表的互联网财富管理、金融创新独步全国,独领风骚……

这就是新的杭州!"精致和谐,大气开放"的人文精神在这里孕育、生成,源远流长,犹如举世闻名的钱江大潮,浩浩荡荡,奔腾向前,气象万千。

三十多年来,我们一直生活在这个城市,参与和见证了杭州的发展变化,对她有太深的感情,太多的感悟。穿行在这精致和谐、大气开放的城市之中,我们视接千载,神通万里。该以什么方式表达我们对杭州的热爱与赞美?《微观中国》系列丛书及时提供了范本和机遇。这本《微观杭州》以420余条微博、190多幅照片,从不同侧面,讲述杭州的历史文化、经济发展、社会生活、科技创新、生态环境、旅游休闲、时尚精神。虽是碎片式呈现,但每一条微博都力求言之有物,独立呈现一个事实,传递一种情感,见人、见事、见情,描绘出细腻、真实、变化中的杭州,展示杭州人的日常生活,发掘他们的内心世界、人文情怀。希望这些汉英双语、图文并茂的微博表达,能比其他的表达形式更有吸引力和表现力,为中外读者所接受和喜爱。

"你若盛开,清风自来。"《微观杭州》乘春风而来,于仲夏绽放。让我们在G20杭州峰会到来之际,开启"天城"之门,迎接八方来客,汇聚世界目光!

王建华
2016年4月

Preface

The Most Luxurious City in the World

In September of 2016, Hangzhou will become a major site for foreign relations, as it hosts the G20 summit. The city of Hangzhou, so significant in history, is now welcoming a new opportunity. How should it display itself to friends from around the world? This is a pressing and serious affair for the city of Hangzhou.

When describing Hangzhou, everyone knows the saying: "Up there is heaven, and down here are Hangzhou and Suzhou", as well as Tang Dynasty poet Bai Juyi's description of Hangzhou as the most memorable city in the Jiangnan area (the area south of the Yangtze River), and Su Dongpo's description of the West Lake in the rain. Hangzhou is the former capital of the Southern Song Dynasty, a cultural capital, the birthplace of the Liangzhu and Wuyue cultures, and a famously warm and prosperous spot. Hangzhou is the seat of Zhejiang Province, a modern city that is beautiful, fashionable, trendy, and inclusive. Hangzhou is a synonym for the Jiangnan area, and has long been seen as the "most liveable city". Hangzhou is an international city that was once praised by Marco Polo as "the most luxurious city in the world" centuries ago.

After three decades of opening up and reform, Hangzhou has evolved even further. The city has received a number of honours: a national-level forest city, a national-level city of environmental protection, an international garden city, a UN habitat scroll of honour... the West Lake and Beijing-Hangzhou Grand Canal have both been listed as UNESCO world heritage sites. In the future plans of the Chinese government, Hangzhou's position is to be one of a famous cultural centre, a city of innovation, a famous oriental metropolis, an example of a beautiful Chinese city, an international travel destination, a haven for innovation and entrepreneurship, and a first-rate international city. It's rare to see a city that can incorporate so many different aspects.

Understanding all aspects of Hangzhou is not easy, and introducing the city to people from both a foreign and Chinese perspective at the same time is even more difficult. It's important to approach from different angles and simultaneously employ different expository techniques. Speaking broadly, "the most luxurious city in the world" is a good characterisation. We could describe it from four main aspects: refined, harmonious, generous and open-minded.

The refinement of Hangzhou: all know about the beauty of the West Lake, beautiful against the clear sky and even more so when it rains. In recent years, the West Lake has been extended towards the west, and Yang Gong Causeway complements the Su Causeway now. The West Creek Wetlands area has been developed, showing their beautiful natural state to all. From the rivers to the traditional houses that sit upon their banks, people live comfortably along the waterways. Tea houses are located upon Santai Mountain sitting both to peaks and water, elegant and quiet, these structures with upturned eaves and pretty pavillions. One can eat a lotus cake with rice in it that's been flavoured with osmanthus, and savour the soft texture and fragrant complexities of the flavour. The girls of Hangzhou are beautiful and refined. The maple forest near the Xiling Bridge brings views of red leaves against purple mists in autumn. At the Prince Harbour Park, sunlight through the moist air shines over visitors' shoulders with fragrance all around. A poem, a bridge, a tower, a bolt of silk, a tea leaf – these are all exquisite, beautiful objects that show off the high quality of Chinese cities at modern times.

The harmony of Hangzhou: Hangzhou is said to be clouds and mountains on three sides, and the city the rest. Mountains, waterways, the city and the people all go well together. The West Lake, that takes running water from the Qiantang River is clear and surrounded by mountains which one can view from near or afar. With the water of the lake nourishing them, they are beautiful beyond compare. A train station built on an intercontinental scale, a city enjoys underground rails and high-speed rails, and a green-car rail line is preserved among them for workers and residents to commute. Income disparity here is the lowest in the country, which speaks to the harmonious development of city and countryside at the same time. The Running Tiger Temple is where the monk Hong Yi cast off worldly desires, and is an excellent site to visit for its austere scenery, just as there is the Jesus Alley of John Leighton Stuart, who was born and buried here. A number of century-old stores continue handcraft traditions that are on the verge of extinction, their crafts passed down through the ages. A creative base in the West Creek Industrial Park provides opportunities for entrepreneurship, and gives hope to youths who wish to participate. You can see free bicycle rental points throughout the city, which is a new addition. Cars yield to pedestrians at crosswalks by habit now, which is another nice addition to an already cultured and harmonious city.

The generosity of Hangzhou: "There are many lakes like the West Lake, But the West Lake in Hangzhou is the best". Visitors from other places flow in to line the banks of the West Lake as it has been open to tourists for free for a number of years, which makes people call Hangzhou the most generous city. New construction along the Qiantang River has transformed quaint old buildings into modern constructions along the banks, with the Binjiang District and Dajiangdong District being home to operations of enterprises such as Alibaba, Netease, Samsung, Siemens, ABB and others as they push along high-tech progress. The Hangzhou Grand Theatre offers 60-Yuan discount tickets that allow the normal residents of the city to freely enjoy plays, operas, performances and other high art. At the Qianjiang New City, the modern Hangzhou Library admits homeless people to read books, and there are travelling bookcases at tourist spots that give everyone a surprise when taking a rest. It's an amazing city that appreciates human rights and is full of warmth and welcome.

The openness of Hangzhou: the K155 city bus line, with its route number resembling the English word "KISS", has sparked the imaginations of many people, causing the bus line to be officially dubbed "Hangzhou's most romantic bus". When the middle-aged women dance in the squares, the younger generation joins in too, bringing rhythm, style to the scene. A great march happens every year in which visitors from around the world join the people of Hangzhou, young and old, to walk the entire city. Zhejiang University is approaching its goal to become a world-class university. Architect Wang Shu won the Pritzker Architecture Prize in 2012, and designed every aspect of the new campus. Under the i-hangzhou scheme, WiFi covers the entire city, making it the first scheme to offer citywide WiFi coverage to a major city nationwide. "West Lake Announcement" deliver all kinds of useful information to everyone on topics such as government, finance, medicine, and education, from car parks at shopping centres and public transport information, which makes Hangzhou a lively smart city.

Innovation and entrepreneurship have already become a new trend in Hangzhou, with the future technology centre and west-of-city technological innovation corridor complimenting each other, and the Alibaba group's operations becoming one of the 5 strongest in the industry worldwide. Internet wealth management and finance innovation companies representing by Alipay outpace any other area in the country.

This is the new Hangzhou, being refined, harmonious, generous and open-minded. This sums up how this city nurtures and grows its constituents, its fame and influence reaching far and wide, like the strong current of the Qiantang River.

Over the past three decades we have all lived in this city and have participated in and witnessed its development and changes. We have deep feelings for her, a strong emotional bond. When we wander through this refined, harmonious, generous and open-minded city, its history and scenery unfolds before us like a panorama. How should we convey our love and admiration for this city? The Microblog China series has given us an excellent opportunity. This book has more than 420 stories and 190 pictures. Looking at the city from different angles, exploring history, culture, economic development, society, life, technology, innovation, the environment, travel, leisure, and fashion, we assemble a picture from these fragments that as a whole gives us a good feeling of and for the city. We see people, things and emotions that give us a precise, true and changing picture of Hangzhou. We showcase the everyday lives of the people of Hangzhou, showing their inner-heart worlds, their humanity and feelings. We hope this bilingual English-Chinese volume full of pictures will have a special attraction to audiences, convey our ideas well, and be accepted and loved by both Chinese and foreign readers.

"If you build it, they will come." This book arrives on the spring wind and blooms in the summer. We hope as we await the G20 summit that the door of our heavenly city will open up and welcome guests from all over the world!

Wang Jianhua
April 2016

目 录 | Contents

都市・乐活	1	City and Leisure
轶史・钩沉	25	History and Reflections
地域・物产	47	Areas and Products
西湖・印象	67	West Lake and Impressions
互联・创新	93	Internet and Innovation
古城・寻踪	115	Ancient City and Traces
舌尖・记忆	141	Taste and Memories
吴越・包融	157	Wu-Yue and Inclusiveness
佛国・诗话	181	Buddhas and Stories
时尚・潮涌	197	Fashion and Waves
索引	223	Index

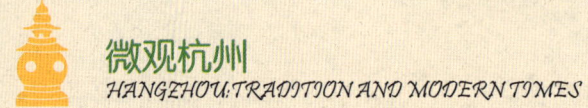

今日西湖
The West Lake Today

2001年起,杭州市政府实施新湖滨和湖西景区建设,西湖西进,扩大了6.5平方公里。引配水工程使西湖与钱塘江沟通,每天引入钱塘江水约30万立方米,让西湖水变活。而老百姓最能感受到的是西湖变大了,走在湖滨,步行桥将西湖水扩展到路边;西湖也走不尽了,沿着复建的杨公堤西望,十万人家在那一头。

In 2001, the Hangzhou city government carried out construction works on the lakeside and West Lake Scenic Area, extending the lake further west for an expansion of 6.5 square kilometres. Water supply work was performed and the lake was connected to the Qiantang River. It now pulls in 300,000 cubic metres of water from the river each day, and now the lake water supports a living ecosystem. The most apparent effect of the expansion work on everyday people's lives is that the lake is bigger, and taking a walk around the entire circumference of the lake, its pedestrian bridges would be a rather extended affair. The reconstructed Yang Gong Causeway affords quite a nice view.

摄影:李选

都市・乐活
City and Leisure

摄影：郑若琪

西溪湿地
The West Creek Wetlands

杭城规模不断扩大，固定人口从上世纪80年代初的100万，增加了6倍，外来人口几百万。周边的农田和蔬菜基地都变成了高楼大厦，唯独西溪湿地得以保留。西溪湿地内原本有几个村落，种桑养蚕，盛产鱼蟹，果树以柿子树为主。政府保留了西溪湿地原貌，开辟成旅游景点。真是应了宋高宗的一句话："西溪且留下。"

Hangzhou is expanding continuously. From a population of 1 million in the early 1980's to seven times that, millions of people have come to Hangzhou from other places. The surrounding fields and vegetable patches have been replaced by high-rise buildings, with only the West Creek Wetlands being left untouched. There are a number of villages in the area, the residents of which are involved in raising mulberry trees and silkworms, fish and crabs, and growing persimmons. The government has kept the area in its original state, and also opened it up to tourism. Just as the Gaozong Emperor of the Song Dynasty said in the 12th century, "the West Creek area shall remain as it is".

娟娟饭馆
Juanjuan Restaurant

娟娟饭馆的老板是一对江山夫妇，为人勤快老实。饭馆开业多年，一直有好口碑，"杭城螺蛳王"就是饭馆的别称。老板娘娟娟认为，"食材是第一个不能马虎的地方"。他们家所用的食材，都是老板亲自挑选的，生怕客人吃到坏的。至于配菜，也是托人从江山老家采集运送过来的。很多人就是奔着叠螺蛳来吃宵夜的。

The Juanjuan Restaurant is owned by a hard-working couple from Jiangshan. It has been open for a number of years and has a great reputation. It's also known for being the "King of Spiral Shells" in Hangzhou. The owners believe that they can't skimp on ingredients, so they select all of them themselves, performing quality control. Even the vegetables are imported from their hometown in Jiangshan. The restaurant is a popular destination for midnight snacking.

微观杭州
HANGZHOU: TRADITION AND MODERN TIMES

办张公园年卡
A Yearly Park Pass

杭州的免费景点多，但有些还是要收费。对于杭州居民来说，办张40元的年卡是明智的选择。凭这张卡可以免费通行13个主要景区。如果对佛教感兴趣，还可以办张40元的庙卡。有趣的是，上海人也有权办理这两张卡。甚至有人戏称"杭州是上海人的后花园"——哪怕再不起眼的景点，你都能听到"阿拉上海人"的声音。

Hangzhou has a number of free tourist attractions, but there are some at which a ticket must be purchased. For a Hangzhou resident, spending 40 RMB for a yearly park pass is a good choice. With the card, one can enjoy free access to 13 different scenic areas. If you are interested in Buddhism, you can also spend 40 RMB to buy a Temple Pass. What's interesting is that Shanghai residents can also obtain these two passes. People have previously remarked that "Hangzhou is Shanghai's back garden". You can hear people speaking Shanghainese at these attractions frequently.

爱情之都
The City of Love

世界上有"浪漫之都""动感之都"，杭州则希望打造"爱情之都"，使"美丽杭州"充满浪漫爱意。确实！许仙白娘子在断桥相识，梁山伯祝英台于万松书院结同窗情谊，苏小小阮郁邂逅西泠桥后互结同心，还有郁达夫和王映霞，史量才与沈秋水，徐志摩并陆小曼，每一段都印证了杭州的爱情味。

Cities like Hong Kong and Paris have titles like "The City of Dynamism" and "The City of Romance". Hangzhou seeks to be "The City of Love", and overflow with romance and passion. In fact, when Lady Bai and Xu Xian famously met at the Broken Bridge, when Liang Shanbo and Zhu Yingtai met at the Wansong Academy, when Su Xiaoxiao and Ruan Yu met at the Xiling Bridge, when Yu Dafu and Wang Yingxia, Shi Liangcai and Shen Qiushui, Xu Zhimo and Lu Xiaoman all met, these were the beginnings of Hangzhou love stories.

摄影：陈心远

都市・乐活
City and Leisure

主编供稿

西湖龙井
Longjing Tea

西湖龙井，中国十大名茶之一，素有"绿茶皇后"之称，色绿、香郁、味甘、形美。细雨天里，临窗而坐，沏一杯龙井，手执书卷，静听窗外游丝般的雨声，欣闻龙井轻幽幽的茶香，实在是人生一大享受。如有机会来杭州，一定要到西湖的茶坊里坐一坐，品着西湖龙井，赏着西湖美景，诗意人生不过如此。

The Longjing Tea of Hangzhou's West Lake is one of China's ten most famous teas, and has the nickname "The Empress of Green Teas". The leaves are known for four qualities: being green, fragrant, sweet in taste, and beautiful in shape. Sitting by a window on an overcast day, making a cup of Longjing Tea, with a book in hand to enjoy with the tea against the background noise of light rain outside is one of the great pleasures in life. If you have the opportunity to come to Hangzhou, you must visit a tea house by the West Lake and try some Longjing Tea while enjoying a view of the lake – a slice of the poet's life.

让洞于民
Into the Caves

每年夏天，杭州市都会开展"让洞于民，避暑纳凉"活动，将一些平时管制的防空洞开放给市民避暑。这项活动至今持续了13年。防空洞内一般都有桌椅、电视机、茶水。来纳凉的人多是当地的老人小孩和外来务工人员，并有保安维持秩序。据说这一惠民活动每年能节电80万度左右。

Every year in summer, Hangzhou puts on an activity called "Into the caves to avoid the heat". The city opens up a number of underground air raid shelters which are normally closed. It's already been going on for 13 years. Within the shelters there are tables, chairs, TV, and tea. Most of the people that come are elderly, children, or workers from other regions of China. There are security guards to maintain order. Apparently, these activities save 800,000 KWh of electricity that would otherwise be spent on AC each year.

微观杭州
HANGZHOU: TRADITION AND MODERN TIMES

问路
Asking for Direction

到武林门会同学，查了地图却也坐错了车，懒得再查，就问一美女。"可以百度的，"她说。但并不等我自己搜，拿出手机搜了，然后带我过去，到了路口她说朝前走就是了，还担心地看着我，唯恐我不明白。这种礼遇，已不是第一次。若是碰到赋闲的老年人，他们甚至会带你过去。杭州景美，人心更美啊！

On my way to Wulinmen to meet classmates, I checked the map and saw that I'd taken the wrong route. I didn't feel like rechecking, so I asked a pretty girl. She said I could look it up on my phone, but didn't wait for me to do so. She took her phone, found the place for me and then took me there, pointing me down a road in front and saying that it was right up there. She looked at me worriedly, afraid I hadn't understood. This wasn't my first time receiving this kind of treatment. If you ask an elderly person with free time, you'll almost always be escorted part of the way. Hangzhou is a nice place and the people are nice, too!

小吃街夫妻档
Husband-and-Wife Snack Street

宿舍后面有一条小吃街，里面有大大小小的各种小吃和饭店。每次过来吃饭，总能看到夫妻档：鸡蛋灌饼的河南老夫妇，总是夸他家的鸡蛋饼独门秘制，无人能比；二层小阁楼的胖哥夫妻面馆，每每过去总是座无虚席；一胖一瘦夫妻的水果摊，推销的水果总是那么讨人喜……幸福就是简简单单一起相伴的日子。

Behind the dormitory there is a snack street, upon which there are all kinds of snack shops and restaurants, large and small. Every time you come, you will see husband-and-wife operations, a couple from Henan that makes fried egg-filled savoury pancakes. They say that theirs are the best, and the recipe is secret. On the second floor of a building there is another husband-and-wife affair, "Fat Bro's Noodle Shop". It's always packed. A fat husband and skinny wife run a fruit stand which is extremely popular. Happiness is being to lead a simple life with the one you love.

开茶节
The Tea Festival

"茶为国饮，杭为茶都"，作为西湖龙井的故乡，悠久的茶文化历史积淀和浓厚的茶饮习俗氛围使杭州获得了"中国茶都"的美誉。茶文化和茶习俗早已融入了杭州人的血液中，每年一度的西湖龙井开茶节也已经成为所有爱茶人的盛大节日。你爱茶、懂茶吗？如果你也好这一口儿，一定不要错过这个美丽的节日！

"Tea is the national drink, and Hangzhou is the capital of tea". As the home of West Lake Longjing Tea, a long history of tea culture and a strong preference for the drink among the local population have given Hangzhou the name "China's Tea Capital". Tea culture and tea-drinking customs are in the blood of people from Hangzhou, and every year there is a large "tea festival" for the start of the West Lake tea harvesting season. Do you like and understand tea? If this kind of thing is your jam, make sure to not miss out on this beautiful holiday!

都市・乐活
City and Leisure

翻丝棉大妈
The Women Who Process Silk Floss

每年国庆节一过，来自桐乡的翻丝棉大妈就像候鸟一样准时来到杭州，在老小区的弄堂口、花园旁空地上搭起棚子，戴上老花眼镜开工。不用打任何广告，熟识的老主顾都会带上丝棉袄壳儿，到老地方来找她们。"大妈，今年翻一件丝棉袄多少钞票？""还是15块！"真是实诚的桐乡大妈，价格十年如一日！

Each year as soon as the National Holiday in early October ends, women who process silk floss from Tongxiang (Tongcheng County in Anhui Province) flock to Hangzhou like migrant birds, and set up small stands on the available ground in various complexes, put on their glasses and prepare to work. They post no ads, but their customers know where to find them. They show up, cocoons in hand, to have them processed. "Old lady, how much is the price this year?" "It's still 15 Yuan!" These are very honest women – the price hasn't risen in ten years!

红树醉西泠
Red Leaves at Xiling Bridge

西泠桥，枫树林，秋来霜红雾紫，鲜艳夺目。秋风渐起，午后漫步西泠。和暖的阳光恰好驱散了寒气，举目尽是明艳艳的橙红。在残荷凋零、叶落水寒的萧瑟秋景中，这是一笔浓厚的诗情画意。撷取枫叶把玩手上或压制成书签，把秋天融到书里带回了家，幽情耿耿撩人，别有趣味。

At the Xiling Bridge there is a forest of maple trees, and when autumn turns the leaves red and frost accumulates on the leaves, they are a sign to see. I take a walk at Xiling as the autumn wind blows. Warm sunlight drives away the cold in the air, and the scene is bathed in bright orange-red. The lotuses wilt, leaves fall down – the whole experience feels very poetic. One may pick maple leaves and play with them in hand, or press them into bookmarks, taking a piece of the scene home to keep.

主编供稿

微观杭州
HANGZHOU:TRADITION AND MODERN TIMES

王奶奶的西湖绸伞情缘

The Love Story of Granny Wang and the Silk Umbrella

王奶奶有一把珍藏了五十多年的西湖绸伞，那可是她和王爷爷的定情之物。说起当初与王爷爷因一把西湖绸伞结缘，王奶奶还是一脸害羞："50年代你王爷爷是国营杭州西湖伞厂的制伞工人，第一次相亲就带了一把他自己亲手制作的西湖绸伞送给我，你说我看到能制作这么精美雨伞的巧手工人能不欢喜吗？"

Granny Wang has a West Lake silk umbrella that she's used for more than fifty years – it was a courtship gift from Old Mr. Wang. She blushes even now when she sells the story of how Mr. Wang gave her the umbrella. "Your grandfather worked at a state-owned factory making umbrellas in the 1950's, and the first time that we met on a traditional date, he brought me this West Lake silk umbrella which he'd made himself. How could I not fall in love with him when presented with such a beautiful and exquisitely-made work?"

摄影：丁刘冬

交芦田庄

Jiaolutian Village

交芦田庄位于西溪福堤南入口的西侧，在古色古香的高庄与蜿蜒曲折的溪水围绕下，这片净土自有其农桑耕植的情趣。它是以农事体验为主的农业生态休闲园。在这里，鱼塘密布，男耕女织。在现代化大都市中体验别样的古朴民间农活，未尝不是一件"偷得浮生半日闲"的美事。

Jiaolutian Village is situated on the west side of Fudi (the Embankment of Proseprity) in the West Creek area. It is an antique-looking village that contains a small creek which winds and twists through it, with the soil around it planted with mulberry trees. It's an ecological park where one can experience agricultural activities. The pools are full of fish. Male residents are responsible for tending the fields and women weave. It's a great place to take a half-day trip to experience a lifestyle from a simpler time in the middle of the modern city.

都市·乐活
City and Leisure

创意民宿
Innovative B&B's

在离杭州市区开车不到半小时的青山绿水间，民宿开始流行。正如回味无穷的私房小菜，民宿主人从传统文化中汲取灵感，白墙黛瓦保留了江南建筑的简朴风格。小而雅致的客房、园林、书房、茶室和宽敞的露台，有的还带有碧波荡漾的小湖。在这里无拘无束地喝茶、聊天、看书，体验山水之间的别样生活。

With lush greenery and nice waterscapes less than a half-hour drive from Hangzhou, staying at Bed and Breakfast has become popular in the area. Amazing food and the chance to experience some local culture in the traditional buildings with white walls and black tile roofs characteristic of this region of China. Here you can relax and enjoy drinking tea, chatting, reading books and experience another kind of lifestyle.

排长队的李记酥鱼
A Fish Shop with a Long Queue

李记家的酥鱼卖二十来年了。李老板曾经在卤味店工作过，学到了很多做菜厨艺，加上他的妻子又有卖酥鱼的经验，夫妻俩索性开起小店卖起酥鱼来了。李老板多年研制的卤酱加上妻子的高汤秘方，正是他们家酥鱼独霸一方的秘诀，四面八方的食客纷至沓来。你看，这节假日，过来吃酥鱼的人排队都排到马路中央去了。

The Li shop has sold crispy fish for more than two decades. Boss Li used to work in a braised food shop, and learned how to cook. His wife had experience selling crispy fish, so the couple went and opened up a store to sell the product. Li used his experience at the braised food shop combined with his wife's secret soup recipe to produce a new dish, and customers have flooded in constantly. After the holidays if you go by the shop you will see the queue of customers extending all the way into the middle of the street.

摄影：孙宏茂

微观杭州
HANGZHOU: TRADITION AND MODERN TIMES

"三无"餐厅
The Restaurant Lacking Three Things

屏峰社区有一家素食餐厅，位置偏僻但生意红火。老板星星是陕西小伙，笃信佛教，为人爽气，还有一杭州人谢姐是其助手。餐厅食客多为来自五湖四海的打工青年。餐厅特色有三：一无招牌，初访者常以为不是餐厅；二无餐单，顾客随意配菜，老板随心烹制；三无柜员，所有菜价一律十元，由食客自行投钱结算。

In the Pingfeng Community there is a vegetarian restaurant that is a bit out of the way but always does great business. The boss is a guy from Shaanxi. He faithfully follows Buddhism, and is a bright and open-minded person. He has a female assistant who is a native of Hangzhou. Most of the customers at the restaurant are young people coming from all over to Hangzhou to work. The restaurant lacks three things that most others have: First, there is no sign. First time visitors may miss the fact that there is a restaurant operating there. Second, there is no menu, customers pick the vegetables for the boss to cook. Third, there is no till – all dishes are 10 Yuan, and customers retrieve their own change.

吴山庙会
The Wushan Temple Fair

每年的吴山庙会，是杭州人的狂欢节，庙会上人山人海，而丰富多彩的节目和活动，更是让人流连忘返。祭祀巡游、文艺展演、民间艺人表演、卖书画、变戏法耍杂技、卖花斗鸟、特色小吃展卖、逛街购物……在这里，可以体验到老街的市井民俗，重温儿时的美好记忆，感受盛大节日的气氛。不说了，赶快狂欢去吧。

The Wushan Temple Fair is a joyous affair when it comes around each year. The temple is packed with people, and all kinds of programs and activities take place, making it very memorable. There are ceremonies and parades, performances, folk art, calligraphy and painting sales, juggling and conjury, birds and flowers for sale, exhibitions and sales of unique snacks, all kinds of shopping. Here one can experience the customs of the old city, relive childhood memories, and enjoy a festive atmosphere. It is a day of fun that is definitely not to be missed.

热衷游泳
Passion for Swimming

一次听同事高兴地说，她的孩子被学校游泳队选中，课后每天训练5000米。原来，杭州的家长很喜欢孩子游泳，这应该是名人效应。你看，2002釜山亚运会获三项冠军的吴鹏，2004雅典奥运会100米蛙泳金牌得主罗雪娟，乃至近几年的孙杨、叶诗文等中国泳坛的领军者，都是杭州人啊！

I once heard one of my co-workers excitedly exclaim that her child has been selected for the swimming team and was to practice swimming 5,000 metres a day. Parents in Hangzhou very much like their children participating in swimming, due in part to a celebrity effect. The third-time gold medallist at the 2002 Pusan Olympics Wu Peng, the 100 metre frog-stroke gold medallist at the 2004 Athens games Luo Xuejuan, and in recent years Sun Yang, Ye Shiwen, leaders in Chinese swimming, have all come from Hangzhou!

都市·乐活
City and Leisure

赏桂花
Appreciating Osmanthus Flowers

不知道是九月送来了暗香浮动的桂花，还是桂花带来了凉爽舒适的九月。在初秋的杭城桂花总可以"独占三秋压众芳"。作为杭州的市花，桂花有着富贵的寓意，象征友谊、爱情、荣誉和思念。"满觉陇旁金粟遍，天风吹堕万山丘"，赏桂花的最佳去处就数有着9000多株桂花树的满陇桂雨公园了。

It is hard to say if September brings about the floating fragrance of osmanthus blooms, or if the osmanthus blooms bring about the chilly comfort of September. At the start of autumn in Hangzhou one can always expect the fragrance of osmanthus. As the city flower of Hangzhou, the osmanthus carries connotations of prosperity, friendship, love, honour, and reflection. "Yellow flowers blanket Manjuelong valley, and as the wind blows their fragrance descends upon myriad peaks." The best place for appreciating these beautiful blossoms is Laurel Park in Manjuelong valley, where over 9,000 osmanthus grow.

运河水上巴士
Travelling on the Canal Bus

三十多年前，道路没有这么发达，从运河沿岸的小镇到杭州最适合的交通工具往往是轮船，小镇居民都希望有一天可以坐公交车去杭州。不曾想到的是，因为交通的便捷而一度被废弃的轮船，现在却成为了运河上一道亮丽的风景。运河水上巴士，为旅游的人们提供了不同的交通工具，也提供了不一样的人文感受。

Thirty years ago, the road system wasn't as developed, and the preferred mode of transport for those who lived along the banks of the canal to travel from their small villages into Hangzhou was by boat. At the time, the residents of these villages all hoped that one day they would be able to take buses into the city. When this was implemented, the boats were more or less abandoned by the residents, but surprisingly became valued by others for the scenery that could be enjoyed upon them. Now the canal "buses" still run, and travellers choose to take these boats for a different kind of experience.

摄影：施麟麒

微观杭州
HANGZHOU: TRADITION AND MODERN TIMES

心之向往
The Heart's Direction

来了久了才知道，我所接触到的地道杭州人少之又少。出门坐出租车，司机八成是河南人，做拉面的是新疆人，食堂的小妹是西北人，朋友们更是来自五湖四海……或许"老杭州"从来不像我们这般匆碌，他们会在房檐下沏一壶清茶，和旧友聊几句越乡软语……这倒不是臆测，而是每一个来到这里的人内心里向往的生活。

After being in Hangzhou for a while you will realise how few people are actually natives of the city. When you take a taxi, 4 in 5 of the drivers are from Henan. The makers of hand-pulled noodles are from Xinjiang, the girls working in the cafeterias are from the Northeast of China… there are people from all over here. The "old guard" here isn't as busy running about. You'll see them making tea at home, chatting with old friends in the local dialect. Yet one could say that such is the ideal life for everyone coming here.

时尚的广场舞
Fashionable Dance

傍晚去广场散步，远处传来神曲《小苹果》，脑袋里浮现出一群大妈整齐划一地跳着广场舞。慢慢走近，似乎不一样啊，怎么年轻人也在跟着跳，小伙打扮挺潮。只见他们随着音乐有节奏地跳着，步伐轻快，律动和谐，真是把广场舞跳出了民族舞的意思。原来广场舞不是大妈的专属，舞步也不再老套俗气。

When you go to walk around the square at night, you may hear the song "Small Apple" – China's "Gangnam Style", if you will. What one would normally picture is a large number of middle-aged women doing a coordinated dance in the square, as is common across China. Yet, when you slowly walk closer, you see that there are also young people in the group, dressed fashionably. As you see them dance to the beat of the music, steps quick, rhythm harmonious, the plaza dance seems more like a folk dance. It turns out that dancing in the public plaza is no longer the exclusive domain of old ladies, and is actually becoming fashionable.

摄影：王建华

都市·乐活
City and Leisure

摄影：董思聪

千变杭州
Ever-Changing Hangzhou

一分钟前还是大都会里的琳琅满目，转过一个街角又变成了古色古香的红砖墙与青石路。之前还在踩着山间泥路上的青苔碎石，翻过一个山头又钻入了一方失修的古亭，坐在老式的方木墩上鉴赏亭心驻着的石碑。在杭州城里漫步，永远别去猜下一站你会遇到什么风景，因为它有千万张脸谱，谁也不知道它下一秒想为你展示些什么。

In a minute you can go from the dazzling metropolis, and taking a turn around a corner, you'll be in an ancient-feeling scene of red brick walls and green stone roads. You might be walking over a mud road in the mountains, and green-moss covered cobblestone streets, and after cresting a peak, come upon a dilapidated old pagoda. Sitting on a traditional wooden bench, you can see a stone stele that evokes strong emotions upon looking at it. Taking a walk around Hangzhou, you never know what scenery you might come upon next, because it's a city of a thousand faces. Who knows what the next moment may bring about?

浣纱溪的遗憾
The Sad Story of Huansha Creek

每次经过浣纱路总会联想起词牌名浣溪沙，这么诗意的名字，一定会有浪漫的过去吧。询问浣纱路上一位坐馆老中医，言谈间颇多遗憾："浣纱路原为浣纱溪填平而成。旧时浣纱溪自涌金桥下引入西湖水，流往市区主要做饮用水。溪两旁柳荫夹道，溪水清澈见底，岸旁埠头女人们的捣衣声说笑声，别是一种风土人情哦。"

Every time I go down Huansha Road I always think of a traditional Chinese tune name, Huanxisha – such a poetic name, it must have a romantic past. I asked a doctor of Chinese medicine about it, and he said with lament: "Huansha Road is the filled-in bed of Huansha Creek. In the old times Huansha Creek flowed from Yongjin Bridge into the West Lake, and was mainly used as a source of drinking water for the city. It was lined with willows, and the water was clear. You could hear the sound of women laughing as they washed clothes. It was really something."

微观杭州
HANGZHOU: TRADITION AND MODERN TIMES

放心
Relax

有一次逛商场,看到一些年轻人在做兼职,装载 App 就附送小礼物。一名少妇的机型特殊,兼职的小哥弄了半天也搞不好,她就直接把手机塞到小哥手里,然后就拉着同伴扎进了商场。我吃过午饭出来,刚巧看见她出来取手机,一切理所应当的样子。我不禁纳闷,到底是媒体夸大了社会的不诚信,还是杭州这座城市,是个特例呢?

There was one time that I was at a mall, and saw a young part-time worker giving away small gifs to those who installed an app on their smartphones. A young woman had an unusual phone, and the young part-timer wasn't making any progress. She put the phone in his hand, and pulled her friend away with her to go shopping. After I ate lunch and came out, I happened to see the girl getting her phone back from the young man as if this was perfectly normal. I couldn't help but wonder, is it that the mass media has amplified concerns about dishonesty, or that this is a special characteristic of Hangzhou?

安宁的模样
Models of Calm

每一百个杭州人中就有十七个老人。他们不紧不慢,为这座城市虚掩上浮华的门。晨雾朦胧,他们在林间唱起遥远的歌谣。雨打红桃,他们蘸着西湖水在青石板上随性挥毫。在江南潮湿的阳光下,他们任凭时光从肩头流过,自提鸟笼,落下一地啼鸣的芬芳。他们拥着最朴素的生活和最美好的梦想,那是杭州最安宁的模样。

17% of Hangzhou's native population is elderly. They are calm and cool, as flash and ostentation isn't part of Hangzhou's culture. In the mists of the morning, the sound of them singing traditional songs flows throughout the forest. When the rain falls upon the red peach blossoms, they write with brushes dipping with water of the West Lake on the green stones. In the moist air under the bright sun, they walk around, carrying birdcages and from which emanate all kinds of chirping sounds. They live simple and beautiful lives – they are the models of calm.

摄影:金炫辰

都市·乐活
City and Leisure

摄影：王杰于

服装第一街
The Street for Clothing

第一次走过四季青服装市场一定会被震到：满街的人，人行天桥上是人，往下走的露天过街地道是人，马路两边、马路中央都是人。各人不是提着各色大小包袋，就是推着各式大小拉车：平板的，有俩大轮子的；简易的，带俩小轮的，等等。车上载满包包袋袋，包袋里塞满各式衣裳……这里不愧是中国服装第一街。

I was startled the first time I walked by the Sijiqing Clothing Street – there were people everywhere, with people packing the pedestrian bridges, and underground passages. There were people on both sides and in the centre of the street. If people weren't carrying bags and purses, they were pushing all kinds of carts, large and small: flat-back with two large wheels, simple with two small wheels, and so on. The carts were all packed with bags and packages, inside them all manner of clothes. This may be the street with the most clothes in all China.

夏天到，蝈蝈儿叫
Crickets in the Summer

夏天一到，河北卖蝈蝈儿的农民总会运大量蝈蝈儿来杭城叫卖。他们用自行车装着很多的蝈蝈儿笼沿街溜达，蝈蝈儿响亮的歌唱声自然引来许多市民。酷热难挨的夏天，午休时听着挂在阳台上蝈蝈儿的鸣唱，会朦胧觉得自己来到了清凉的深山老林中，然后迷迷糊糊打个瞌睡。夏天就这样在蝈蝈儿陪伴的惬意慵懒中过去。

When summer arrives, rural cricket-sellers from Hebei Province come in large numbers with larger numbers of crickets to Hangzhou. They ride bikes that have many cricket cages hanging from them, and the sound of their chirping brings many customers to the market. During the very hot summer days, you can hear the sound of these crickets chirping in their cages hung upon the balcony, and hazily imagine that you are in a cool forest deep in the mountains as you drift off to sleep. This is how crickets make pleasant companions on an indolent summer day.

微观杭州
HANGZHOU: TRADITION AND MODERN TIMES

小酒吧老板
The Boss of a Small Bar

阿敏经营着一家小酒吧，店面不大，却温馨有情调。杭城有许多这类很像家庭客厅风格的小酒吧，适合熟人朋友小聚。这个酒吧阿敏经营了十年，不管经济危机、金融风暴，它都不温不火地存在，让阿敏衣食无忧。阿敏说，她喜欢这种生活状态，赚不了大钱，但也没有压力。这很符合很多杭州人的生活观念：知足常乐。

A-Min runs a bar which is small but warm and colourful. Hangzhou has a number of these small bars that resemble restaurants operated out of a home that are suitable for small gatherings of friends. She's run the bar for a decade already, pushing on through the financial crisis with stable business. She says she likes this kind of lifestyle – it may not be hugely profitable, but it's stress free. This conforms well with the outlook on life that Hangzhou people have – be happy with what you have.

美丽校园
A Beautiful Campus

浙江科技学院坐落在城西小和山脚下。校园里有山有湖，真山真水，风光旖旎，不输给任何风景区。坐落在杭州的很多高等院校，得益于杭州得天独厚的自然条件，校园就像一座座公园。难怪有许多外国留学生来到杭州留学以后，就希望能留下来，一直生活在杭州。

The Zhejiang University of Science and Technlogy is situated at the base of Mount Xiaohe in the west of the city. The campus has lakes, real mountains and streams, and charming and gentle scenery that rivals that of any scenic area. Universities in Hangzhou enjoy excellent natural conditions with the campuses resembling parks. It's no wonder that students from abroad who come to study here fall in love with the campus and wish to remain in Hangzhou.

摄影：林杰

都市·乐活
City and Leisure

摄影：程永艳

小区绿化
Greenery in Compounds

杭州小区的绿化水准在中国各大城市中绝对是一流的。大部分小区干道两旁都均匀地种着香樟、桂花之类的树木，杂以其他树种，品类繁多。三春时分，樱花飞舞，桃花斗艳；酷夏之际，凌霄满墙，枇杷压枝；金秋时节，桂花飘香，银杏泛黄；寒冬来临，松柏迎风，墨菊呈祥。每个小区，都是一座花园。

The greenery in housing compounds in Hangzhou is definitely first-rate among large-scale cities nationwide. Most of the small roads in these compounds are lined with camphor, osmanthus, and other trees of many different varieties. In the spring, cherry petals fly about and peaches boom. In the summer, the Chinese trumpet creeper covers the walls all about, and loquats hang from the branches. In the autumn, the smell of sweet osmanthus is about and the gingko turn yellow. In the winter, pine trees greet the wind, and black chrysanthemum make an appearance. Every housing community is a garden.

学院路夜市
Xueyuan Road Night Market

城西的老居民都知道当年的学院路夜市。华灯初上，文一路、学院路口北行，总是热闹非凡。南来北往的小贩、一脸悠闲的市民、青春活泼的大学生、五花八门的廉价商品，到处都是生活的味道。当然，很多人来夜市转转，都是慕文教区美女如云之名而来。如今夜市搬迁，怀旧之人难免平添些许感叹。

The old residents of the western part of the city all remember the Xueyuan Road Night Market of years past. Under bright streetlamps, at Wenyi Road at the north entrance of Xueyuan Road, it was always a bustling affair. Merchants from all over, city-dwellers with relaxed looks on their faces, energetic university students, and all kinds of low-priced articles for sale – there was a feeling of vibrancy throughout. Of course, many of the people who came were there to see the famous beauties of Cultural District. As the market has now been relocated, it's no surprise that many people sigh nostalgically about the old memories.

微观杭州
HANGZHOU: TRADITION AND MODERN TIMES

堵城的交通
A Congested City

杭州的交通相当发达。地下有地铁和隧道；地面东西和南北都有交通要道；还有贯通南北和东西的高架快速道。设立了公交专用通道，配以足够的出租车，还配备了公共自行车。既有水上交通，也有绕城高速，加之以高铁和杭州萧山国际机场。然而，城市人口的剧增和中国人均第一的私家车数，却使杭州成了有名的"堵城"。

Hangzhou's transportation infrastructure is well-developed. There is a subway and underground passages beneath the surface, and upon it there are bus routes running in every direction. There are also elevated carriageways that run throughout the city. There is a bus lane network and adequate taxis. There are also public bicycles available. There are ferries on the waterways, and an expressway that bypasses the city. There is the new high-speed rail, and Hangzhou Xiaoshan International Airport. However, added to the rapidly expanding population and highest rate of private car ownership in the nation, the city is still very congested.

喜"闲"的杭州人
Leisure-Loving Hangzhou

对于很多道地的杭州本地人来讲，"闲"对他们至关重要。或许因为得天独厚的青山秀水，他们与生俱来一种淡淡的满足感，喜欢温和中庸，不喜恶语相向，玩到虚脱的事是绝对不干的。闲暇时喜欢逛逛西湖游游公园，看看花喝喝茶，打打牌搓搓麻将。难怪丰子恺会在《吃酒》一文里说"闲"是杭州人最佳的性格写照了。

For real Hangzhou people, "relaxation" is a key concept. Possibly because of the surrounding beautiful landscapes, everyone has a kind of relaxed satisfaction with life, and enjoys a moderate, friendly lifestyle, eschewing harsh words and conflict. Nobody "parties hardy" here. Popular activities for free time are walking around the West Lake, admiring flowers and drinking tea, playing cards and mah-jong. It's no surprise that in his book *Drinking*, the early 20th century author Feng Zikai said that "leisure" was the true mark of a Hangzhou person's character.

摄影：程永艳

都市·乐活
City and Leisure

主编供稿

适宜散步的城市
A Good City for Walking

沿着钱江,顺着运河,绕行西湖,漫步湿地,想到卢梭《一个散步者的遐想》,充分说明了散步的哲学功能。散步不仅锻炼身体,灵感也会如电光火石般迸发出来。"水光潋滟晴方好,山色空蒙雨亦奇;欲把西湖比西子,淡妆浓抹总相宜。"这几句美轮美奂的诗句,一定是苏轼在西湖边散步时突然从头脑中迸发出来的。

Along the Qianjiang River, down the canal, about the West Lake, walking in the wetlands makes one think of Jean-Jacques Rosseau's *Reveries of the Solitary Walker*. Walking not only is good for your health, it tones your senses, and provides flashes of inspiration. Su Shi must have thought of the lines of his famous poem when walking along the lake. "The brimming waves delight the eye on sunny days. The dimming hills give a rare view in rainy haze. The West Lake looks like the fair lady Xi Shi at her best, whether she is richly adorned or plainly dressed."

杭城小弄堂
Alleyways in Hangzhou

杭州是个现代气息和古典文艺相结合的城市,在车水马龙宽敞的马路背后还有蜿蜒曲折不为人知的小弄堂。杭州人真的很幸福,早上起来就可以在弄堂的拐角处喝一碗热腾腾的豆浆,抬起头就可以跟楼上敞开了窗户浇花的老大爷唠家常,身边会经过一群你追我赶上学校的孩子们,脚下躺着一只眯着眼睛晒着太阳的流浪猫。

Hangzhou is a city that blends the flavour of modern lifestyles with the traditions of times past, with large roads carrying large numbers of large vehicles, and small winding alleyways existing unknown to many. The people of Hangzhou are truly lucky. One can wake up in the morning and stroll through the alleyways drinking a hot bowl of soy milk, look upward to see an old man talking idly as he waters the plants outside of his window, pass a group of hurrying school children, and look down to see a lazy stray cat warming itself in the sun.

微观杭州
HANGZHOU: TRADITION AND MODERN TIMES

摄影：梅莹

火柿映西溪
Fiery Persimmons at the West Creek

柿子树，被誉为"长寿树"，寓意吉祥。金风乍起，火柿盈枝。收获时节，每年西溪都会在此举办"火柿节"。秋高气爽，芦花盛开，西溪水岸，火红的柿子高挂枝头，与美绝的晚霞相映成趣。乘兴而来的人们热热闹闹地采摘着柿子，品尝着甜腻，欣赏着"千树明霞笼柿果，一溪金阳隐芦花"的美景，好不惬意。

The persimmon tree is also known as the "tree of longevity" and has auspicious connotations. When the golden winds blow, the branches are covered in fiery fruit. At harvest time each year, there is a "fiery fruit" festival in the West Creek area. The autumn air is fragrant and the reed catkins are all about as the persimmons decorate the banks of the West Creek, bathed in the warm light of sunset. People in high spirits happily pick the fruit, enjoying sampling the sweet flavour – these scenes are well-known from depictions in classical literature.

热心红娘伍大姐
Lady Wu, a Matchmaker

伍大姐是杭城著名的热心红娘，为了给杭城的大龄男女青年牵线搭桥，她不仅开通了博客，而且还建立了两个千人QQ群，贴财贴力为他们服务牵红线。三年多时间已经成功让几十位男女喜结良缘。每周伍大姐都会为群里的姑娘小伙们找一个不同的聚会场所，相互增进了解。你身边有找不到对象的人吗？快找伍大姐去。

Lady Wu is a famous matchmaker in Hangzhou, and in order to help older single youths in the city find companions, she's set up a microblog, as well as two QQ chat groups of more than 2,000 people. She's hooking people up left and right. In just over three years she's made dozens of matches happen. Every week she organises an activity for young men and women to meet and get to know each other in a different location. If you're looking for a partner, you should go to her.

都市・乐活
City and Leisure

爱心凉茶摊
Friendly with Cold Tea

每逢酷暑，大大小小几十处免费爱心凉茶摊就会默默出现在杭城大街小巷，为路过的人们送上一份清凉。"我们茶摊由14位平均年龄超过60岁的老人轮流值守，两人一班，就想发挥点余热，做点有意义的事。"面对赞扬，江干区濮家新村爱心凉茶摊发起人、义务摆摊13年的王惠玲老人淡淡地说。

When the notoriously hot summers of Hangzhou roll around, a few dozen stands are quietly set up, small and large, on the large streets and narrow alleyways of the city. They give out a cup of cool tea for free to the passers-by. "Our tea stands are manned by 14 volunteers with an average age of 60, two people per shift. We just wanted to do something nice for other people" – Wang Huiling explains simply how he started the first tea stand in Pujia New Village in Jianggan District 13 years ago, in response to praise from others.

林荫隧道
The Shady Tunnel

在火车站随意搭上了去灵隐寺的公交车。了解一座城，从坐公交开始。听着站名，看着窗外，还有专门的司机带你去你想去的地方，这也是一种极好的享受。绕过西湖，进入了那段令我印象深刻的悠长的森林隧道。两旁树木高大，枝繁叶茂，树枝在高高的上空交叉，不留空隙。杭州市民是幸福的，在如此天然氧吧，连散步都很有格调。

From the train station I took a bus on a whim to Lingyin Temple. To understand a city, you can start with its transit network. When I heard the station name, looking out the window, I saw drivers waiting to take me wherever I wanted to go, and felt great. Around the West Lake, through the forest tunnel that left me with such a strong impression. On either side there were tall trees covered in green leaves. The branches intertwined, not leaving any space. The people of Hangzhou are lucky to have this natural source of oxygen and excellent backdrop for taking walks.

摄影：李选

微观杭州
HANGZHOU: TRADITION AND MODERN TIMES

摄影：俞洋

钢镚儿找零
Coins

在杭州每次付钱找零都是给硬币，初来时不太适应，在北方钢镚儿是很少被使用的。后来了解到从1992年起，银行在个别城市开展试点，逐步实行壹元以下小面额货币单一投入硬币，使杭州率先实现了小面额货币的硬币化，所以，如果你来杭州旅行，记得准备好钱袋来装零散的钢镚儿。

Whenever you get small change in Hangzhou it will be coins. Outsiders might not be accustomed to it, as coins are rarely used to make change in the north of China. As the result of a program by the central bank started in 1992, for amounts of 1 Yuan and less, Hangzhou as more of less moved entirely to coins. Thus, when you visit Hangzhou, remember to bring a coin purse.

孝道文化
A Culture of Filial Piety

杭州首家"孝道文化展示体验馆"，位于皋亭山景区千桃园内，分为孝廉广场、文化长廊等展示区域。它以丁兰故事为创作主线，通过动态展示、互动参与孝道艺术文化等方式，展示中华孝文化发展史以及新老二十四孝的故事，突出杭州本土孝文化遗迹及民间的孝文化内容。周末就带上你的孩子去体验吧！

Hangzhou's first "Cultural Experience Centre for the Confucian Doctrine of Filial Piety" is situated in the Peach Garden of the Mount Gaoting Scenic Area, and is divided into the Piet Plaza, Cultural Corridor and exhibition area. It centres around the story of Ding Lan as its main theme, and through a dynamic display and interactive cultural exhibits show the history of the development of the culture of filial piety and the old and new stories of the Twenty-four Filial Exemplars, showing the local cultural heritages and the cultural content of the concept filial piety among the local people. This is a great place to bring your child on the weekend!

都市·乐活
City and Leisure

现代化城市建设
Modernising Urban Construction

2014年开始，杭州比以往更大力度地建设人行过街设施，包括天桥和地道。其他各大路口的天桥作用固然十分重要，但令人感受最深的莫过于医院门前的天桥了，且基本上都配备了电动扶梯。以往每每看到老弱病残患者在医院前的人行道上匆忙地赶着绿灯时，都会有种莫名的着急和担忧。我想以人为本便是如此吧。

At the start of 2014, Hangzhou entered into a new large-scale round of road construction, including that of pedestrian bridges and underground passages. The bridges at major intersections are still very important, but one of the most impressive is most of bridges in front of hospitals are outfitted with escalators. Old and weak hospital patrons previously had to wait nervously at a red light, but this kind of human-centric thinking has now provided them with facilities that allow them to avoid this discomfort.

虎跑泉趣事
The Story of Running Tiger Spring

虎跑泉水是上天的恩赐，和龙井茶是绝配，大伯大妈们凭着公园卡，提着大桶小桶，耐心地在一眼泉水前，排上两三小时的队。忽见一位排队的大伯，从容地拿着一个橘子，边剥边慢慢品尝，润喉、滋养、洗肺、消磨时光，都有了。再回家泡一壶龙井，听着越剧，嗑着瓜子，享受休闲时光。

Running Tiger Spring is a gift from heaven, which is matched with Longjing Tea. Old men and women, park passes in hands, carrying small buckets queue up in groups of two or three in front of the spring. I see an old man take out an orange and peel it. It looks sweet, juicy and healthy. It's a good day to go home, make a pot of Longjing Tea, listen to an opera, crack sunflower seeds and enjoy some leisure time.

摄影：董思聪

微观杭州
HANGZHOU: TRADITION AND MODERN TIMES

免费凉茶
Free Cold Tea

夏季来杭州旅游，不难发现街边或者西湖边的免费凉茶摊。西湖边固然凉快，杭州的夏天却是酷暑难当，这时突然发现一个凉茶摊，不失为杭州给人的又一惊喜。凉茶一般是径山茶，喝上去很是解暑。

Travelling in Hangzhou during the summer, it's not hard to find stands at the West Lake or along the streets giving out free cold tea. Whilst it may be cooler along the West Lake, Hangzhou's summers are notoriously hot, and happening to find some free cold tea is a very nice surprise the city presents you with. The tea is normally Jingshan tea, which is said to have a cooling effect.

城区
The City Area

杭州有五个老城区，还有滨江等五个新秀。上城区是南宋皇城所在地，下城区是以武林广场为核心的市中心，江干区定位是新的中心城区，CBD钱江新城就在此。西湖区是旅游文教中心，拱墅区以前是工业基地，现在运河申遗成功，成为一张金名片。滨江区高新技术产业云集，有阿里、网易、三星、西门子、ABB等。

Hangzhou has five old districts, and five up-and-coming districts. Shangcheng District has the ruins of the residence of the Song Dynasty Emperors, Xiacheng District has Wulin Plaza as its centre. Jianggan District is the new city centre and home to the central business district. Xihu District is the centre of tourism and education, Gongshu District was once an industrial centre, and is seeking to have the Grand Canal recognised as a World Cultural Heritage Site. Binjiang District is an area where high-tech enterprises exist, such as Alibaba, Netease, Samsung, Siemens, and ABB.

摄影：俞燕君

轶史·钩沉
History and Reflections

摄影：石战杰

微观杭州
HANGZHOU: TRADITION AND MODERN TIMES

宋城抛绣球
Throwing an Embroidered Ball

抛绣球这个节目是宋城的一大特色。一阵喜庆的声乐中,王员外上场,把自家的女儿夸得天花乱坠,小姐上台后引起了一阵轰动。待她把绣球抛出后,台下的观众一阵哄抢,最终一位幸运的年轻小伙接到了绣球,得以上台同美貌的小姐喝交杯酒,入洞房。虽说是戏剧,但大家都玩得很开心,体验了一次古时的风情。

Throwing an embroidered ball is one of the big activities at Hangzhou's Songcheng Park. Amid joyous music, a landlord surnamed Wang takes the stage and talks up his daughter's ball game. She takes the stage and the crowd goes wild. After she throws out the embroidered ball, the audience shouts and jostles for the ball. A young man finally takes hold of it, and takes the stage to have a drink with the beautiful young woman, before they retreat to the bridal chamber. Although it's just a play, everyone has a great time watching and experiencing a bit of ancient culture.

月老和月老祠
The Matchmaker and Matchmaker's Temple

雷峰塔边的月老祠,因发源于杭州的月老故事而成为香火极盛的卜婚场所。金庸为此曾比较月老和爱神丘比特,认为小孩拿箭乱射是鲁莽,月老稽考簿籍,红线缚人,则温柔、文明。而月老祠的楹联"愿天下有情人,都成了眷属;是前身注定事,莫错过姻缘",更是东方哲学和"爱情之都"浪漫气息的体现。

Next to the Leifeng Pagoda is the Matchmaker's Temple. Because of the classical story of the matchmaker under the moon at this site in Hangzhou, the place has become a famous site for fortunetelling regarding marriages. Jin Yong (a well-known writer) once compared the matchmaker under the moon of China and the god of love Cupid, thinking of the child as hot-headed and rash, whereas the matchmaker checking record is gentle and cultured. The set of couplets hanging on the wall of the Matchmaker's Temple says: "Let the lovers of the world become spouses. This is set in previous lives – do not miss your match." This is the romantic meeting of oriental philosophy and "the city of love".

摄影:王嫱

轶史·钩沉
History and Reflections

摄影：施麟麒

相亲圣地
A Place for Meeting One's Love

万松书院是明清时杭州规模最大、历时最久、影响最广的文人汇集地。王阳明、齐召南等大咖曾在此讲学，袁枚也曾在此就读。但现在它是一个相亲场所。每周六上午，四面八方的大妈大爷都会带着自己子女的信息过来，为其物色对象。这种功能的变化，源于一个经典爱情故事——梁祝。这两位正是在此地读书而结缘的。

The Wansong Academy of the Qing and Ming dynasties is the site of cultural exchange largest in scale, with the longest history and biggest impact. The famous Wang Yangming and Qi Zhaonan, among others, gave talks here, and Yuan Mei also studied in this place. Now it's a spot for people to meet their lover. Every Saturday morning, old ladies and gentlemen from all over bright their children's information to find them a potential spouse. This kind of functional shift has its origins in a classical love story – the *Butterfly Lovers*. The two are said to have met here.

秦始皇和杭州
Emperor Qin Shihuang and Hangzhou

公元前221年，秦灭六国，秦始皇率领船队出游东南。据《史记·秦始皇本纪》记载："至钱塘，临浙江（钱塘江），水波恶。乃西百二十里从狭中渡。"面对汹涌的钱塘潮，逆行120里，秦始皇派人将大船缆系在保俶山一块巨石上，自己登上山顶眺望江面。他就这样，于两千多年前在杭州留下了自己的印记。

In 221 BC, when the Qin Dynasty destroyed the six kingdoms, Emperor Qin Shihuang lead an expedition to the southeast of China. According to historical records on the emperor: "When arriving at the Qiantang, near the Qiantang River, the water was rough. Thus, the party travelled west 120 li to cross". The emperor had the boats tied to a rock at Mount Baochu, and ascended the mountaintop to look over the river, leaving his footprints in Hangzhou more than two millennia ago.

微观杭州
HANGZHOU: TRADITION AND MODERN TIMES

此为胜处
A Nice Place

花港观鱼中有一个马一浮纪念馆,是国学大师马一浮晚年蛰居17年的蒋庄。大师被周恩来誉为"当代理学大师",与好友梁漱溟、熊十力并称为中国新儒学的"三驾马车"。新中国建立初期陈毅曾登门拜访,为见其面而在雨中静候多时,留下"马门立雨"的佳话。而马一浮对蒋庄也钟爱有加,曾撰文作记,言"此为胜处矣"。

The Flower Harbor Park has a memorial hall for Ma Yifu, one of the pillars of the studies of classical Chinese culture who lived here at Jiangzhuang in seclusion for seventeen years. He was praised as a great scholar by the former Prime Minister Zhou Enlai himself. With his friends Liang Shuming and Xiong Shili, he was praised as one of the three giants of new Confucianism. At the start of the founding of the People's Republic, the Marshal Chen Yi came to visit him, and waited in the rain for a long time, later writing a poem on the subject. Ma Yifu liked Jiangzhuang very much, and wrote a treatise once, titled "This Is a Nice Place".

荷花与美酒
Lotus Blossoms and Fine Wine

许多游客观览曲院风荷,都为其近四十亩荷田美景所醉,却往往忽略了此处本是宫廷酒坊。南宋皇帝赵构为了花天酒地的生活,在洪春桥设立了这所曲院,召集天下酒匠酿制美酒。院中池塘引入西湖水,遍种荷花。一到夏天,荷花粉吹入新酿之酒,使得酒中带有荷花的香味,最终形成了杭州的一大名酒——"荷香酒"。

A number of visitors like to visit Quyuan Fenghe near the West Lake. People are intoxicated by the 40-mu fields of lotus blossoms, yet frequently miss out here was once the imperial distillery. The Emperor of the Southern Song Dynasty Zhao Gou, in order to get his hands on better liquor, built a distillery at the Hongchun Bridge, and summoned the best distillers from around the empire. A pond in the distillery draws in water from the West Lake and lotuses grow around it. As summer arrives, the pollen from these flowers enters into the freshly distilled liquor, imparting upon it a lotus fragrance, finally making the most famous liquor in Hangzhou – "lotus fragrance liquor".

摄影:夏利亚

杭州通司徒雷登
John Leighton Stuart

司徒雷登是杭州通，而且可说是杭州话讲得最好的美国名人了，因为他生在杭州，长在杭州，在美国去世后也如愿魂归故里安息在杭州。据说当年他去河坊街王润兴饭庄吃饭时点菜："件儿要瘦，肥了倒胃；木郎豆腐多放胡椒，要烧得入味；响铃儿要熬稍……"正宗的杭州土话直把饭店伙计听得一愣一愣的。

John Leighton Stuart was an "old Hangzhou hand", and was the best American speaker of Hangzhou dialect, as he was born and grew up in Hangzhou. After he died in the United States, he wanted his remains returned to Hangzhou to be buried. It's said that one time he ordered at the Wangrunxing restaurant at Hefang Street: "Make it thin, 'cause fat messes up my stomach, y'all. Gimme more spice in the beans, that's how I likes it. Cook it up right…" his fluent use of the vernacular shocked the waiters.

小热昏的第六代传人
A Sixth-Generation Xiaorehun Singer

"小锣一敲唱开场，今朝唱点啥名堂。不唱短来不唱长，今朝唱唱杭州老街的孩儿巷……"小热昏第六代传人周志华"开心茶馆"中一开唱，就吸引了电视机前的许多老杭州。"可惜这种起源于清末杭州街头'说朝报'的'小锣书'现在会唱的还不到5人，真怕我们这些老家伙走后就失传了。"周志华的担心不无道理。

"The bell sounds out when tapped, what song shall I sing this morning? Not a long one nor a short one, today I will sing about an alleyway of old Hangzhou…" A sixth-generation of songs in the xiaorehun style, Zhou Zhihua sings on "Happy Teahouse", holding the attention of a number of aged Hangzhou residents in front of the TV. "Sadly, this kind of song from the late Qing, in which people would 'sing the morning news' only has 5 remaining practitioners. I'm afraid when we pass so will our craft, too." Zhou Zhihua's worries aren't unfounded.

传说中的才女
A Talented Woman of Legend

相传苏小小是古时钱塘第一名妓，中国古代最有名的才女佳人。死后葬于西泠桥畔，能够时时刻刻欣赏西湖美景。不论她是否真实地存在过，也不论由她引发的关于道德、人性美丑的悖论。红颜多薄命，一缕芳魂终究是飘散了。"生在西泠，死在西泠，葬在西泠，不负一生爱好山水"的遗愿能够完成，也算不枉此生。

The famous Su Xiaoxiao was the most famous courtesan in Qiantang (Hangzhou today) in ancient times, and one of the most famous talented women in ancient China. She was buried in the fields near Xiling Bridge after her passing, so that she could always appreciate the views of the West Lake. Whether or not she truly existed, or the stories on the beauty and ugliness of human nature attributed to her are in fact hers is unknown. She was a classic beauty whose life was made difficult by her looks. "To be born at Xiling, die at Xiling, be buried at Xiling as a lifelong lover of nice scenery" – her wish is said to have come true.

不应忘却的范市长
A Mayor that Should Not Be Forgotten

历代"市长"中，北宋范仲淹是不容忘却的一位。他担任杭州知府仅一年多，恰逢"两浙路大饥荒，道有饿殍，饥民流移满路"。范公大胆实行"荒政三策"：大兴土木、发展旅游、招商引粮。三策条条奏效，饥荒顿除。范公死后，百姓为纪念其惠政，曾在孤山建范公祠，在梅东高桥建范府君庙，甚至一度奉其为土地神。

Among the "mayors" of history, Fan Zhongyan of the Northen Song Dynasty is one that deserves remembering. He served for only a little more than a year in Hangzhou, but at the time the city ran into a severe famine during which many people starved to death. He boldly implemented a three-point policy combating the famine, where many buildings were constructed, tourism was developed, and merchants were courted to import grain. The three points were all effective, and the famine was eradicated. After he died, to thank him for his excellent work, at Mount Gu a shrine was constructed for him, at the Meidong Bridge a temple was built, and some revered him as a local deity.

为何西溪鳞塘多
Lakes around the West Creek

传说大圣孙悟空从石头缝里蹦出来后，大闹天宫。他来到蟠桃盛宴上，一边喝美酒，一边尝仙果，仙果只吃大的，小的都扔掉，那些扔掉的仙果都掉在了西溪。这些天上的东西掉下来，把西溪这块湿地砸出了大小不一的上千个鳞塘，这就是西溪鳞塘星罗棋布的原因。

Legend holds that when the Monkey King Sun Wukong jumped out from a crack in a stone, he caused an uproar in heaven. When he arrived at the banquet of the heavenly peach, he drank fine liquor and ate the forbidden fruits, only choosing the biggest. The smaller ones, he threw out, and they landed around the West Creek area. When they fell from heaven, they carved big lake beds in the ground, which is the reason or the wide distribution of small lakes around the West Creek.

胡适的烟霞洞
Hu Shi's Cave of Smoky Red Clouds

"睡醒时，残月在天，正照在我头上，时已三点了。这是在烟霞洞看月的末一次了……今当离别，月又来照我……不知何日再能继续这三个月的烟霞山月的'神仙生活'了！"这是胡适1923年10月3日的日记。烟霞洞寄寓过胡适生命中罕有的欢情，游人从洞里看来，也免不了唏嘘：相悦而不能相守，纵使智者也会痛的。

"When I wake up, the moon is still in the sky, shining over my head. It's still very early in the morning. This is the last time I see the moon at the cave of smoky red clouds. Today I leave, and the moon comes to shine upon me. I don't know when I will be able to watch this beautiful moon for a three-month stretch again." This is the journal written by Hu Shi on October 3, 1923. The cave of smoky red clouds was a rare spot of happiness for Hu Shi in his life. Upon seeing the cave, one cannot help but exclaim: being true to each other yet unable to be together must be painful for intellectuals, too.

铁史·钩沉
History and Reflections

摄影：杜红英

东、西穆坞的方向为什么是反的
Why West and East Muwu are Reversed

到西溪游玩，很奇怪东穆坞村在西穆坞村的西面，而西穆坞村在东穆坞村的东面。打听之下，原来跟皇帝选妃有关。说是皇帝在东、西穆坞分别选取的两位妃子深得其欢心，就赐匾给她们家乡。使官被当地景色迷得乱了方向，赐匾时竟把两者搞反了。因是皇帝御赐，乡亲们也只好将错就错。于是，东、西穆坞方向就反了。

When you travel the West Creek area, you will find that oddly, East Muwu is to the west of West Muwu, and West Muwu is to the east of East Muwu. If you ask, you will find that this had to do with the emperor's selection of concubines. The emperor very much liked two concubines from East and West Muwu, and made a move to officially display his gratitude to the two villages. However, when the officials came to deliver the emperor's thanks, they were confused by the scenery, and mixed the two villages up. As this was an official move of the emperor, the village residents decided to simply keep the names reversed.

苏东坡的红颜知己
Su Dongpo's Red-faced Companion

什么叫红颜知己，让一个杭州姑娘来告诉你。苏东坡来杭做官，收了个娇娘在书房，叫朝云。朝云伺候苏东坡读书写诗，做些红袖添香的事。苏东坡很喜欢她。一日东坡问众人自己是怎样的人，众人都哄他高兴，唯独朝云说他是"一肚皮的不合时宜"。东坡吃惊。后来，东坡果然因"不合时宜"地批评朝政坐牢了。

What is a "red-faced companion"? Let a girl from Hangzhou explain it to you. When Su Dongpo came to Hangzhou to serve as an official he took on a young girl to assist him in his study, named Zhao Yun. She accompanied Su Dongpo when he wrote and read poems, as was a common practice in classical China. Su Dongpo liked her very much. One day, he asked the people what they thought of him, and they all said nice things to please him. Only Zhao Yun told him: "You are definitely not with the times." Su Dongpo was shocked. Later, he was imprisoned by the imperial government for "not being with the times".

望仙桥上盼仙归

Waiting for the Return of a Sage on Wangxian Bridge

望仙桥早先只是一座无名石桥。桥边有个衣衫褴褛的郎中,因为治好了一种怪病而名声大振,生意受了影响的其他医家便贿赂知府赶走他。知府审讯时忽生疔疮,求他医治,后不治而亡。他因此被判死刑。在押赴刑场的桥上,郎中跳河随波漂去。大家在桥上期盼他再来治病,时间久了,这座无名小桥就被称为"望仙桥"。

Wangxian Bridge was originally a nameless small bridge. Near it there resided a doctor dressed in poor clothing, who had come to fame for curing a strange disease. Other doctors whose business had been damaged by competition with his sudden popularity bribed local officials to drive him out. When the magistrate of the district was interrogating him, he was suddenly afflicted all over with malignant boils. He asked the doctor to cure him, but he refused, leaving the magistrate to his fate. He was sentenced to death for this. When he was being transported to the execution ground over the bridge, he jumped into the river and drifted off. The common people hoped for him to return to treat illnesses, and after a long time the bridge became known as Wangxian Bridge – "wangxian" means "looking for a sage".

摄影:夏利亚

History and Reflections
铁史·钩沉

摄影：夏利亚

斗富不成成"豆腐"
The Un-prosperous "Tofu"

"豆腐桥"在建国南路，由北到南有三座。名字跟豆腐渣工程无关。传说王佐劝陆文龙归宋有功，被封为安乐王，在东河边建造王府，因此占用了仅有的一艘船，百姓怨言四起。王佐用建造王府的材料造了一座桥，百姓称颂。秦桧知后心生嫉妒，连造三桥与王佐斗富，起名斗富桥，但百姓不买账，叫它们"豆腐桥"。

There are three "Tofu Bridges" at Jianguo South Road. Legend says that Wang Zuo was appointed as the Anle King for successfully persuading Lu Wenlong to return to the Song Dynasty. He established a residence by the East River. As he made use of the only boat available, the local residents were upset and complained. A bridge was built with materials from the official residence, and the people appreciated it. Qin Hui, a famously execrated capitulationist of the time, envied him and thus built three bridges to compete, naming them the Dofu ("prosperous") Bridge. The common people had none of it, however, and adopted another, similar-sounding name to make a mockery of him: "Tofu Bridge".

油条的起源
The Origin of Youtiao

南宋宰相秦桧加害抗金名将岳飞，招致国人愤恨。众安桥有个面点店主，把两根面条并一起扔进油锅炸，说，一根是秦桧一根是他老婆王氏，众人大笑。面条炸了就膨胀得又粗又黄了。一人说，我吃了他们。一吃，味道还不错。大家都说要吃"油炸桧"，店主干脆就做起了油炸桧。油条小吃就这样诞生了。

As Qin Hui of the Southern Song Dynasty did harm to the famous anti-Jin general Yue Fei, people were furious with him. The boss of a bread shop threw two strips of flour into a pot of boiling oil, saying one was Qin Hui and the other, his wife. Everyone laughed. The dough bloated and turned thick and yellow. One person volunteered to try eating them, and said the flavour was not bad. Everyone afterwards said they wanted to eat "Youzhahui" ("fried Hui", another name for youtiao), and the boss of the shop continued to use the name for youtiao.

微观杭州
HANGZHOU: TRADITION AND MODERN TIMES

主编供稿

杭城故事
A Hangzhou Story

拥有丰富感情的杭州人，创造了许多动人的故事。许仙白娘子的惊世之恋；苏小小的芳魂不断；济公的醉观尘世……每一个故事都表达着杭州人的爱恨情仇。他们有"杨柳岸晓风残月"的缠绵悱恻，也有"舍得一身剐，敢把皇帝拉下马"的侠肝义胆。他们是可爱真实的杭州人。

The Hangzhou people, full of feeling, have made many moving stories. Xu Xian, Lady Bai and their story of love, Su Xiaoxiao and her beautiful soul, the famous mad monk Ji Gong's drunken view of the world… every story reflects the strong emotions of the people of Hangzhou. They have the poetic feeling of willows on the banks of a river under moonlight, as well as a dashing bravery that knows no bounds. These are the characters of Hangzhou people.

风雨茅庐
Wind and Rain over the Thatched Cottage

大学路的郁达夫故居风雨茅庐近日开放。1927年，原居上海的郁达夫遇见了杭州女人王映霞，一见倾心，与其相恋。不久，他移居杭州，与王过起了神仙眷侣生活，并于1936年建成了这个爱巢。郁达夫因此举债，离家谋职，先后遭遇抗战爆发、妻子偷情、老母亡故，最后远赴重洋。备受打击后，杭州成了他的伤心地。

Situated upon University Road is the Thatched Cottage of Wind and Rain of Yu Dafu, recently opened to the public. In 1927, Yu Dafu, originally from Shanghai, met Wang Yingxia of Hangzhou. They instantly fell in love. Not long after, he moved to Hangzhou, and they lived happily together, to be formally united under one roof in 1936. Yu Dafu took on debts because of this and left to work. The war broke out, his wife had an affair, his mother died, and he himself had to go abroad. After all these hardships, Hangzhou became a place of sorrow that he refused to talk about.

轶史·钩沉
History and Reflections

梅妻鹤子的传说
The Legend of the Plum Wife and Crane Children

传说宋代诗人林逋，不愿为官，就隐居于杭州，结庐孤山北麓，沉浸于歌山画水。他终身未娶，没有子嗣。种了一株梅花，把梅花当做妻子；还养了两只鹤，就把鹤当做自己的孩子。于是就有了梅妻鹤子的故事。你可以解释为清高自闲，也可以理解为逃避现实生活。如今，只留下林逋之墓在灌木杂草之间。

Legend holds that Song poet Lin Bu was unwilling to become an official, and instead chose to become a hermit in Hangzhou, living on the north side of Mount Gu and involving himself in songs and paintings. He never married, and had no heir. He planted a plum tree and treated it as his wife, and raised two cranes as his children. He may be seen as either aloof, or avoiding real life. Today, only Lin Bu's grave remains among tangled vines and bushes.

摄影：董思聪

微观杭州
HANGZHOU: TRADITION AND MODERN TIMES

西溪且留下
Let the West Creek Remain

关于"西溪且留下",坊间有这样一种说法。宋高宗赵构南逃,路过西溪,想把皇宫建在这里。大臣劝说此地不宜做都城,赵构只得说,好吧,那就留下吧。大臣不知道西溪的地名,就把此地记录为"留下"。最后赵构和大臣们选定了凤凰山脚建造皇宫,南宋由此开始。有历史学家考评,赵构从未到过西溪,认为这只是个美丽的传说。

About letting the West Creek remain, legend says that when the Gaozong Emperor of the Song Dynasty, Zhao Gou, fled south, he came upon the West Creek area and wanted to build his palace there. His ministers advised him against it, saying it was not a good place to build a city. Zhao Gou simply said OK, then "let it remain". The ministers didn't know what the place was called, so they simply recorded it as "let it remain". They later built the capital at the base of Phoenix Peak and the Southern Song Dynasty then began. According to historians, Zhao Gou had never been to the West Creek, which is just a beautiful legend.

主编供稿

铁史·钩沉
History and Reflections

摄影：武欣

岳王庙里忆岳飞
Remembering Yue Fei

岳王庙位于西湖边的北山路上。南宋著名爱国将领岳飞堪称是一个完美的男人，他既是军事家又是诗人。"莫等闲，白了少年头，空悲切！"他所写的《满江红》壮怀激烈，文采斐然，激励了一代又一代的爱国青年。这样的男人到了今天或许就该称为男神了。

The Yue Fei Temple is situated on Beishan Road on the side of the West Lake. Yue Fei was a patriotic general of the Southern Song Dynasty and is widely praised even now as a great man. He excelled at military affairs as well as poetry. A famous poem written by him is full of passion and has motivated generation after generation of patriotic youths.

微观杭州
HANGZHOU: TRADITION AND MODERN TIMES

"受降镇"小史
The History of Shouxiang Village

1937年抗日战争全面爆发，杭州富阳沦陷。日军以宋殿村为据点，烧杀淫掠，无恶不作。他们在村南挖坑，把无辜被害的中国民众抛尸坑内，形成"千人坑"。1945年，日本宣布无条件投降，宋殿村被指定为侵驻浙江地区日军投降地点。1950年，富阳县人民政府将原宋殿村所在地长新乡更名为受降乡，以志纪念。1987年受降撤乡建镇。

In 1937 when the war erupted, the Japanese occupied Hangzhou and Fuyang. They used Songdian Village as a base, and committed all manner of atrocities. They dug pits at the south of the village, and used them for mass graves. In 1945, when the Japanese surrendered unconditionally, Songdian Village was named as the site of surrender for Japanese forces in the Zhejiang area. In 1950, the village was renamed by the People's Government of Fuyang County as Shouxiang ("accepting surrender") Village as an act of remembrance. In 1987 the status of the village was upgraded as a town.

李渔操办文化产业
Li Yu's Involvement in Cultural Industry

清初，李渔就办起了文化产业。他是个文人，写剧本卖给戏班赚稿费，后来发觉自己写戏自己演能赚更多，于是到杭州组建家庭戏班。杭州城里演出场次不多，他就雇船游走四方巡回演出。他还写小说，卖给出版商后再改成剧本一鸡两吃。那个时候文人经商还不成气候，他如此精明经营还是落得老来穷。

At the start of the Qing Dynasty, Li Yu helped started the cultural industry. He was a man of letters, and able to sell his scripts for plays for high prices to theatre groups. He later discovered that he could earn more money writing and performing himself, and so built a base for a theatrical group in Hangzhou. They didn't perform much in Hangzhou, but rather rented boats and performed all over. He also wrote novels which he sold to publishing houses and also used to turn into scripts to double his profits. Sadly, he ended up in poverty in old age, as cultural industry was less developed at that time.

摄影：陈晓红

铁史·钩沉
History and Reflections

摄影：陈波

昌化石缘
The Stones of Changhua

浙江工艺美术大师邵城鑫作为土生土长的临安人，一出生就带着昌化鸡血石的烙印，并且注定要为临安的传统工艺美术昌化石雕做贡献。他爱石如命，为石成痴，石头的生命和灵魂就这样在他的一雕一刻中，在他的《踏雪寻梅》《后羿射日》《女娲补天》《挣扎的灵魂》《钟馗醉酒》等国宝级作品中被唤醒和重生。

Eminent Zhejiang artist Shao Chengxin is a native of Lin'an, and has long worked making sculptures from the red stones of Changhua to represent for Lin'an. He loves stones and is deeply passionate about working with them. A number of his works such as "Searching for Plums in the Snow", "Struggling Soul", "Drunken Chung Kuei" and others have achieved National Treasure status and have been highly praised.

钱塘第一井
The First Well at Qiantang

"钱塘第一井"位于杭州大井巷，旧名寒泉，是杭城现存古井中唯一能使用的。古井坐东朝西，总体布局呈"凹"字形。天井中分布五井，旁有界碑镌刻为"古大井墙界"，历千年不竭，泽被民生，惠及百姓。井水"不杂江湖之味，泓深莹洁"，掬一捧来喝，清甜甘冽直入心脾，真不愧为"杭州之圣水"。

The "First Well at Qiantang" is situated at Dajing Lane in Hangzhou, and was formerly called the Winter Spring. It is the only well still usable among the ancient wells of Hangzhou. It sits at the east and faces west, for an overall U shape. The courtyard has five well shafts, and there is a carved stele that marks the location as the site of the old wells. These wells have been in service for more than a millennium, and the water they yield is clear, sparkling and pure. Upon trying it, anyone will remark that it is the best water in Hangzhou.

微观杭州
HANGZHOU: TRADITION AND MODERN TIMES

立马回头
Limahuitou

"下一站,立马回头",去往灵隐寺的公交,多会路经此站。"立马回头"是杭州一个特别的公交站。据说清乾隆帝出游杭州,第一次路过此处,对这里破败的山路非常不满。当地官员得知后,赶紧为皇上专修了一条新路。乾隆再经过普福岭时,路况已大为改观,乾隆龙颜大悦,立马驻足,从而有了"立马回头"的说法。

"Next stop, limahuitou (meaning stop the horse and look back)." This is something that many people encounter on the way to Lingyin Temple. "Limahuitou" is a special stop in Hangzhou's transportation network. It's said that when the Qianlong Emperor of the Qing Dynasty visited for his first time, he was displeased with the state of the road which was in disrepair, and after the local officials were notified, they quickly redid the road for the emperor. When he reached the Pufu Peak, he discovered that the road had been widened and improved, and was greatly pleased. He ordered the horses stopped, from which the phrase "turn back immediately" became famous.

广济桥
The Guangji Bridge

塘栖广济桥是京杭大运河仅有的七孔石拱桥和最大的薄墩联拱石桥。桥体高耸,从桥下拾级而上,宛如登山。在桥顶可欣赏古镇全景。以前,这里还有元宵节"走桥"的民俗。据说元宵晚上走的桥越多,福分就越多。所以到了当天晚上,人们手提花灯,成群结队在河边、桥上游走,远看星火点点,蔚为壮观。

The Tangqi Guangji Bridge is the only seven-arched stone bridge on the Beijing-Hangzhou Grand Canal, and the only thin-pier combined arch bridge as well. It is a high bridge, and ascending it step by step is like climbing a mountain. From the top of the bridge you can see all of the old town scenery. During the Lantern Festival, there is a folk tradition of "walking the bridge" here. It is said that the more you walk on the bridge during the festival, the more prosperous you will be. Thus, on the day of the festival, people will take a lantern and form a long queue upon the river, climbing up the bridge and looking at the views and the lanterns below.

摄影:施麟麒

History and Reflections

摄影：许雷梅

外婆的同学录
Grandmother's Yearbook

如果不是为外婆整理房间，张哲可能永远不会看到这本同学录。蓝色布面的小册子，仅用褐色麻绳穿了穿。翻开一看，竟是外婆少女时代从湘湖师范毕业时的同学录，每一页都是毛笔书写的赠言，有投身时代洪流的豪言壮志，也有依依惜别的同学深情。笔迹工整得可以媲美书法作品，饱含一个时代独有的气度和烙印。

If it weren't for him cleaning his grandmother's room, Zhang Zhe may have never discovered this yearbook. A small blue book bound only with light brown cord, he found when he opened it that it was a yearbook from when his grandmother graduated from Xianghu Normal University in Zhejiang. Every page is inscribed with notes written in a brush pen from classmates, with sentiments of the time personal goodbyes penned in excellent calligraphic hand. The book carries the marks of the special atmosphere at the time.

宋江路
Songjiang Road

坐 B 支 4 到长途车站，听到报站："宋江路"，一时很是好奇，不由地说："为什么叫'宋江路'呢？"好友一时哑然，旁边一民工模样的人接茬说："是因为宋江在此打败了方腊，就取名叫宋江路。"一查历史，果然。一时之间对那个民工模样的人顿生敬意。

As I was taking the bus, I heard the announcement "Next Stop: Songjiang Road". My curiosity was piqued, and I wondered aloud why it was so called. My friend had no reply, but a migrant labourer suddenly spoke up: "It's because this is the place where general Song Jiang defeated Fang La." I checked the historical records, and he was right. All of a sudden, I feel I should show respect to that labourer.

桃花错
The Missed Peach Blossom

吴山有一岩石叫感花岩。相传唐代诗人崔护吴山游春，因口渴叩一柴扉求饮，巧遇一桃花般明媚的女子。次年再访，佳人却杳无影踪，遂于壁间题下"去年今日此门中，人面桃花相映红。人面不知何处去，桃花依旧笑春风"一诗。200年后苏轼游吴山念及崔护其诗其事，亦于壁间写下《赏牡丹诗》附之，感伤这场桃花错。

At Mount Wu there is a "sentimental peach blossom rock". Legend has it that Tang Dynasty poet Cui Hu visited Mount Wu in the spring and knocked on a door to ask for a drink because of thirst. He was greeted by a maiden beautiful as a peach blossom. When he visited the next year, there was no trace of this beauty. He wrote a poem: "A whole year ago to the gate I did pace, with blooming peaches shining upon her face. Now the smiling face which I saw and miss has gone nowhere, the peaches are still coming into bloom in spring breeze here." 200 years later Su Shi travelled here and read Cui Hu's poem. He wrote his own poem, "Admiring the Peonies", to acknowledge this missed meeting between Cui Hu and the peach beauty.

未央村
Weiyang Village

上城孝女路上有个未央村，"未央"二字历来备受争议。有人认为"央"和"阳"同音，该名字的寓意应为"没有阳光的村子"。其实，"未央"是"未尽""未达"之意。既然"未央"，那就是未到尽头。因此，人们经常特意跑来此处，以便沾沾运气，讨个好彩头。

On Xiaonü Road in Shangcheng District, there is a "Weiyang Village", the name of which has historically been a topic of debate. Some people believe that the "yang" is the same as in "yin-yang" (meaning sun), taking it to mean "village with no sunlight", as "wei" means "not". However, it in fact means "unfinished" or "unexhausted". So people come here to boost their luck.

知味之余，知音不断
Zhiweiguan Restaurant

"知味停车，闻香下马；欲知我味，观料便知"说的是杭州百年老店知味观，它是国家首批认定的中华老字号和中国十大餐饮品牌。1913年由孙翼斋建立，开张之初生意并没他想象中的红火，他想着自己的点心不比别人差，就在门楣上写下了"欲知我味，观料便知"，不料竟引起了人们的好奇。从此知味之余，知音不断。

One of the major classical food and beverage brands as recognised by China, Zhiweiguan is a famous restaurant in Hangzhou. Founded by Sun Yizhai in 1913, the business wasn't originally that good as he imagined, As he thought the pastries he produced could compete with other brands, he hung a sign at the doorhead saying "If you want to know how the product is, come see how it's made". It attracted curious people, and the brand became famous since then.

摄影：杜红英

杭城雅号
Nicknames for Hangzhou

对于杭州的雅号——文化之都、旅游之都、休闲之都，相信很多人没有什么异议。但大多数人可能还不知道，杭州还是个动漫之都。每年的春天，杭州都有一个固定的节目——中国国际动漫节，自2005年开办，迄今已有11届，越办越成熟。如果你是个动漫爱好者，一定不能错过哦。

Everyone agrees with common nicknames for Hangzhou – the City of Culture, the City of Travel, the City of Leisure, but what many people may not know that it is also a city of cartoon and animation. Every year in spring, there is a festival on a set day – the China International Cartoon and Animation Festival, held since 2005 and now in its 11th year, it increases in scope with each occurrence. If you're interested in anime and manga, you shouldn't miss it.

子久草堂
Zijiu Thatched Cottage

都以为黄公望只在富春山间徘徊，未曾想杭州的浴鹄湾也有他的足迹，他的足迹留在子久草堂。草堂临水，背山而还可望山，倚门眺望，雷峰塔可一收眼底。他画的《富春山居图》，无论你赶到台北故宫还是浙博，都只能看到半幅，但坐于这草堂，你可以轻轻松松地把他六百年前见过的风景一一看来。

We all think that Yuan Dynasty painter Huang Gongwang only walked around the Fuchun Mountain Range, but in fact his footprints also set upon Yuhu Bay in Hangzhou at the Zijiu Thatched Cottage. The cottage lies near the water, and has a view of mountains. If you stand at the door and look far off, you can see the Leifeng Pagoda. You can see one half each of his painting *Living in the Fuchun Mountains* at the Zhejiang Provincial Museum and the Palace Museum in Taipei, but sitting here, you can take the entire thing in.

微观杭州
HANGZHOU: TRADITION AND MODERN TIMES

摄影：刘天捷

杭州话里的"爹爹"
"Diedie" in Hangzhou Dialect

在北方，称呼父亲一般用"爸爸"，也有人叫"爹"或者是"爹爹"。杭州话里，却叫祖父"爹爹"。您确实没有看错，同一个词语，表示两种不同的意思，因此它们的发音也是不同的，在北方指称父亲时是"diedie"，而在杭州话称呼祖父时是"diadia"。这一称呼承袭了上古语音与称谓特征，专指祖父。

In the north, it's common to call your father "baba" "die" or "diedie". In Hangzhou, however, this term is used to refer to one's grandfather, however it is pronounced as "diadia" – these are the pronunciation and meaning of the word at an earlier stage in Chinese history.

碑林
Forest of Steles

某日席间，一老北京问一老杭州，"你们有个碑林，你知道吗？"老杭州愕然无答，觉得很丢面子，居然叫一个外地人这样问倒。回后多处打听，终在吴山边的劳动路上找着这碑林，一看更汗颜，竟有如此多宝贝：二王、苏米等历代书家的手笔刻石，理宗、康熙、乾隆的御书石碑……五百多方，由唐至清，十分壮观。

One day, an old Beijing man asked an old Hangzhou native, "You have a forest of steles, you know that?" The Hangzhou native was surprised, and felt ashamed that an outsider would ask him this. After he returned and made inquiries, he finally found this forest of steles near Laodong Road, next to Mount Wu. He blushed with shame when he saw so many steles: the Two Wangs(Wang Xizhi & Wang Xianzhi), Northern Song calligraphers Su Shi and Mi Fu, and others, the Lizong, Kangxi and Qianlong emperors… more than 500 in total, from the Tang to the Qing Dynasty, all a sight to behold.

铁史 · 钩沉
History and Reflections

十门城谣
A City of Ten Gates

"百官门外鱼担儿，坝子门外丝篮儿，太平门外粪担儿，螺蛳门外盐担儿，草桥门外菜担儿，候潮门外酒坛儿，正阳门外跑马儿，清波门外柴担儿，涌金门外划船儿，钱塘门外香篮儿。"随着时代的变迁，民谣中描写的昔日杭州运河两岸集市盛况的十大城门均已湮没历史中，如今只剩下代表古城门遗址的石碑，令人扼腕。

"Fish at the Baiguan Gate, silk at the Bazi Gate, faeces at the Taiping Gate, salt at the Luosi Gate, vegetables at the Caoqiao Gate, liquor at the Houchao Gate, horses at the Zhengyang Gate, firewood at the Qingbo Gate, boats at the Yongjin Gate, incense at the Qiantang Gate". While preserved in the folk songs of Hangzhou, the ten city gates on the two sides of the Grand Canal have not stood the test of time, and now only a stele remains at the ruins of the Gucheng Gate, which is a pity.

浣纱路
Huansha Road

走过浣纱路，未见浣纱河。听老杭州说这是在浣纱河上筑的路。浣纱河古称清湖河，又因在这里浣纱洗衣的杵捣声终日不绝，而得名浣纱河。昔日的浣纱河，沿岸杨柳低垂，小桥流水人家，夏日里，小伢儿在河里游泳、抓鱼、嬉闹。由浣纱河变成浣纱路，对多数老杭州来说，是一段难以割舍的记忆。

Walking along Huansha Road, I don't see the Huansha River. An old resident says that Huansha Road was built over the Huansha River. The Huansha River was originally called the Qinghu River, but its name was changed due to associations with washing clothing. Huansha River in the old days was lined by willows, featured many bridges, and had people who would wash clothes and children playing in it in summer days, fishing and having fun. It's a nostalgic memory for those old enough to remember it.

凤凰展翅越千年
The Phoenix Spreads its Wings to Cross Milennia

杭州凤凰寺创建于唐代，因寺院建筑结构似凤凰展翅而得名，是我国著名的伊斯兰教清真古寺之一。1400多年来，它成了中国和阿拉伯文化交流的历史见证。浙江科技学院来自也门的留学生阿伟每周五都会和其他七八百名穆斯林一样来寺里参加主麻聚礼。他说，在异域他乡，还可以每周有地方做礼拜，真好！

The Phoenix Mosque in Hangzhou was built during the Tang Dynasty, and gets is name as its shape resembles a phoenix spreading its wings. It is one of the most famous Islamic mosques in China. For more than 1400 years, it has served as proof of the friendship between Chinese and Arabic cultures. Awayim, an exchange student from Yemen studying in Hangzhou, comes here every Friday to pray with seven hundred to eight hundred Muslim friends. He says that it's nice to be able to worship here although he's away from home.

微观杭州
HANGZHOU: TRADITION AND MODERN TIMES

摄影：朱琦

八卦田
Field of the Eight Diagrams

玉皇山南麓的八卦田，是由南宋皇帝赵构所建，距今有近900年了，保存完好。这是根据伏羲氏所作的太极阴阳八卦图案建造的。按一年二十四节气四季轮回在"八丘田"里种植不同的庄稼，表示对农事的尊重，祈求风调雨顺、五谷丰登，也表示赵构重整旗鼓、收复江山的决心。现开辟为公园，成为人们学习农事和休闲的地方了。

At the southern foot of Jade Emperor Mountain there is a Field of the Eight Diagrams, which was built under the reign of Southern Song Emperor Zhao Gou, and almost 900 years later it remains in good shape. It is built in the shape of the Eight Diagrams of Yin and Yang defined by legendary leader Fu Xi. It consists of sections that are planted in accordance with the twenty-four Solar Periods as defined in the traditional Chinese lunar calendar, to show respect for agricultural affairs and pray for good rains and harvest. It was also built as a display of Zhao Gou's determination to rally force again and recover the lost territory. It is now open as a park, for both relaxation and learning about agriculture.

古韵书香
文澜阁
Ancient Books in the Wenlan Pavillion

文澜阁位于西湖孤山南麓，是1782年为珍藏《四库全书》而建的皇家藏书楼。阁内东南侧和东侧的石碑，分别刻有清乾隆帝题诗、颁发《四库全书》上谕和清光绪帝所题"文澜阁"。阁内的《四库全书》历经沧桑，是浙江几代人的侠肝义胆才使得它能躲过战乱而幸存。而文澜阁日积月累的古书香气，一直浸润着杭城人的心灵。

The Wenlan Pavilion is situated at the southern foot of Mount Gu near the West Lake. For saving the *Complete Library of the Four Branches of Literature*, it was constructed in 1782 by the emperor. Inside, at the southeast and east sides there are steles, with inscriptions by the Qianlong Emperor as well as the Guangxu Emperor. The books within have been preserved through wars and conflicts due to the bravery and heroic efforts of generations of people in Zhejiang. The collected works in this place reflect the spirit of the people of Hangzhou.

地域·物产
Areas and Products

摄影：许敬

微观杭州
HANGZHOU: TRADITION AND MODERN TIMES

王星记"杭扇"
Wangxingji's "Hangzhou Fans"

王星记的扇子与丝绸、龙井茶一同誉为"杭三绝"。扇面或山水风光或峰峦叠石,妙笔丹青无所不包。杭扇与拱桥的结合,既是桥与山景的结合,又有月下西湖的意境。扇面以丝绸为原料,体现出杭州作为丝绸之府的特色,包含了浓郁的江南文化内涵。

Wangxingji's fans, silk, and Longjing Tea are known as the "three best" of Hangzhou. The faces of the fans are decorated with rivers and hills or rocky ridges and peaks, depicted in exquisite detail which is the combination of Hangzhou fans and arched bridges, the combination of arched bridges and mountain scenery, and the West Lake under moonlight are also common themes. The fans are made of silk, and reflect Hangzhou's role as a capital of silk production, as well as the subtle and refined culture of the region.

摄影:王端

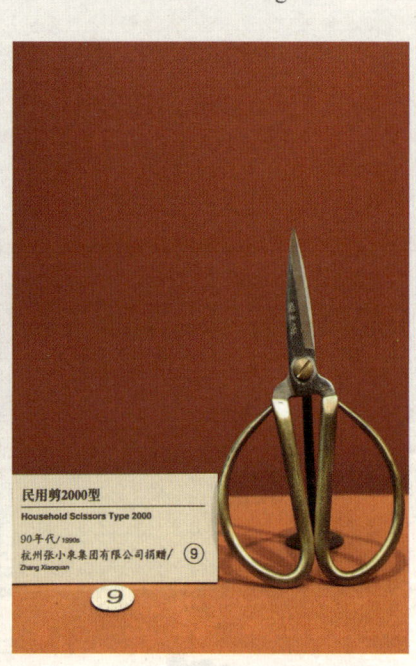

摄影:丁刘冬

快似风走的张小泉剪刀
Zhangxiaoquan Scissors

"快似风走润如油,钢铁分明品种稠,裁剪江山成锦绣,杭州何止如并州。"这首诗赞美的就是杭州知名的张小泉剪刀。1915年在"万国博览会"上获奖后,张小泉剪刀就远销南洋和欧美一带,成为国际友人的"新宠"。据统计,张小泉剪刀在海外的销量月均上万把。

The Zhangxiaoquan scissors manufactured in Hangzhou have long been fabled for their quality and beauty, even referenced in poems. After winning a prize at the 1915 Panama Exposition, the scissors sold widely across the world. Statistics show that more than ten thousand are sold abroad per month.

地域・物产
Areas and Products

摄影：李选

轻车熟驾
Sightseeing by Bike

在杭州，骑行成了别具一格的风景线。随处可见红色的自行车租借点，马路上也是各种小电摩。找个好天气，独自一个人或者约上几个好伙伴一起骑车去西湖，一路上欢声笑语，时而大声放歌，时而驻足拍照，时而来一场自行车的速度与激情，这一切的惬意不正来自于杭州这座旅游城市所推崇的绿色出行吗？

In Hangzhou, riding a bike itself is a nice scenery. One can see red bike rental shops all around, and the streets have all kinds of bikes and scooters upon them. Wait for a day with nice weather and head out on your own or with some friends to the West Lake, enjoying pleasant sounds and songs, stopping to take pictures, or getting fast and furious on the pedals. This is a great way to enjoy Hangzhou in a green format.

地铁站纳凉
Cooling off in the Subway Station

作为一座"火炉"城市，如何避暑是令杭州人头疼的问题。有一回坐地铁到终点站临平，发现了一道奇景：车站大厅沿墙整齐地铺着凉席，上面散放着枕头、毛毯，许多当地的老人和小孩儿坐地乘凉，神情惬意。不时有乘警和保安路过，也只是维持秩序，并无驱赶之意。整个场面有些凌乱，却又不失温馨。

As one of China's "oven cities", avoiding the summer heat is a big topic in the minds of Hangzhou residents. One time I took the subway to the terminal at Linping, and discovered that all along the walls of the station were people with cooling bamboo mats out, accompanied by blankets and pillows – locals both young and old taking advantage of the cool air in the station. Sometimes the transit police or guards would come around, but just to keep order, without hassling the locals. The scene was disorderly, but still friendly.

微观杭州
HANGZHOU: TRADITION AND MODERN TIMES

摄影：范晶晶

塘栖的枇杷

Loquats at Tangqi

枇杷是江南小镇塘栖的特产，没有吃过塘栖枇杷的朋友说现在水果超市都有卖枇杷的，个头还比你们的大，不稀罕。可是塘栖人会告诉你，那个是福建那边的枇杷，品种不同，没有我们塘栖枇杷好吃，也没有我们塘栖枇杷金贵。塘栖枇杷上市期仅一个月左右，不易储存，所以想吃的话就来明年六月的中国杭州塘栖枇杷节吧！

Loquats are a local specialty of Tangqi. Those who haven't tried them will say that loquats are readily available at supermarkets, and that they're even larger than those grown in Tangqi. However, the people of Tangqi will tell you that those are from Fujian, and are of a different variety, not as good as the Tangqi variety, and not as precious. As soon as they go on the market, all stores are depleted within a month, so if you want to try these loquats out, come to Hangzhou for the Tangqi Loquat Festival next June!

地域·物产
Areas and Products

湖滨"呆萌"小松鼠
Lakeside Squirrels

"西湖边的松鼠好呆萌可爱，玩它的尾巴都没有关系哦。"看到湖滨公园一名男子正握着树上松鼠的尾巴，任由那条大尾巴在他的脸上、口鼻间轻扫，任小姐赶快拿起手机拍照发微信告诉她的朋友。而这边呢，小松鼠已经跳下地来享用这位男子带给它的玉米大餐了。看来，西湖边的松鼠与人类相处越来越和谐了。

"The squirrels at the side of the lake are so adorable," remarks a man as he pulls on the tail of one climbing a tree at the lakeside park. Amidst this relaxing scene, a girl quickly pulls out her phone and snaps a picture to share with her friends. By the time she finishes, the squirrel has already jumped back down onto the ground and is enjoying a meal of corn that the man has brought him. Humans and squirrels are coming to exist in harmony on the sides of the West Lake.

摄影：李选

酱一酱再吃
Sauce it up

用酱油腌制风干，所制成的酱菜是杭帮菜的一大亮点。鸡、鸭、鱼、肉、萝卜、黄瓜……都可以拿来酱一酱再吃。以酱鸭最为有名，好的酱鸭色泽油亮红艳，咸淡适宜，香甜可口，是下饭佐酒的佳肴。酱鸭适宜保存，路过杭州，寻一只好的酱鸭带回家，是不会让人失望的。

Using soy sauce to make meat jerky or preserved vegetables is popular in Hangzhou. Chicken, duck, fish, beef, carrots, cucumbers… all of these things can be processed in this way. Soy sauce duck is the most popular, with good product having an oily lustre and red colour, light in flavour with a hint of sweetness. It's perfect to eat with a meal or when drinking liquor. It stores well, so if you're visiting Hangzhou you can buy some to take home with you.

微观杭州
HANGZHOU: TRADITION AND MODERN TIMES

摄影：郑若琪

市井纳凉
Cooling off at the Alleyways

汗背心一件、破蒲扇一把，弄堂口一坐，俭朴的杭州人，在家家户户已经安上空调的今天，依旧会选择老底子留下来的纳凉方式。在夜色未至、凉风已起的傍晚，吆喝一声，"熬烧熬烧"（快点儿），几个老友相约摆上一局象棋，杀个热火朝天。而观战的，往往比战场上的更为激动，已全然忘却夏日的炎热。

With an under shirt and a busted palm-leaf fan, sitting at the end of an alleyway, thrifty and simple locals select to keep cool in this way even though all their houses now have air conditioners installed. As night arrives, the air begins to cool down, and someone calls out "all right, hurry up". A group of friends come out to play chess. The battle on the board is as fierce as that on the battleground, and the heat is forgotten.

吴山夜市
Night Market at Mount Wu

在杭州城里，吴山夜市大概是最具市井气息和烟火风味的地方。坐地铁到龙翔桥站，沿仁和路走400多米就到了。既是夜市，自然是晚上最热闹。九点之后，吴山夜市早已是一片人海，叫卖声，讨价还价声，情侣嬉闹声，好一片生机勃勃的景象。在这里，可以淘到很多心仪的小商品，但是要记住，可别忘了杀价哦！

In the city of Hangzhou, the Mount Wu Night Market has the best atmosphere and ambience among markets. Taking the subway to Longxiang Bridge, I walk along Renhe Road for about 400 metres before I arrive. As a night market, it's most boisterous at night. By 9 p.m., the market is flooded with people, merchants hawking wares, people bargaining, lovers chatting playfully, sights to see all around. You can find all kinds of nice little things to buy, but don't forget to bargain over the price!

地域·物产
Areas and Products

美景美食的西溪
Nice Scenery and Food at West Creek

1000多年前，宋高宗赵构看到了小桥流水、芦花似雪的西溪美景。近日得空进去，简直要被绿色砸晕了脑袋。浅的，深的，绿得发亮，阳光洒下来，斑斑点点，渐欲迷人眼，煞是好看。美景往往不乏美食。白嫩滑溜的豆腐撒上虾米、紫菜、碎榨菜。红墙绿瓦，一碗豆腐脑，满满都是童年的记忆。

1,000 years ago, Emperor Zhao Gou of the Song Dynasty saw the beautiful water, bridges, and reed catkins swaying in the wind at the West Creek area. If you visit today, you will see that there is enough green there to make your head spin. Pale, deep, bright and dazzling greens, speckles and patches will gradually make you dizzy with their beauty. To go with the beautiful scenery there is also excellent food. Pale, smooth tofu sprinkled with dried shrimps, laver, and shredded mustard. Red walls, green bricks, and a bowl full of tofu, these are all memories of childhood.

书吧
Book Bar

穿过北山路边的民国大宅，登上宝石山，迈过几百级台阶，一家名为"纯真年代"的书吧就跃然眼前。招牌是艺术家韩美林写的，迎客对联是莫言送的。余华、张抗抗、陈忠实、阿来、北岛等著名作家和诗人都在这里留下过足迹。读书，品茶，文化交流，这家受到市政府资助的民营书店，现在已成为杭州的文化地标。

Passing through a Republican-era mansion on Beishan Road, you may climb Gem Mountain and after a few hundred steps you will arrive at a book bar called "Pure Era". The sign was written by famous artist Han Meilin, and the pair of couplets to welcome customers was a gift from Mo Yan. Yu Hua, Zhang Kangkang, Chen Zhongshi, Ar-lai, Bei Dao and other famous authors and poets have all left their footprints here. Reading books, drinking tea, cultural exchange – this government-supported private bookstore is a major cultural landmark in Hangzhou now.

摄影：杜鹃花

微观杭州
HANGZHOU: TRADITION AND MODERN TIMES

炒新茶
New Tea

西湖开茶节，刚好在清明节前。龙井茶当然是好茶，价格也是好价格。炒茶师傅的手上满是老茧，不怕高温，徒手炒制，凭手感来炒制茶叶，手也被茶叶熏得黑黑的。他感应炒制时的温度、干湿度，靠手掌压制出茶叶。传统的手艺，传统的味道。

The West Lake Tea Festival comes before the Tomb-Sweeping Holiday. Longjing is of course a great tea, and the price is good, too. The tea-frier's hands are covered in callouses and can withstand high temperatures. As he fries the tea bare-handed, his hands are blackened by the smoke. He uses his hands to feel when the tea is done, taking into account temperature, moisture, and yield to pressure. It's a traditional craft that produces a traditional flavour.

摄影：郑若琪

龙井白露私房茶
Dragon Well, White Dew

很多杭州老茶腔最爱的还是龙井白露新茶。秋天桂花盛开，约上几位好友围坐树下，品上一杯茶农自留的白露私房茶，那才叫神仙日子。"春茶苦，夏茶涩，要好喝，秋白露"，此话不假，经过春夏两季磨砺，秋茶喝起来自有一种独特浓烈的甘醇味道。"这茶包治百病，我们不卖的，只留给自己喝，"老茶农实话实说。

A favourite of many tea-drinkers in Hangzhou is Longjing ("dragon well") Bailu ("white dew") tea. In autumn when the osmanthus flowers bloom, meet with a few of your friends and try some tea from a grower's private store to have a really nice day. "Spring tea is bitter, summer tea is astringent. If you want something nice, have white dew tea in the autumn." This is truth. After the trials of the spring and summer, the plants produce a strong yet smooth tea in the autumn. A tea grower spoke about it honestly: "This tea can cure all kinds of diseases. I don't sell it; I keep it to drink myself."

地域·物产
Areas and Products

蒸谷米
Parboiled Rice

杭州人有吃蒸谷米的食俗。蒸谷米是将稻谷蒸熟晒干，经砻、舂后食用。由于食后易消化，因此尤其适合老年人。相传是吴越相争时，越国大臣文种献计将种谷蒸熟后献给吴国，结果吴国人种不出秧苗，造成大荒年，民心大乱，越国趁机灭了吴国。越国臣民遂以余下蒸谷加工成米，食之相庆，从此吃蒸谷米习俗相沿至今。

The people of Hangzhou enjoy eating parboiled rice. To make the dish, unhulled rice is boiled and then dried, hulled, and then ground. As it's good for disgestion, it is commonly eaten by the elderly. It's said that when the kingdoms of Wu and Yue were at war, Wen Zhong of the Yue Kingdom gave a large amount of unhulled rice that had already been boiled to the Wu Kingdom. When the people of the Wu Kingdom planted these grains, they didn't grow and a great famine ensued. The kingdom fell into disarray, and was defeated by the Yue Kingdom. The people of the Yue Kingdom processed their boiled unhulled rice and ate it, and continue the custom to this day.

天空之镜——千岛湖
The Mirror of the Sky – the Thousand Island Lake

要选一处代表杭州山水气质的景观，相信千岛湖可以名列其中。千岛湖水在中国大江大湖中位居优质水之首，不经任何处理即达饮用水标准，被誉为"天下第一秀水"。在湖央划船，仿佛一不小心就会掉进千岛湖的蓝镜中。傍晚彩霞在平静的湖面轻轻地移动，海天一色，如梦如幻，此时的千岛湖幻若一面天空之镜。

If you want to pick a representative scenic spot in Hangzhou, the Thousand Island Lake will definitely be on your list. It has the best water among the large lakes and rivers of China. It's drinkable without any kind of processing, and is known as the best water in China. Rowing a boat on the lake, you may fall into the blue mirror of the Thousand Island Lake. At night, the red clouds gently move around in the reflections on the lake like a dream – at this time the lake is like a mirror of the sky.

摄影：俞洋

微观杭州
HANGZHOU: TRADITION AND MODERN TIMES

摄影：郦文娟

小朋友的小天堂
Heaven for Little Kids

但凡来杭州都会选择一览西湖之美，每逢节假日总是要上演一幕"断桥不断"的剧目。但这绝非小朋友们的第一选择，较之西湖，他们的心头爱是浙江省自然博物馆，在那儿可以看到恐龙、古生物等8个专题。每天都会有络绎不绝的孩子在这里排队通过互动设施感受恐龙的大力气，这里才是他们心目中的人间小天堂吧。

When visiting Hangzhou the first choice is always the West Lake, the Broken Bridge is always packed with people at every holiday. However, for children, this definitely isn't the go-to destination – their choice is the Zhejiang Natural History Museum. There they can see dinosaurs, ancient animals and six other main topics. Every day the venue is packed with children queuing for the interactive dinosaur exhibits – this is where you should take your kids in the city.

塘栖"土灶月饼"香
The Fragrance of Mooncakes Baked in Tangqi

土灶月饼源于塘栖一带农村。老底子过中秋，大部分人家买不起月饼，便就地取材，用番薯、南瓜、芋艿做馅，纯手工摊皮，再用土灶火烧烘烤，做成各种味道的土饼，当成中秋月饼。因为是用白炭、木屑、泥混制而成的煤球当燃料，因此烤出来的月饼，皮很酥，咬一口外皮纷纷往下掉，真是又香又脆，满满的旧时味道。

Mooncakes baked in mud stoves originate from villages in the Tangqi area. Originally when the Mid-Autumn Festival came around, the local inhabitants didn't have money to buy mooncakes, so they used what they had available, such as sweet potatoes, pumpkins and taros for the filling, making the wrappers themselves too, and then bake them with fire of a mud stove for a unique kind of flavour. They ate these as mooncakes. Because the mud stoves use balls of coal made of hard charcoal, sawdust and mud, the cakes have a very crispy skin which will flake off when bitten, both fragrant and crunchy.

地域·物产
Areas and Products

餐厨垃圾处理的"杭州模式"
Kitchen Waste in the "Hangzhou Model"

一条专"吃"餐厨垃圾的生产线年底将在天子岭建成。以往，餐厨垃圾基本是被人买走，有的喂猪，有的被不法商贩利用，回流到餐桌上。天子岭"餐厨垃圾"处理生产线采用"三相分离+厌氧产沼"处理工艺，把餐厨垃圾变废为宝，既让地沟油不再回桌，又合理利用餐厨垃圾制造生物柴油和发电，一举两得。

A processing channel for kitchen waste is to be established in Tianziling at the end of the year. Previously, kitchen waste was sold, as feed for pigs, or to illegal merchants who extracted "gutter oil" from it to be used by unscrupulous restaurants. Tianziling's kitchen waste program will employ three-phase separation and anaerobic biogas generation to fully utilise the waste, keep gutter oil off restaurant tables, and contribute biofuel and power generation benefits.

杭州最美骑行道
The Nicest Bike Ride in Hangzhou

三江两岸绿道建设是杭州市政府"十二五"重点工程，它北岸东起钱江二桥，西至珊瑚沙水库；南岸东起钱江二桥，西至闻涛路东信大道路口，是离杭州城区最近的绿道。秋高气爽之时，迎着凉爽的钱塘江风，追着钱江潮从江东大桥一直骑到彭埠大桥，看着蔚蓝天空、滔滔江水，再看看这气势磅礴的大桥，心胸不禁开阔起来。

Beautification and addition of greenery to the "three rivers and two coasts" is a major project of the 12th Five-Year Plan of the Hangzhou municipal government. On the north coast, it starts from the No.2 Qianjiang Bridge in the east, to the Shanhusha Reservoir in the west. On the south coast, it starts from the No.2 Qianjiang Bridge in the east, to the crossroad of Wentao Road and Dongxin Road, this is the closest "green corridor" to downtown Hangzhou. During autumn, as the cool air over the Qiantang River sweeps in on a breeze, following the flow of the Qiantang River, Pengbu Bridge, looking at the blue sky and river water, then to the majestic bridge, you will feel open and free.

摄影：李选

微观杭州
HANGZHOU: TRADITION AND MODERN TIMES

摄影：朱法华

里西湖的划艇
Rowboats in the Inner West Lake

不同于外西湖的熙攘，里西湖是安静的，沿苏堤向前，过望山桥西望即是。天好的日子，常可见三两只皮划艇离弦箭般地争流，那是国家皮划艇队在训练。赛场一分钟，场下十年功，聚光灯背后流过多少血汗只有自己最清楚。夕阳西下，远山连绵，湖光粼粼，百舸竞舟。问今朝谁主沉浮，劈波斩浪，惟我中国少年！

Unlike the boisterous outer West Lake, the inner West Lake is calm, and when progressing towards the Su Causeway, you will pass Wangshan Bridge and find it. On days with nice weather, you will see some rowboats on the river, cutting arcs through the water – this is the national canoeing team practicing. A minute's game takes ten-year practice. Only they themselves know what this means. Under the setting sun, with the mountain peaks in the distance, the water clear, boats race about. The youth of China are not to be messed with when it comes to rowing a boat!

孔凤春
Kong Fengchun

记得小时候一到冬天，早上都会擦一点桂花香的雪花膏或者蛤蜊油来防冻，它们有一个共同的牌子——孔凤春。这家创建于清同治元年的老店，是中国历史上记载的第一家化妆品企业，是中华"百年老字号"企业。它的"鹅蛋粉"曾是清代皇家贡品，慈禧专用，甚至南极考察队的防冻专用品也选了这个牌子。

I remember when I was a child, when winter arrived we would apply some vanishing cream with osmanthus fragrance or clam oil to protect us from the cold – they were both of the same brand, Kong Fengchun. The store was established in the first year of the Tongzhi period of the Qing Dynasty (1862), and is the first make-up brand in China. Their "goose egg powder" was used by the imperial household, and by Empress Dowager Cixi herself. Even the Antarctic expedition chose this brand as their choice for anti-cold make-up products.

地域·物产
Areas and Products

民间绝技 "翻九楼"
Fanjiulou, a Unique Skill

在杭州萧山民间流传着一种"翻九楼"的绝技。据说源于2000多年前孟姜女搭台祭夫的典故。它要求表演者在毫无保护下逢双向上翻跟斗至由9张八仙桌叠成的高约11米的"舞台",并在上面进行金鸡独立、童子拜观音、老鹰扑飞等表演。翻九楼虽已于2008年入选国际非遗名录,但传承者只有钱小占师傅一人了。

There is a unique skill among the people of Xiaoshan in Hangzhou, called Fanjiulou ("climbing to the ninth floor"). Legend says that more than 2,000 years ago, Meng Jiang was holding a ceremony for her lost husband, which required performers to climb a tower that had been made of nine stacked square tables to perform all manner of stunts. Performances on this kind of 11-metre high platform were recognised as an intangible cultural heritage in 2008, but there remains only one true performer in modern times, Qian Xiaozhan.

城市文化墙
Cultural Wall

走在杭城大街小巷,一面面大大小小的文化墙都在向你展示着杭州浓厚的文化气息,讲述着一个个美丽动人的故事:有清新亮丽的西湖风景,有描写杭州的古诗词和历史故事,有杭州的各种"最美"……城市文化墙,成了城市文化的一部分。真乃一堵墙话一座城,一面墙绘一座城。

Along both the small lanes and wide streets of Hangzhou there are cultural walls, which are painted with beautiful stories about Hangzhou. There are bright scenes of the West Lake, stories that talk about the old poems and histories of Hangzhou, all kinds of depictions of the most beautiful sights in Hangzhou. These cultural walls have become a part of the culture of the city, and are an integral part of life here. Each wall speaks about a city, and each wall paints with sights of the city beautifies.

摄影:徐骋

微观杭州
HANGZHOU: TRADITION AND MODERN TIMES

市树
City Trees

2005年来杭州读研时,英语课上听到的第一个单词就是 camphor trees(香樟树),是杭州的市树。后来发现它在杭州随处可见,民间把它看成风水树、祖宗树,寓意避邪、长寿、吉祥如意。它在四五月份开花,秋天结果,花香浓郁,果香诱人。据说因樟木上有许多纹路,像是大有文章,故在"章"字旁加一个木字为树名。

In 2005 when I came to Hangzhou to do my graduate studies, the first word in English class was "camphor trees", which is Hangzhou's city tree. Later on I discovered that I could find these trees all over Hangzhou, as the people use them as scenery, sites of worship, to fend off evil, and symbols of long life and prosperity. They bloom in April and May, bear fruit in autumn, and have a strong, enticing fragrance.

摄影:夏利亚

蒋村船拳
Jiang Village Boat Boxing

在船只上练拳?是的,蒋村船拳就是这样一种以强身健体、保家护院为目的的拳术,这可是明末清初三位少林高手传下来的哦。如今的船拳除保留古朴的武术套路外,还与民俗节庆、祭祀庙会、舞龙、舞狮、走高跷等民间文体活动融为一体,成了各大节日表演节目单上的常客。现在蒋村船拳班队伍有200多人,兴旺着呢。

Practicing martial arts on a boat? This is Jiang Village Boat Boxing, a martial art that focuses on strengthening the body and protecting the home. It is passed down from three Shaolin monks at the start of the Qing Dynasty. The modern-day Boat Boxing preserves the martial arts skills of old time, and integrate with folk festivals, rites, temple fairs, dragon dances, lion dances and stilts, among other traditional performance forms. It's a regular sight at performances for large holidays. The Jiang Village Boat Boxing Team has over 200 members even now, and is quite active.

地域·物产
Areas and Products

民间圣音"楼塔细十番"
Ten Pieces of Instruments at the Tower

杭州萧山楼塔细十番是明朝宫廷御医楼英辞官返乡，和一批善音律乐器的文人雅士，以笛、管、箫、弦、提琴、云锣、汤锣、木鱼、檀板、大鼓十种乐器共同演奏各种古典套曲产生的。凡逢年过节均免费为百姓演出，曲牌主要为歌颂大禹治水之功德。如果你去楼塔亲耳听一听，那么一定会有"余音绕梁，三日不绝"之感。

Performances at the tower in Xiaoshan of Hangzhou date from the time a retiring royal doctor of the Ming Dynasty was back to his hometown. He organized a group of musicians and performed with ten instruments, namely three kinds of flutes, two stringed instruments, an array of small gongs, a large gong, a wooden fish, a hardwood clapper, and a large drum. They performed all manner of songs. In later years the tradition continued, with the musicians performing for free at holidays for the common people, usually songs extolling the merits of King Yu taming the flood. If you have the opportunity to go to the tower and listen for yourself, you'll definitely not be disappointed.

萧山萝卜干
Dried Carrots of Xiaoshan

萝卜干是萧山农业传统名产，至今已有一百多年历史。传统萝卜干采用"风脱水"加工法，原料以"一刀切"萝卜品种为主。制作工艺包括清洗切条、翻晒、拌料腌制和储藏。近年来，当地企业又开发出甜萝卜干、辣萝卜干和盐渍萝卜干等新品，还引进了日韩优质萝卜品种作为原料。生产方式也完全规模化、标准化。

Carrots are one of the traditional agricultural specialties of Xiaoshan, with more than a hundred years of history. Traditionally, the carrots were air-dried, with a specific "one-knife-cut" variety being used. They were first cleaned and then cut into strips before being dried and seasoned. In recent years, sweet, spicy and salted dried carrots have appeared, and some have been made with premium carrots imported from Japan and Korea. The production has been completely scaled and standardised.

摄影：施麟麒

微观杭州
HANGZHOU: TRADITION AND MODERN TIMES

虎跑的铁杆粉
Running Tiger

凌晨4点半,天蒙蒙亮,80岁的杭州人沈寅初已早早起床。5点钟,他手拎水壶,坐上公交车前往虎跑公园取水。沈老回忆说,60年前,尚无公交车直达,每天早晨他步行3小时来此打水。这些年,陪伴他的家人从父母变成了儿女,唯一不变的是每天一桶虎跑水。"虎跑水水质纯,味道好,我家泡茶、烧饭都用这水。"

At 4 in the morning, before the sun's started to rise, the 80-year-old Hangzhou native Shen Yinchu has already awoken. At 5, kettle in hand, he takes the bus to Running Tiger Park to retrieve water. He remembers that 60 years before, when there were still no public transit systems, he would walk a three-hour round trip each day for water. These years, rather than his parents accompanying him it is his children. The only thing that hasn't changed is the daily pot of water from Running Tiger. "It's good quality water, it tastes nice. For making tea, making rice, this is the stuff I always use."

主编供稿

玉兰花
Magnolia Flowers

很多城市都种植玉兰,但杭州的玉兰貌似与众不同。杭州地处江南,日光不强,雨水充足;几千年的文化沉淀,让这座城市多了一份典雅与含蓄之气。而这些都让杭州的玉兰显得格外空灵、多变。开心时,她是灿烂的天使;忧郁时,她是幽怨的女子;你送她一颦,她还你一笑。一切都与城市的诗化气质暗合。

Many cities plant magnolias, but those in Hangzhou are different. As a southern city without strong sunlight yet with plentiful rain, millennia of cultural development have turned the city to a refined and reserved metropolis. This has made the magnolias of Hangzhou flexible and varied. When happy, they are shimmering angels; when sad, they are young girls with bitterness in their hearts; when you smile they will smile back. They are in sync with the poetic nature of the city.

江南铜屋
Copper House

这里没有铜金属，有的只是艺术品。江南铜屋又名朱炳仁铜雕艺术博物馆，坐落于杭州历史名街——河坊街上。馆内各厅独具匠心，颂雅厅、福荫厅、佛香阁、琳宇厅，处处都是铜的海洋。这里的每一扇门窗、每一件家具或装饰品所闪烁的铜光，不仅是艺术的闪光点，更是对创作者精湛、超人技艺的充分肯定与高度认可。

The Hangzhou region doesn't yield copper, and it's only seen in artistic works. The Jiangnan "Copper House" is also known as the Zhu Bingren Copper Sculpture Museum, and is located on the famous artistic Hefang Street in Hangzhou. Each hall inside displays unique ingenuity, from the Songya and Fuyin to Foxiang and Linyu halls – an ocean of copper. Each door, window, each piece of furniture and accessory is shining with the light of copper. They are not simply nice pieces to look at, but are also testaments to the meticulousness, artistic skill and high degree of expertise held by their makers.

摄影：梅莹

微观杭州
HANGZHOU: TRADITION AND MODERN TIMES

杭州天堂伞
Heavenly Umbrellas of Hangzhou

伞这个名词，出现在我国南北朝时期，在此之前，都称为"盖"。人们常说"上有天堂，下有苏杭"，那么在有"人间天堂"之称的杭州，自然就要用"天堂伞"了。天堂伞素以轻、新、牢、美著称，产品质量和技术工艺代表了当今世界先进水平。如此好伞，大家又怎肯轻易错过呢。所以，不仅仅杭州人在用天堂伞，全世界都在用。

The now-modern nomenclature for umbrellas came into use in China at the time of the Northern and Southern Dynasties. A well-known phrase "Heaven in the sky, Hangzhou and Suzhou on Earth" would point to the fact that Hangzhou is "heaven on earth", so of course the umbrellas produced there are heavenly, too. They are light, up-to-date, strong, and beautiful, and are testaments to the state-of-the-art technical and artistic expertise. You shouldn't miss out on the opportunity to try one of them. They're not just for people of Hangzhou, they can be enjoyed by anyone in the world.

"小阿六头"
Little Liu Tou

要说杭州的"小阿六头""老豇豆"，不少杭州市民都非常熟悉，老熟人啦。翁屹涛，小小伢儿是童星。他两岁就会对着电视模仿说杭州话，嘴巴甜得不得了，特别招人喜欢。再加上外公是地地道道的杭州人，见外孙这般有天赋，索性做起了专门的"写手"。有关老杭州的故事，经"小阿六头"一说，还真是乐趣无穷。

Many people in Hangzhou are familiar with "Little Liu Tou" and "Old Cowpea". Weng Yitao is a child star – when he was only two years old he would imitate the Hangzhou dialect while watching TV, which others found quite cute. When his grandfather, who is a Hangzhou native, saw his performance, he decided to take up writing stories for his grandson to perform. They have become quite popular in recent years.

杭州竹篮
Hangzhou's Bamboo Baskets

要说杭州的土特产，竹篮得算上。在没有塑料袋之前，江沪地区使用的竹篮都产自杭州，"黄山篮"就是杭州的一个品牌。老杭州人对竹篮多少都了解。西溪盛产竹子，编竹篮是这一带村民的拿手活儿。村民挑着竹篮进城售卖曾是一道流动的风景，随着塑料袋的出现，这道风景已经消逝了。

Bamboo baskets are one of the first few things to come to mind when talking about Hangzhou's traditional products. Before the advent of plastics, the bamboo baskets used in the region were products of Hangzhou, with "Huangshan Basket" being a popular Hangzhou brand. Old people of Hangzhou know all about these baskets. The West Creek produces large amounts of bamboo, and producing baskets was a specialty of the villagers around there. Villagers walking into the city with baskets for hawking was a common scence, but as plastic bags became available, this industry gradually fell to the wayside.

摄影：林国强

微观杭州
HANGZHOU: TRADITION AND MODERN TIMES

江南雨伞
Jiangnan Umbrellas

都说烟雨蒙蒙的江南处处是故事。"她彷徨在寂寥的雨巷,撑着油纸伞……"这样的诗句总让人情不自禁想起江南。近日,抽时间来到杭州中国伞博物馆,放眼望去,果然别有韵味。不同于北方伞的粗犷,烟雨江南衍生出来的伞更加轻巧、细致,不带一丝市井之气。难怪它会成为诗人的宠儿,成为众多爱情故事的见证者。

There are many stories of the mist and rain in the Jiangnan region. "As she wandered towards a desolate rainy alley, she held an oil-paper umbrella…" These kinds of works always make one think of Jiangnan. These days, one may take some time to visit the China Umbrella Museum in Hangzhou and be swept away with poetic feelings when looking around inside. Unlike the rough, coarse umbrellas of the north, those derived from the needs of the Jiangnan area are lighter, more delicate, and free of an urban feel. It's no wonder they've become popular topics for poetry and frequently appear in love stories.

大井巷
Dajing Lane

大井巷与河坊街只一墙之隔,却是喧嚣与宁静两个世界。大井巷的房子大多依山而建,面街而筑。翻新的老街中,灰黑的电线和电表箱以及灰泥剥落的老墙,是时间经过留下的脚印。在这里还增添了许多现代元素,那就是极具文艺范儿的小店以及咖啡馆。巷内的钱塘第一井见证着这现代和古老的矛盾体。

A wall is all that separates Dajing Lane and Hefang Street, but the difference between the bustle of one and quiet of the other is two worlds. Most of the houses on Dajing Lane are built into mountains, facing the street. Upon the renovated old street, black and grey cables and electricity boxes and the old wall scraped of dust and mud serve as reminders of different eras. There are a number of modern elements in the scene, too, such as cute little shops and cafes. The existence of the first well in the Qiantang area serves as evidence of the contrast between modern and old.

杭帮菜
Hangzhou Cuisine

近几年来杭帮菜大行其道,北京、上海的高档酒店,都打出杭帮菜这面旗帜。何谓杭帮菜?它的内涵和特点是什么?以杭帮菜式中几款代表素菜烧二冬、油焖笋、干炸响铃等为例,可以用苏东坡的词来概括杭帮菜的内涵:"蓼茸蒿笋试春盘,人间有味是清欢!"杭帮菜不刺激,不讲噱头,追求平淡、简单和真实。

In recent years Hangzhou cuisine has gained popularity, with high-end restaurants in Beijing and Shanghai claiming to serve it. Just what is Hangzhou cuisine? What is it about, what does it contain? There are a few representative dishes you can try out: braised black mushrooms with bamboo shoots, yellow braised fresh mushroom, fried stuffed bean curd paste, to name a few. Even the famous Su Dongpo praised the vegetable dishes of Hangzhou in his poetry. Hangzhou cuisine eschews strong and pungent flavours for a mild, simple and real flavour.

西湖·印象
West Lake and Impressions

摄影：陈心远

微观杭州
HANGZHOU: TRADITION AND MODERN TIMES

夜西湖
The West Lake at Night

"晴湖不如雨湖，雨湖不如夜湖"，这是老辈杭州人说到西湖的一句话，其实今日也如此。春日夜雨，游人多半寥寥，撑一把不大的伞，从断桥沿白堤一路缓缓走去，看两边楼阁暖暖的灯在波光里闪烁，再回首望，不远处宝石山上的华灯衬着树梢俏影。或独自漫步，或约二三好友漫天闲话，都别有趣味。

The lake on a clear day isn't as nice as on a rainy one, and the lake on a rainy day isn't as nice as the lake at night – this is something that the older generation in Hangzhou all says, and it's true. On a rainy spring night travellers decorate the lake, holding small umbrellas in hand, walking from the Broken Bridge to the White Cuaseway at a leisurely pace, light from the buildings on both sides reflecting in the ripples on the water, with the lamplight among the trees on Gem Mountain visible in the distance. Some walk alone, some a couple of friends, chatting idly. It rivals walking among the shade of the green poplars.

摄影：杜红英

浴鹄湾
Yuhu Bay

这不是个"一旦相逢，就会刻骨铭心"的地方，但是一个看一眼就一辈子不会忘记的地方。茅亭，浅流，平静的湖水，不高峻的青黛黛的平和的山，罕见游人，也没有行人。坐在茅亭里，你可以发思古之幽情，也可以什么都不想，就看看山，看看水，看看水里的你自己。

Not a place bathed in poetic poignancy that will carve itself upon your heart at first gaze, this is still an unforgettable site to visit. Pavilions among rushes, shallow flows and calm lake waters among low-lying verdant peaks – travellers are rare here, and pedestrians absent. Sitting in an old-style pavilion, you can muse over things of ancient times, or you can clear your mind and simply look at the scenery and your reflection in the lake water.

西湖·印象
West Lake and Impressions

雪湖热游
Snowy Lake, Hot Trip

崇祯五年，张岱记西湖："大雪三日，湖中人鸟声俱绝……惟长堤一痕，湖心亭一点。"今日若大雪，湖中鸟声必绝，人声则必日夜不绝。白日，湖边亭桥水榭人满无插足处；夜晚，张岱的"余舟一芥，舟中人两三粒而已"的幽寂也无存。不过，现今杭人均好这雪湖热游，自誉曰："杭儿风。"

In 1632, the 15th year of the reign of Chongzhen Emperor, Zhang Dai wrote of the West Lake: "After three days of snow, there are no people on the lake, not even the sound of birds... Only a long causeway and some traces of the pagodas are reflected in the lake". In present days, when it snows the birds stop singing but there are still people there, day and night. On the bridges, in the pagodas, and on the waterside pavilions there are people everywhere. Zhang Dai's accounts of "only two or three boats on the lake" no longer apply. Don't be discouraged, however, as it's a lively scene and not to be missed.

十里荷花
Lotus Flower

"三秋桂子，十里荷花"，柳永这句引金主投鞭南下的词是写实的。杭州荷花确乎多。夏日逛西湖，看荷是必须的。走在桐荫蔽日的北山路，放眼看去，成片的荷叶荷花随路直路转，一会儿浓密得翠盖压湖，一会儿又疏散错落，不似"无穷碧"那么单调。紫禁城的荷花养在缸里，不过再大再多的缸，也养不出这十里的风情。

"The osmanthus blooms in the autumn, and the lotus flowers extend for miles" – this is a description written of the area by Northern Song poet Liu Yong, and it remains true today. Hangzhou has many lotus blossoms. When visiting the West Lake in summer, you must admire the lotus blossoms. Walking in the shade of the paulownia trees along Beishan Road, you can see lotus plants and blossoms all along, sometimes in dense patches upon the lake, sometimes growing sparsely – more character than simple "endless green". The lotus of the Forbidden City in the capital are raised in pots, but no matter how large of a pot you have, you can't recreate such a scene as in Hangzhou.

摄影：俞燕君

微观杭州
HANGZHOU: TRADITION AND MODERN TIMES

主编供稿

西湖记忆
Memories of the West Lake

立于柳浪闻莺的深处,望着远处的西湖。当年摘花的孩提,如今已成为种花的青年;而当年种花的青年,现在却背上行囊,志在八方;时光荏苒,白驹过隙,当年远走他方的青年,早已经成为耄耋老人,在夕阳下垂垂老去。湖仍是那片湖,树仍是这些树,到底谁才是这里的主人?

I remember standing at the West Lake, at a site known for being suited to listening to orioles singing in the willows, looking far out over the West Lake. From being a young child picking flowers to a youth planting them to me now, walking with a travelling pack upon my back. Time passes quickly, and the youths of then are now old me, living under the setting sun. The lake is still there, as are the trees – who is the owner of this place?

桥未断,为何叫断桥?
The Unbroken Broken Bridge

西湖白堤东段有一座桥,叫断桥,很有名。桥未断,却叫断桥,为什么呢?或曰冬雪之时桥面无雪,形似断桥。窃以为,是晴日阳光照射水面,波光潋滟,反射到桥身,明暗晃动,桥似乎断裂了,因此呼其为"断桥"。加上传奇的爱情故事《白蛇传》的主人公白娘子和许仙在此缘断,增强了"断"的悲剧色彩。

There is a bridge on the White Causeway of the West Lake called the Broken Bridge which is quite famous. What is the reason for its name? On snowy winter days, no snow lies on the bridge, making it appear broken. In my humble opinion, it's that on clear days sunlight reflects off the water and spills on to the bridge, and the light and dark contrast makes it look like a part broken. Added to this is the love story of Lady Bai, in which the two characters part at this bridge – the bridge may appear broken, but their feelings for each other are not.

西湖·印象
WEST LAKE AND IMPRESSIONS

孤山，孤还是不孤?
Is the Lonely Mountain Lonely?

西湖西北部有一个孤岛，称为孤山。不知何时，人们在孤山的西边造了座西泠桥，与宝石山脚的北山路西段衔接；向着东边，造了条白堤，在断桥与北山路东段连接，于是，孤山也就不再孤了。从原本的孤独，到现在的不再孤单，寄托着世人不愿孤单的情怀，于是就有了"孤山不孤"的说法，成全了人们美好的愿望。

To the northwest of the West Lake lies an island, called Mount Gu ("Lonely Mountain"). At some time, the Xiling Bridge was built, connecting the foot of Gem Mountain to the western portion of Beishan Road. To the east, the White Causeway was constructed, connecting the Broken Bridge to the eastern portion of Beishan Road. Therefore, the Lonely Mountain was no longer lonely. The relief of the loneliness of the mountain reflects the human desire to not be alone, and the well-known phrase "the Lonely Mountain is not lonely" is a reminder of this sentiment.

杨公堤
Yang Gong Causeway

毕业时，和好友来了兴致，决定步行绕西湖走一圈，最后走到一处长堤边，累得丢盔卸甲的老友执意休息，借口是想让我知道这条长堤的来历。传说这条长堤是当年杭州一杨姓郡守，看西湖被围造田，几近毁灭，就开始疏浚，挖出的淤泥除了修补苏堤，都堆积起来，筑起一条与苏堤相对的长堤，便是今天的"杨公堤"。

When I graduated, my friends and I decided to take a walk around the West Lake. When we got to this long causeway, one of my very tired friends insisted we rest, saying that he wanted to tell me the origin of the causeway as an excuse. It's said that an official surnamed Yang looked over the fields around the West Lake, and seeing their encroachment, started to dredge and deepen the waterways to repair the Su Causeway, and build a new causeway to pair with it. It is thus called Yang Gong Causeway.

摄影：夏利亚

微观杭州
HANGZHOU: TRADITION AND MODERN TIMES

西湖的水，我的泪
My Tears Are the Water of the West Lake

白蛇传里的这句歌词如今都成了这个漫长雨季的吐槽必备了，几个同学打趣说道："白素贞，许仙他不在这里，就别再下雨了。洗了一个星期的背心，现在还没晾干呢？"小师妹说："杭州真是一座水做的城市，你说这雨会不会把杭州的水都下没了？"我笑道："古有杞人忧天，今有你脑洞大开啊。"

The words of the famous song attributed to Lady Bai have become a common phrase to complain about the long-lasting rainfalls in the area. Students jokingly compose verses: "Lady Bai Suzhen, Xu Xian is not here, so please do not cry. We've washed our vestments for a week, shall you not give them time to dry in the sun?" A female classmate of mine says: "Hangzhou is a city made of water, with this rain do you not fear drowning it?" I smile as I think of my classmate worrying about the weather just as the person in ancient times thought the sky might fall.

北山路秋梧桐的震撼
Parasol Trees along Beishan Road in Autumn

最爱北山街的秋，尤爱那湖边美得令人窒息的法国梧桐，它用满树的金黄与湖中残荷互相映照，然后在风起时恋恋不舍地飘落，拥抱大地。而眼前这一排密密交织在一起的梧桐叶子，就如火烧过一般，是半焦的黄褐色，如漫天云霞，又如飘荡的火苗，呈现出无与伦比的美丽，令人有生命辉煌之震撼而绝无秋日萧条之感！

I love autumn of Beishan Road the most, and especially love the beautiful parasol trees along the road at the time. The lake reflects their golden leaves among the fading lotuses, and when the wind blows their leaves fall gracefully upon the ground. The trees before my eyes, branches intertwined, look like they are on fire, a mass of brown-yellow like a sky of fiery clouds. Their beauty isn't one of desolation or wilting as one might normally think of the fall, but rather a vibrant, fiery life.

摄影：俞燕君

西湖·印象
West Lake and Impressions

摄影：郑若琪

白娘子的雷峰塔
Leifeng Pagoda and Lady Bai

虽然现在的雷峰塔是那么摩登、现代，全然没有人们记忆中"雷峰夕照"应有的历史沉淀和岁月侵蚀的痕迹，但人们似乎并不在意。他们更多的是为了追忆白娘子而来到这里，并不在乎旧时的雷峰塔是怎样的，只要它在这里，只要它叫雷峰塔就可以了。有塔在，心中白娘子和许仙千年忠贞的爱情就在。

The Leifeng Pagoda is now quite modern; in current times nobody thinks of the "sun setting over Leifeng" and the historical significance or saga of the ravages of time. Instead, people come here to seek out Lady Bai, or the Lady of the White Snake. People don't worry about how the Leifeng Pagoda looked in times past – as long as it is there, and it's called Leifeng Pagoda, well, then Lady Bai and Xu Xian's love a thousand years ago was real, as it is a famous site in the story.

西湖船娘
The Girl's Boat of the West Lake

到西湖坐船，一定要叫船娘的手摇船。无论是水光潋滟的晴日，还是山色空蒙的雨天，坐着手摇船在西湖上慢慢欣赏美景。船尾，是身着水绿色的窄长袖、白底蓝花的前襟后背，头戴蓝色头巾的船娘。恍惚间，让人感觉像是穿越到了"西湖水滑多娇娘"的宋朝。西湖船娘与手摇船，构筑了柔美西湖的独特风景。

If you take a boat on the West Lake, you should definitely try a kind of paddleboat called the "Girl's Boat". Whether it's during a bright, sunlight day or rainy day with the hills shrouded in mist, taking one of these boats on the lake is a great way to enjoy the beautiful scenery upon the West Lake. At the aft of the boat, there is a girl with narrow long green sleeves, a white blouse decorated with blue flowers, and a blue scarf upon her head. It reminds one of the descriptions of beautiful maidens upon the waters of the West Lake in the Song Dynasty. These "Girl's Boats" and paddleboats are a part of the uniquely beautiful scenery upon the West Lake.

微观杭州
HANGZHOU: TRADITION AND MODERN TIMES

长桥不长，为何叫长桥？
The Not-long Long Bridge

杭州西湖，有一座桥，叫长桥。为什么叫长桥？长桥有多长？无从考证了。传说梁山伯与祝英台在万松书院读书，分手时十八里相送，就在这桥上作别。你送我，我送你，缠缠绵绵，在桥上不知道走了多少个来回，一座小桥，走成了长桥，故此就叫"长桥"了。"长"就是情深意长的意思吧。

On the West Lake in Hangzhou there is a bridge called the "Long Bridge", but why? How long is it? There is no textual evidence for this name. According to stories, when Liang Shanbo and Zhu Yingtai studied at the Wansong Academy, they accompanied each other for 18 li when parting, and said their final farewells at this bridge. They walked the bridge many times back and forth, having a long journey upon a short structure, making the distance feel greater. Thus we can see "long" is to be taken to mean having deep feelings.

摄影：俞燕君

西湖的山
The Mountains of the West Lake

山有两大类：一是高峻险拔隐居于世外的，如闽西的高山，终年云雾缭绕，美则美矣，却只能惊鸿一瞥；一是像西湖周围的山，海拔从几十米到五百米不等，可远观，可近昵。我更喜欢后者。西湖周围比较有名的山有烟霞岭、凤凰山、吴山、灵隐山、北高峰、栖霞岭、宝石山等，它们在西湖水的滋养下，灵秀无比。

There are two main kinds of mountains: the first are high-peaked mountains that are far from our noisy modern world, such as those in western Fujian, surrounded by clouds and mist all year long. They are beautiful, but we only rarely get glimpses of them. The second is the kind of mountain that surrounds the West Lake, with heights of a few dozen to less than five hundred metres. They afford nice view and are approachable. I prefer the latter kind of mountain. The more famous of the peaks around the West Lake, such as the Yanxia Peak, Phoenix Mountain, Mount Wu, Lingyin Mountain, Beigao Peak, Qixia Peak, Gem Mountain and the like are nourished by the water of the lake, delicately beautiful and elegant.

西湖·印象
West Lake and Impressions

花港红鲤
Red Carp in the Flower Harbour

说起"花港",马上就会想到成千上万条金红色的鲤鱼。传说它们是鱼龙公主的后代。鱼龙是南海龙王之女,因贪恋西湖美景被捕,好心的渔夫将她放生,为报恩与渔夫成亲。后被龙王抓回,渔夫思念妻子,日夜对海呼唤,鱼龙把一双儿女(红鲤鱼)送来陪伴渔夫。从此鲤鱼代代繁衍,"花港观鱼"成为西湖十景之一。

When one mentions the "flower harbour" the first thing that comes to mind are the thousands upon thousands of red carp that swim in it. According to legend, they are the descendants of the Fish Princess. The Fish Princess was the daughter of the Dragon King of the South Sea, who was arrested for being covetous of the beautiful scenery of the West Lake. A good-hearted fisherman set her free, and to thank him, she married him. She was later abducted by the Dragon King, and the fisher, longing for her called out to the sea day and night. The Fish Princess sent a pair of red carp to accompany him. The descendants of these fish are the ones that fill the Flower Harbour.

一树桃花一树柳
Peach Blossoms and Willows

桃红柳绿,西湖的春天,美不胜收。"一树桃花一树柳,落红尽在水波中。"西湖的苏堤、白堤及周边,莫不是一树桃花一树柳。柳树长得高大,柳枝婆娑飘逸,两株柳树之间,会有很大的距离,显得空荡荡的。桃树比较矮小,种在中间,弥补了空隙,增添了色彩,真是绝妙。何时形成了这独特风景,则无从考究了。

The red of peaches and green of willows, the West Lake in the spring – these are beautiful sights. Classical poems have been written that praise the reflections of the trees in the lake. Around the Su Causeway and White Causeway, these trees are everywhere. Willows are tall, with long handing branches that sway elegantly. Between two willows there is a large gap, which may feel empty. Peach trees, by contrast, are shorter, and can be planted between them to fill this space and add some colour for a nice effect. Who knows when this beautiful scene was created?

摄影:俞燕君

微观杭州
HANGZHOU: TRADITION AND MODERN TIMES

风月无边
Gentle Breeze and Bright Moonlight

船在西湖湖心亭靠岸，游走之下，石头上"虫二"两字引起大家的注意，原来该字为当年乾隆所题，寓意"风月无边"。"虫二"取自"风月"二字的繁体。风月二字的繁体去掉外面轮廓后剩下虫字加一撇和二，因为没有"一虫加一撇"这个字，便口口相传读作"虫二"，用来形容风景优美，景色宜人。

Docking a boat at the mid-lake pavilion of the West lake, stepping out, there is an inscription that everyone will notice: "Chong'er" – meaning *insect two*. They come from a saying in the Qianlong period of the Qing Dynasty, *The wonders of the natural scenery, the gentle breeze and bright moonlight, are boundless*. The characters for "breeze" and "moonlight" contain the characters of "insect" and "two", and thus the inscription is a kind of play on words or riddle that reminds people of the saying and the natural beauty that surrounds.

西湖又叫什么湖？
Other Names of the West Lake

湖在城的西部，人们习惯称它为西湖。杭州最早叫钱塘，也曾叫钱塘湖。郦道元的《水经注》记载，涌金门外湖中有金牛出现，于是又叫它金牛湖。苏轼写道"欲把西湖比西子，淡妆浓抹总相宜"，所以又叫西子湖，也叫情人湖。还有不少其他名称，可见人们爱西湖的程度。

The lake is situated in the west of the city, and is commonly known as the West Lake. Hangzhou was originally called Qiantang, and the lake was called the Qiantang Lake. Li Daoyuan of the Northern Wei Dynasty in his *Commentary on the Waterways* wrote that the lake outside of the Yongjin Gate had yellow cows appear, and thus it was called the Yellow Cow Lake. Su Shi compared the lake to famous classical beauty Xi Shi in his poem "The West Lake looks like the fair lady Xi Shi at her best. Whether she is richly adorned or plainly dressed." It was then called Xi Zi Lake, or Lover's Lake. It has also been known by a number of other names, which shows how popular it is.

摄影：许雷梅

西湖·印象
WEST LAKE AND IMPRESSIONS

摄影：俞燕君

丰子恺与西湖杨柳
Feng Zikai and the Willows of the West Lake

丰子恺有处旧居名为"小杨柳屋"，其漫画随处可见杨柳的点缀，可见他对杨柳的偏爱。但真正让画家悟出其精神意蕴的，却是西湖杨柳。他在西湖边长椅上休息时，看见湖岸杨柳树"好像挂着几万串嫩绿的珠子，在温暖的春风中飘来飘去，飘出许多弯度微微的S线"，感其"高而不忘本"的精神，于是写下《杨柳》一文加以盛赞。

Feng Zikai used to live in a house called the "Small Willow House." His drawings frequently include willows, which show his love for this tree. However, what really the artist came to realise their spirits was the willows of the West Lake. As he would sit by the West Lake in a long chair, he would look upon the willows. He once wrote of them in a piece he called *Willows* – "It's as if one looks upon myriad strings of green pearls, swaying back and forth in the warm spring wind."

南宋御街
Southern Song Imperial Street

南宋御街是南宋都城铺设的一条主要街道。这里有很多仿古建筑，建筑里面是现代化的店铺，还有很多老字号的店，像胡庆余堂、方回春堂、张小泉剪刀坊等。在这里你可以品品茶，把把古玩，逛逛特色店，吃遍小吃一条街。古老的建筑、百年老店都在以自己的方式向你诉说着前尘过往。

The Southern Song Imperial Street is a major road of the Southern Song Capital. There are many replica antique buildings here, and some modern shops in them, and many locations of famous old Chinese brands, such as Hu Qingyu Tang, Fang Huichun Tang, both pharmacies, Zhang Xiaoquan, a manufacturer of scissors, and others. Here you can try tea, see antiques, visit specialty shops and visit the snack street. The antique buildings and brands of centuries past give you a feeling of a former time.

微观杭州
HANGZHOU: TRADITION AND MODERN TIMES

摄影：李选

莲滩鹭影
Herons on the Lotus Beach

此次出行正值夏末，只收获了莲滩鹭影中的"莲滩"胜景，无幸得见鹭鸟飞翔天际。那静静的水面上铺的几片荷叶安然地托着几朵睡莲，心里的喧嚣瞬间被净化。虽未得见鹭影，但这里的莲花滩生态保护区，绿水萦绕，野趣纷呈，已然成为了各种湿地生物的天堂。

This time I visited the Lotus Beach, it was at the end of summer. I was only able to see the beautiful scenery of the beach, but missed out on the birds flying against the sky. A few lotuses sat upon the still water surface, blossoms upon them. The disquiet of my heart was calmed. Although I was unable to see the herons, the ecological reserve was still a great site to see. With its green water, here becomes a heaven for numerous wetland animals.

十里锒铛
Ten-Li Chain

人人尽说江南好，我问江南哪里好？是啊，江南的美景灵秀多端，但是总觉少了脊梁。直到来到十里锒铛岭，在这九曲十八弯的山岭中，我才体验到南宋王城的龙脉。崇山峻岭，茂林修竹，清流激湍。找个闲暇的日子，登锒铛，瞰西子，远离喧嚣，呼吸点绿树间的负氧离子。真是饱足了眼福，惊叹江南美如画！

People all speak well of the Jiangnan area, I return there and ask how so? Yes, there are many beautiful sceneries in the area, but I always feel it lacks a backbone. It was only when I went to the Ten-Li Chain Peak, and walked through all the curving peaks and ridges that I found that backbone. The peaks are numerous and tall, the forests and bamboo are thick, and the feeling is one of mightiness and austerity. Wait for a day you've free time, climb the mountain, look down upon the city and enjoy being away from the clamour of it all. Breathe in clean air among green trees, and you'll think: "My, this really is a great sight, the Jiangnan region truly has sights to see!"

西湖·印象
WEST LAKE AND IMPRESSIONS

夜探宝石
Searching for Gems in the Night

听闻杭州有一座山名曰宝石山，因此名而对之向往颇深。世间自然不会有镶满宝石的山，只因山上之石含氧化铁，在日光映照下仿佛满山皆是玛瑙，故得此名。但在我心中，宝石山的美名更得之于夜晚时分的她，夜游宝石山是杭州人民的一大爱，与三五友人相约，登山而坐，饮茶赏月，灯光之下此山便犹如宝石林立。

There is a famous "Gem Mountain" in Hangzhou, and there is a deep meaning to the name. It isn't covered in gemstones, but as the mountain contains large quantities of ferric oxide, under the sunlight it glimmers as if made of agate. This is the reason for the ancient name. However, in my heart, Gem Mountain's name is more suited to it at night. Walking the mountain at night is an activity beloved by the people of Hangzhou. Meeting with a few friends, climbing the mountain and observing the moon, one feels the mountain is even more like a gem under its light.

秋芦飞雪
Rushes in the Autumn, Flying Snow

如果你面前是一片水光粼粼的芦苇荡，那片片芦花定能让你心平如水。西溪有二绝——芦花与梅花，观芦花最佳的地点在秋雪庵。它位于蒹葭深处，四面曲水环绕，东面和南面有大面积的芦苇。每至秋季，秋雪滩上的芦花随风肆意飘荡，颇有漫天飞雪之影。若在月下，则此景更甚。

The sight of rushes swaying upon clear water is one that will surely calm your soul. The West Creek area is known for its rushes and plum blossoms, and the best place from which to view them is the Qiuxue Hut ("hut of autumn snow"). It's situated in a secluded area, surrounded by water, with a large amount of rushes to both the east and south faces. Every fall, when the wind blows, the air is filled with reed catkins, so numerous as to seem almost a blizzard. This makes the scene even more beautiful to behold.

摄影：俞蒸君

微观杭州
HANGZHOU: TRADITION AND MODERN TIMES

摄影：俞燕君

曲水寻梅
Looking for Plums among the Water

"疏影横斜水清浅，暗香浮动月黄昏"，想必梅花的倩影让古往今来的诗人大家们念念不忘。清代龚自珍曾将西溪推为江南三大赏梅区之一。这里梅树与曲岸相映，重点分布在梅竹山庄、西溪梅墅一带。因小环境的影响，这里的梅花要比城区的花时迟，等西湖梅花败落，这里的梅花才娇羞吐艳。

"The sparse shadows of plum trees are cast across the shallow water as their blossoms fall, and a fragrance floats in the air as the scene is lit by the yellow moon." Such enchanting scenes continue to delight us today as they did when the poem was penned more than a thousand years ago. Qing dynasty writer Gong Zizhen named the West Creek as one of the best places to appreciate plum blossoms in the Jiangnan area. The curved coast and plum trees here complement each other well. The trees are mainly disturbed in two areas, known as the Plum and Bamboo Mountain Village, and the West Creek Plum Tree Villa. Because of very local environmental factors, these plum trees bloom later than those in the city, showing their beautiful colours only after the blossoms upon the West Lake have already fallen.

回归富春山居的恬静
Tranquility on Mount Fuchun

看过《富春山居图》的人肯定对电影中的画面有深刻的印象，那恬静的山水就存在于富春山桃源之中，富春山桃源位于杭州富阳，景区以"山之清、水之秀、林之茂、洞之奇、村之静"让人充分享受桃花源式的休闲生活乐趣。苍翠欲滴的山峦，诗画般的村落田园，碧波万顷的湖面，每一个场景都让人沉醉。

Those who have seen the *A Residence upon Mount Fuchun* are impressed by the scenery in the film, the quiet which exists upon Mount Fuchun in the Taoyuan area. It is located in Fuyang District in Hangzhou, and is known for its mountains, water, forests, caves, and villages. People enjoy a relaxed lifestyle here, surrounded by excellent natural landscapes, green mountains, picturesque villages, and stunning lake, all sights intoxicate the viewers.

西湖·印象
West Lake and Impressions

摄影：陈心远

一座山的守望
Mountain View

一座山守望着一座城，见证着城市的发展变迁，从白天的忙碌到夜晚的宁静。站在宝石山山顶，可将杭州的美景一览无余，山的一面是西湖边宁静的景色，一面是城西万家灯火的风貌。夜晚的宝石山被盘山路灯照亮，保俶塔则像一把银剑直指夜空。虽然山高仅 78 米，但夜爬宝石山却是杭州人民热衷的休闲方式。

There is a mountain that watches over the city, observing its developments and changes, from the busy day to the quiet night. Standing on the peak, you can take a view of all of Hangzhou at once. To one side of the mountain is the calm view of the West Lake, and to the other side are the lamps and lights of a myriad families in the western portion of the city. Gem Mountain at night is lit by the streetlights of roads circling it, and the Baochu Pagoda appears like a silver sword pointing towards the sky. Gem Mountain is only 78 metres tall, and climbing it at night is a means of relaxing for the residents of the city.

西湖的观法
Viewing the West Lake

明人汪珂玉曾说："西湖之胜，晴湖不如雨湖，雨湖不如月湖，月湖不如雪湖，能真正领山水之绝者，尘世有几人哉！"仿佛西湖知音唯他一人。此语流传甚广，后人也以为西湖之美有时令之差。其实通达如苏轼早已有诗："欲把西湖比西子，淡妆浓抹总相宜。"可见观西湖之法，只可境随心转，切不可执着于外境。

Wang Keyu of the Ming Dynasty once said, "What's nice about the West Lake is that it looks better in the rain than on a clear day, and even better under moonlight, yet better still among the snow. How many others could comprehend this scenery in this world?" He was one of the best appreciators of the West Lake. His words were disseminated, and it became known that the beauty of the lake was seasonal. However, Su Shi made his observation in his poem many centuries before, when he remarked that "the West Lake looks like the fair lady Xi Shi at her best. Whether she is richly adorned or plainly dressed". To appreciate the lake one must take it in with the heart rather than just the eyes.

微观杭州
HANGZHOU: TRADITION AND MODERN TIMES

摄影：梅莹

音乐喷泉
Musical Fountains

见过很多音乐喷泉，都没杭州的好看。西湖边的音乐喷泉是多彩的，但各种颜色并不同时发出。它踏着舞步整齐、优雅地、一波一波地亮起，而这些彩色水柱宛如一个个身材曼妙、舞技高超的艺术家，随着音乐婉转起舞，或站起或后仰或踢腿或弯腰或缓或急，让人恍若置身一座大舞台。难怪每天都有那么多人围观呢！

I've seen a number of musical fountains, but none rivals that of Hangzhou. The one on the West Lake is multi-coloured, but not all the colours appear at once. The action of the fountain is synchronised with the music, elegant and enticing as wave after wave of bright water burst forth. The pillars of illuminated water resemble the lithe and graceful body of a skilled dancer, moving with the music, standing, reclining, kicking or bending, slowly or rapidly, making the lake scene look like a stage of its own. It's no wonder so many people turn up to watch each day!

纳凉圣地 紫来洞
The Best Place to Cool off

位于玉皇山半山腰上的紫来洞是西湖景区中夏天最凉快的地方，洞中气温只有十四五度。老杭州们会带上自制的各种卤味、水果、花生等，在这里一待就是一天。"不要说我们这些年纪大的喜欢来这里乘凉，就连小年轻也喜欢来这里度周末呢，因为洞中开通了无线网络了，"一周最少要来这里五天的陈奶奶如是说。

Situated upon the mid-level reaches of the Jade Emperor Mountain, the Purple Cave is the best place in the West Lake Scenic Area to cool off in summer. The temperature inside the cave reaches only fourteen or fifteen degrees. Locals of Hangzhou will bring braised dishes, fruits, peanuts and other snacks and spend an entire summer day here. "Don't say that cooling off here is just for the elderly, as young people like to come here too and pass the weekend. We even have WiFi here" – so remarks an older woman surnamed Chen, who will spend at least five days a week at the Purple Cave.

西湖·印象
West Lake and Impressions

西湖猫
The Cats of the West Lake

一股香味飘来,才发现树的后面有一位中年大妈,正温声细语说着什么。诧异走近,原来她正在喂养两只花猫。嘴角扬起,继续西湖之行。即将迈上苏堤,又看到一位游客正轻声唤着几只黑猫,原来他要把食物分享给这些小家伙儿。我想:西湖边的猫是铁定不怕人的,很可能那高傲的性子也是西湖边上的人惯出来的呢。

A fragrant breeze blows, and I notice a middle-aged woman behind some of the trees, speaking in soft tones about something. I curiously approach, and see that she is feeding two calico cats. I smile as I continue walking along the West Lake. When I'm almost at the Su Causeway, I see a traveller calling softly to a black cat, with food to give it. I think about how the cats of the West Lake don't fear people at all, and that maybe their confident demeanour has been instilled in them by the people who frequent the lake.

摄影:董思聪

微观杭州
HANGZHOU: TRADITION AND MODERN TIMES

坐画舫和看画舫
Painted Pleasure Boats

不论晴天雨天,只要到了西湖边,一片水天中游弋的画舫是标准景象。此景常引得从没坐过船的外地游客心痒难耐,急猴猴地想立马坐上去。于是,花45块坐上画舫,先为找得临窗之座庆幸,继而便悠然满足地看起近岸远岸的游人。而近岸远岸的游人呢,也悠悠然不用买票就可看起这水天中的画舫来了。

Rain or shine, if you visit the West Lake you will see many gaily-painted pleasure boats upon it, forming a scene of their own. This scene invariably intrigues tourists from elsewhere who have never been upon one, and then rush to do so. For 45 Yuan, you can take a ride on one of these boats, and rejoice at getting a window seat as you look at the travellers all over the banks of the lake. And as you look at them, they too, on both the near and far coast, can have the pleasure of looking at your boat upon the water set against the sky.

白堤
White Causeway

当年白居易任杭州刺史时,在钱塘门外修了一条白公堤。"春桃夏柳,秋桂冬香"是白堤四季风景的写照。杭州的灵动秀丽,从一条长约两里的白堤便可得见一斑。每到三四月,白堤两侧垂柳枝条随风飘摇,柳色碧绿,映入清澄的湖面。环顾四周,山水清婉的气息恰似缕缕幽香袅袅飘来,让人有步入画中世界的感觉。

When Bai Juyi served as the feudal governor of Hangzhou, he constructed a causeway at the Qiantang Gate. "Spring sees peaches; summer, willows. Osmanthus bloom in the autumn, and winter is a time of fragrance" – this is a description of what the White Causeway has to offer in each season. The beauty and natural vitality of Hangzhou can be viewed along the approximately 1km-long causeway. Every year in March and April, the causeway is flanked on both sides by the swaying branches of willows, dark green, reflected in the clear water of the lake. The beautiful scenery will make you feel almost like stepping into a painting.

摄影:刘俊

西湖·印象
WEST LAKE AND IMPRESSIONS

摄影：程永艳

扬帆西湖
Setting Sail on the West Lake

"快看快看，梁祝化成蝴蝶向我们飞来啦。"正一起荡舟西湖上的朋友小孩忽然大喊。可不，只见远处一艘五彩缤纷的帆板正穿过桥洞向我们飞驶过来。"那是省帆板队的孩子们正在训练呢，你们今天运气好，可以看到他们扬帆西湖的身影。"碧水蓝天间，看着一艘艘越驶越近的帆板，真感觉他们像是梁祝化蝶飞回人间。

The child of a friend I'm rowing a boat with suddenly calls out: "Look, look, the butterfly lovers are flying towards us!" I look out across the lake and see the brightly coloured sails of a boat making its way towards us. "That's the boat of the provincial sailing team, currently at practice. You're lucky today to be able to see them on the lake." Against starkly blue water and sky, seeing the colourful sails of the boat approaching, I feel like the butterfly lovers really have come back to the human realm.

夜骑西湖"六吊桥"
Six Drawbridges

曾经最爱夜骑西湖"六吊桥"。晚风里，铆足劲，依次冲上映波桥、锁澜桥、望山桥、压堤桥、东浦桥、跨虹桥。一座、两座……六座，筋疲力尽时终于奋力骑过这六座桥，气喘吁吁中回望，一种人生的感慨油然而生："人生，不也如翻桥吗？翻过了一座，前面还有无数座在等着你，但只要坚持，就一定会到达彼岸。"

I used to love to ride over the "six drawbridges" of the West Lake at night. As the night breeze blew, I'd muster my strength as I rode over the Yingbo, Suolan, Wangshan, Yadi, Dongpu, and Kuahong bridges. One bridge, two bridges… six bridges, and I'd have finished the route, tired yet satisfied. One time, I looked, breathing heavily, back over the route I traced, and suddenly was gripped with emotion, thinking: "Isn't life just crossing bridges? You cross one, and see so many more ahead of you, but you have to keep going – you must make it to the other side."

微观杭州
HANGZHOU: TRADITION AND MODERN TIMES

临安大明山赏枫叶红
Red Maple Leaves

从杭州驱车一小时,就可以看到和北京香山枫叶一样美的枫叶。随着秋的盛宴完全拉开帷幕,山峦展示着热烈的风姿,令人仿佛进入了"车行十里画屏上,身走四方红叶中"的梦幻童话世界。此时的大明山,经过阳光、雨露、秋风,树都开始披上红纱,一片片叶子火红,娇艳妩媚,行走山间,可以领悟秋山的寂静。

One can enjoy views of red leaves on par with those of Beijing's famous Fragrant Hills only an hour's drive away from Hangzhou. The scene unfolds every autumn. Seeing so many peaks covered in bright red, it resembles a painted screen many miles long. Mount Daming at this time, under the sunlight, rain, mist and autumn wind is a sight which will lead you to comprehend the silence of a mountain in fall, surrounded by fiery red on all sides.

雨纷纷
Abundant Rain

杭州的雨,连连绵绵地,一下就是好几天,偶尔的晴天,燥热难当的样子,显然预告着下一场雨。尤其在六七月,赶上梅雨季节,台风横行,更是每天出门必须带伞,否则不是被暴晒就是遭雨淋。然而这时候,空气质量却是最好的,也正是欣赏烟雨中杭州的好时候,真是别有一番风情呢。

When it rains in Hangzhou, it lasts for a couple of days, and a blazingly hot day can be a harbinger of a rain to come. In June and July, during the plum rain season, typhoons pass through, and one must carry an umbrella daily to avoid both sunburn and being soaked by a storm. What's nice is at times like this the air quality is great, and the city looks wonderful in the downpour.

主编供稿

西湖·印象
West Lake and Impressions

灵峰探梅
Searching for Plums among the Sacred Peaks

"她在丛中笑"的"她"是毛主席说的梅。除了塞外苦寒之地，梅都不少。梅也一直是文人圣影，关乎气节，即使成泥成尘，也是"香如故"的。杭州的梅多聚在灵峰，永远不会"开无主"。花季一到，三五亩地的园子，红梅、白梅、粉梅、绿梅，挤得满满，游人也挤得满满。"灵峰探梅"，新十景之一，不过多半"探"不成。

"She will smile in the midst of blooms." "She" in this sense is Mao Zedong speaking of plums. Except in very cold places beyond the Great Wall, there are many plums elsewhere. They have always served as the spirit of men of letters, and have been praised in all manners. The plums of the mountains in Hangzhou will never bloom without someone to see them. When the flowering season arrives, gardens are invariably full of tourists admiring the red, white, pink and green plums. "Searching for Plums among the Sacred Peaks" is one of the "New Ten Sights" of the West Lake, yet not all will be able to find them.

西泠印社
Xiling Society of Seal Arts

湖山最佳处，天下第一社。百年历史的西泠印社坐落于西湖景区孤山南麓，因光绪年间创社四英"人以印集、社以地名"，故而取名西泠印社。印社以幽雅的园林建筑、错落的亭台楼阁、典藏的印章字画、悠久的人文历史而成为中国研究金石篆刻最负盛名的民间学术团体。

"The nicest place in the lakeside mountains, and the best seals in the world". The Xiling Society of Seal Arts, with more than a century of history, is situated in the West Lake Scenic Area of Hangzhou at the foot of Mount Gu on the southern side. It was founded in the Emperor Guangxu period of the Qing Dyansty, and its ground contain large elegant gardens and scattered pavilions and pagodas. Its collection of seals and calligraphy and long history have made it foremost civilian group involved in the research of stone-carved seals in China.

摄影：王嫱

微观杭州
HANGZHOU: TRADITION AND MODERN TIMES

徐志摩的丑西湖
Xu Zhimo's Ugly West Lake

徐志摩曾撰文《丑西湖》讥讽民国西湖的俗化:"断桥折成了汽车桥,哈得在湖心里造房子,某家大少爷的汽油船在三尺的柔波里兴风作浪,工厂的烟替代了出岫的霞,大世界以及什么舞台的锣鼓充当了湖上的啼莺。"扫兴的还有满湖的鱼腥、平湖秋月的聒噪和楼外楼的市井。如今此恶相已大为改善。

Xu Zhimo in his essay *Ugly West Lake* ridiculed the decay of the West Lake during the Republican era: "The Broken Bridge is now the Auto Bridge, people build houses upon the lake, operate petrol-fuelled boats upon the lake kicking up waves everywhere. The smoke of factories has replaced red clouds at sunset, and the noise of gongs and drums from stages of performers has replaced the song of birds." The smell of fish guts permeated the lake, the site of the Autumn Moon over the Calm Lake was ruined by noise, and the Louwailou restaurant was vulgar. These ugly phenomena have been corrected in modern China.

泛舟湖上
Boating upon the Lake

几天的持续阴雨之后,西湖的天开始放晴。约一好友,泛舟湖上,看岸边人潮拥挤,游湖心水波荡漾!船头的船夫摆桨划船,满心欢喜,不停地给我们介绍着西湖各景,"那边是保俶塔,她就像是一位娇羞的少女屹立在西湖边;看,和她隔江相望的是雷峰塔,我们都喜欢称他'老衲'呢……"哈哈,这样的介绍才地道呢!

After a number of days of continuous rain, the sun comes back to the West Lake. I meet up with a friend to go boating on the lake, and see the banks packed with people, and ripples over the lake! The man at the front of our boat paddles away. He's filled with happiness as he introduces all kinds of sights upon the lake to us. "That's the Baochu Pagoda, like a shy girl standing beside the lake; look, she looks out over the lake at the Leifeng Pagoda, which we call 'old monk'..." This is a great introduction!

摄影:陈心远

西湖·印象
West Lake and Impressions

摄影：董思聪

傍晚江南
Jiangnan at Dusk

"欲把西湖比西子，淡妆浓抹总相宜。"烟雨蒙蒙的傍晚，西湖像极了涂抹淡妆的小家碧玉。雾气腾腾的湖面使远处的山水风物或隐或现，让人极想走过去一探究竟。沿湖走到断桥边，路上的行人依然很多，不用急，更不用浮躁，这江南水乡的特点便是轻柔。你只管带着烦恼来，西湖的轻柔会悄悄涤荡尽你内心的浮躁。

"The West Lake looks like the fair lady Xi Shi at her best, whether she is richly adorned or plainly dressed." At dusk of a rainy day the lake looks like a girl with little make-up. Structures and sights drift in and out of view among the mist when viewed across the lake, enticing one to walk over to get a better view. Walking along the lake over to the Broken Bridge, there are still many people out. There's no reason to hurry or be restless, as the Jiangnan region is characterised by gentle demeanour. If you're vexed or irritated, the soft scenery of the West Lake will ease your worries.

雨巷觅浪漫
Looking for Romance in a Rainy Lane

雨天，撑着伞徜徉在小巷里，幻想着自己是戴望舒《雨巷》中那名丁香一样的姑娘，在雨巷中寻觅浪漫。大塔儿巷是戴望舒的出生地，戴望舒以前居住在大塔儿巷11号。或许诗人真的独自撑着油纸伞，走在寂寥的雨巷中，幻想着出现一个丁香一样结着愁怨的姑娘。现在又有谁会想逢着这样的女孩呢？

On a rainy day as I wander through a small lane, umbrella in hand, I imagine that I'm the girl like a bouquet of lilacs from Dai Wangshu's *Rainy Lane*. Datar Lane is Dai's birthplace; he used to live at number 11 of the lane. Maybe the poet really did wander alone along the solitary lane in the rain with an oiled-paper umbrella, and hope to meet a girl like a bouquet of lilacs gnawed by anxiety and resentment. How many others must think of meeting a girl like this?

微观杭州
HANGZHOU: TRADITION AND MODERN TIMES

摄影：潘益青

王澍的世外桃源
Wang Shu's Paradise

杭州有座象山，一湾清水环绕。依山傍水，有人筑起楼房。这楼房无规则地错落在那里，似乎是从山脚下生长出来的。这里就是中国美院象山校区。而象山，因为校园的存在，为人熟知。设计师王澍是2012年建筑界诺贝尔大奖——普利茨克奖得主。象山校区，作为他最大规模的建筑实验，一砖一瓦间，皆可见其个性。

Hangzhou has a Mount Xiang which is circled by clear flowing water. People have built residences upon it next to the waterway, distributed haphazardly without any master plan, yet seemingly growing out of the mountain. This is the seat of the China Academy of Art Mount Xiang campus, the existence of which in turn has led to Mount Xiang being well-known. It's designer Wang Shu was awarded the prestigious Pritzker Prize, said to be the Nobel Prize of architecture in 2012. The campus, his largest work in terms of scale, shows his character in every brick and stone.

高庄之秋
Autumn Scenes in Gaozhuang

杭州城里，处处是自然生态的味道。即便是随意的等车，也会有意外的惊喜，高庄就这样闯入我的世界。满眼红色的枫叶夹杂着黄色的银杏，绿色的植被也欣欣地过来帮忙，三色交融，秋天的气息扑面而来。正赶上太阳快要下山，阳光透过枝丫洒在它们身上，温暖，绽放，我的心也跟着这幅美景融入画中！

In Hangzhou, there's natural flavour everywhere. Even just waiting for a bus, you may encounter surprises, this is how Gaozhuang came into my mind. Red leaves surround the yellow of gingko trees everywhere, as green underbrush lends a hand to create a splendid tricolour autumn scene. As the sun quickly sets, its last rays squeeze through the branches to shine upon them. Warm and comfortable, my heart melts with this scene as if it were a painting.

西湖·印象
West Lake and Impressions

满陇桂雨
Sweet Osmanthus Rain at Manjuelong Village

说到杭州的市花——桂花,想必每个杭州人都为它的花香所沉醉。杭州最能感受桂花香的地方,要数满陇桂雨了。满觉陇因五代所建的圆兴院得名,北宋时改名满觉院,寓意"圆满的觉悟"。陇道上种满了七千多株桂花,每遇露水重时,花随风洒落,陇道中如逢桂花雨,沐"雨"飘香,各类品种的桂花味瞬间浸透你的肌肤。

Hangzhou's city flower – the osmanthus – is one whose fragrance any local person of Hangzhou will become intoxicated with. The best place to see and feel this is at Manjuelong village. Its name is from the Yuanxing Temple built during the Five Dynasties period, which was renamed Manjuelong (meaning "consummate consciousness") during the Northern Song Dynasty. The ridges there are flanked with more than seven thousand osmanthus, and when there is plenty of dew, osmanthus flowers will fall off in great numbers, creating a "rain" of blooms. You will find your surroundings permeated by the scent of all kinds of osmanthus.

冬日西湖美妙的音符
Musical Notes upon the West Lake on Winter Days

来杭越冬的鸟儿是越来越多了,你看,成群结队的鸳鸯、鸬鹚、䴙䴘等野生水鸟一会儿停留在特为它们设置的树桩上休息,一会儿在枯荷围网间游弋觅食、追逐嬉戏,俨然成了冬日西湖一道生动的风景线,成了西湖景区冬季特有的标志!"妈妈快看,它们像不像西湖上的五线谱音符?"朋友小孩的叫声也好有内涵。

More and more birds come to Hangzhou to spend winter – you will see mandarin ducks, cormorants, grebes and other kinds of aquatic fowl coming to rest in tree stumps set there specifically for them. They forage for food among the wilted lotuses and play with each other. They have become a part of the natural scenery of the winter days at the West Lake, and a new marker of winter itself there. "Look here mummy, aren't they like musical notes upon the lake?" A young child calls out upon seeing them.

摄影:杜红英

摄影：李选

互联·创新

Internet and Innovation

微观杭州
HANGZHOU: TRADITION AND MODERN TIMES

摄影:郑若琪

智慧城市
A Smart City

2012 年,杭州 WiFi "i-hangzhou" 免费向公众开放,杭州成为全国首个免费开放 WiFi 的城市。如今,大到涵盖金融、政务、医疗、教育的城市一卡通,小到商场的"智能停车"系统、公交站牌的实时路况,一个充满生机的智慧城市已颇具规模。就连为学术研究不可或缺的"中国知网"之类的资源库,在杭州市 IP 范围内也可免费享用!

In 2012, the "i-hangzhou" Wifi Scheme was launched at no cost to the public, making Hangzhou the first city to have free WiFi. Today, from the City Pass used in financial, government, medical, and education sectors to smaller ones such as smart car parks at shopping centres and public transit stops have been connected in a smart gird that allows interchange of information. The academic-based National Knowledge Infrastructure and other large-scale data resources are also available for free for users with IPs in the Hangzhou range!

鲁冠球与万向集团
Lu Guanqiu and the Wanxiang Group

习大大访美带了两位浙江企业家。一位是马云,另一位是鲁冠球。鲁冠球萧山人,儿时家贫,初中辍学后做过铁器社学徒,办过米面加工厂,摆过自行车修理摊,然后集资 4000 元办铁匠铺,即万向集团前身。万向集团从汽车上一个不起眼的零件——万向节做起,发展成第一个为美国通用汽车提供零部件的中国代工厂。

When Chinese President Xi Jinping visited the United States he brought with him two businesspeople. One was Jack Ma of Alibaba Group, the other was Lu Guanqiu. Lu Guanqiu is a native of Xiaoshan, and lived in poverty as a child. In middle school, he dropped out and interned at a forge, opened a noodle factory, repaired bikes, and later gathered 4,000 Yuan to open a blacksmith's shop, the predecessor of the Wanxiang Group. The Wanxiang Group went on to become the largest Chinese producer of automotive parts for the United States' General Motors Corporation.

"农夫山泉有点甜"
"Nongfu Spring Water is a Bit Sweet"

外国友人初到中国,随身携带的饮用水往往是农夫山泉。这个牌子的国际口碑已深入人心,被美国《读者文摘》评选为中国瓶装水中唯一的"白金品牌"。农夫山泉股份有限公司,这个家在杭州千岛湖的辛勤的"大自然的搬运工",已在中国的饮用水行业市场占了四分之一的份额,在世界饮用水市场中位居前三名。

When a foreign friend of mine first visited China, he always carried a bottle of Nongfu Spring with him. This brand's reputation is strong internationally, with the United States-based *Reader's Digest* having designated it as China's only "platinum" level bottled water. The Nongfu Spring Company is based at Hangzhou's Thousand Island Lake, and bills itself as "movers for nature". It holds a quarter of the market share for bottled water in China, and is third worldwide for drinking water.

自来水管将放出"农夫山泉"
Purified Water from the Tap

2014年,浙江省政府做出一个重要决定,将千岛湖的水通过隧道引到杭州市区,成为杭州市饮用水的主水源。这个计划酝酿了十年,争议不断,终因近年来接二连三发生的饮用水源污染问题而获批,六成的主体工程将于三年内完工。看来,杭州百姓从自来水管放出"农夫山泉"的日子不远了。

In 2014, the Zhejiang provincial government published a major decision, that the water from the Thousand Island Lake was to be transported through a tunnel to Hangzhou to provide a main source of drinking water for Hangzhou city. This is a plan that was in development for a decade, and saw a lot of debate in the process of its birth. The end result was that the water system saw incidents of polluted water occurring, and the plan was approved. More than 60% of the work on the new system will be completed within three years. Very soon, Hangzhou residents will be able to enjoy very pure water from the tap.

摄影:金炫辰

微观杭州
HANGZHOU: TRADITION AND MODERN TIMES

诺贝尔奖背后的华立集团
Nobel Prize and Huali Group

说起屠呦呦及其诺贝尔奖,有一家杭州余杭的公司不得不提——华立集团。它是全世界最大的青蒿素生产企业,也是全球唯一掌握产业链的企业。这家公司原本主要生产仪表,从事电力自动化,之所以投资发展不太赚钱的青蒿素产业链近二十年,既是被科学家的献身精神所感动,也是为了履行民族企业的社会责任。

When talking about Tu Youyou and the Nobel Prize, there is a company based in Yuhang District, Hangzhou, that must be mentioned – the Huali Group. It's the biggest producer of artemisinin, and the only one in its field with an industry chain. The company originally started off producing metering equipment and working in electric automation, but during the past 20 years or so, it has been involved in producing artemisinin with slim profit margins for being touched by the devotion of the scientist and bearing its social responsibility as a civil enterprise.

微公交
Microtransit

刚到杭州,路边一辆辆同款小汽车引起我的注意。这种车白绿相间,色彩淡雅,比一般的小轿车小三分之一,很轻便的样子。仔细一看,车身写着"微公交"三字。原来这就是传说中专门供出租用的纯电动车"微公交"啊。租用方便,即使是外地游客,凭身份证和驾驶证,预刷1000元,都可租用。电费都是免的。

When I first arrived in Hangzhou, a row of identical cars at the roodside caught my attention. Painted in white and green, these pale cars represented almost a third of the sedans I saw. They looked light and portable. When I looked closer, I saw they had upon them the word "microtransit" – so these were the electric rental vehicles I'd heard about. They're convenient to rent, even for an out-of-town visitor. Simply provide your citizen's ID and driving license, pay a deposit of 1,000 Yuan, and you can use one. What's more, the electricity is free!

摄影:夏利亚

互联·创新
Internet and Innovation

阿里巴巴
Alibaba

说起杭州最有名的企业，第一个浮在大众脑海的词估计是"阿里巴巴"。曾有人戏称香港是"李家城"，现如今，不仅是杭州，大半个中国老百姓的日常生活与马云的虚拟帝国都有着千丝万缕的联系。买东西不去实体店了，在淘宝上买；购物不拿现金和银行卡，刷支付宝……

When talking about famous enterprises from Hangzhou, the number one word in everyone's mind is "Alibaba". Hong Kong has previously been called Lee Ka-shing city; in present day, not just Hangzhou but the daily life of most of Chinese people live to some extent in Jack Ma's virtual empire or have a connection to it. Merchants don't waste time with brick-and-mortar stores, they buy from virtual shops on Taobao.com. Buyers don't use bank cards or cash, they use Alipay instead.

"互联网+"和老店采芝斋
Internet+ and Caizhizhai

正当许多百年老店为新经济环境下如何转型而苦苦探寻时，采芝斋却早已尝到了拥抱互联网的甜头。糯米网、拉手网、大众点评网等国内一线团购网站页面都有他们的糕点、月饼、粽子等产品，网络团购让他们找到了新的生机，找到了传统食品行业与时代接轨之路。互联网+的营销模式值得很多传统行业转型时效仿。

When a number of centuries-old famous brands in China are struggling to adapt to a new economic environment, Caizhizhai, an old and famous confectionery store, is already enjoying the sweet benefits of internet commerce. On well-known websites like Nuomi, Lashou, Dazhongdianping and other first-tier domestic shopping portals, their cakes, pastries, zongzi(cooked rice) and other products are all available for sale. Group buying has also given them further business opportunities. They have found a way to link traditional Chinese food products with the modern age – the Internet + model is one that many traditional industries are trying to replicate.

城市阳台
Hangzhou Balconies

在杭州，不仅住楼房的人家有阳台，整个杭州市还有个阳台，这阳台不附于楼，而是拔地而起，玻璃造就，光亮通透。乘三层自动扶梯而上，低头俯瞰，钱塘江水在脚下涌动着；抬眼望去，宽宽的江面，还有江对岸似蝴蝶片片并叠的奥体中心对着你看。晚风拂襟，纵使不酗酒，这样的临江也不由得不生豪情呢。

In Hangzhou, not just people in apartment buildings have balconies, the entire city has a balcony. It's not attached to a building, but rises out of the ground. It's made out of glass and is transparent. Ride a three-storey escalator, and look down and you will see the Qiantang River flowing; look up, you'll see a river scene, and the Olympic Centre across the river. You can't help but feel bold and generous looking out over it.

微观杭州
HANGZHOU: TRADITION AND MODERN TIMES

智慧医疗
Smart Medicine

什么？看病不用排队？怎么可能？如果你在杭州，那么一切皆有可能！2012年杭州开始推出智慧医疗，现已有250万人员开通了市民卡"智慧医疗"诊间结算功能，曾经让你对医院望而却步、想而生怯的挂号和收费窗口前的排队长龙、B超室门口的熙熙攘攘都已成为过去。看病真的很难吗？杭州人民告诉你，排队其实真不难。

What? You can see a doctor without having to wait? If you're in Hangzhou, that's perfectly possible! In 2012, Hangzhou rolled out its smart medicine initiative, and now more than 2.5 million of its citizens have set themselves up with a "smart medicine" doctor visit and account settlement program. With this, all the things that made you want to stay far away from the hospital, such as waiting for a number to get a number to queue up, then the queues snaking out from the counter where you prepay, before you stand in another queue are things of the past. Whereas people in other cities say that seeing the doctor is a nightmare, it's not the case in Hangzhou.

G20平安志愿者
G20 Peace Volunteers

和许许多多志愿者一样，王女士一有空，就会骑着自行车在景区转悠。"帮助景区的巡逻队巡逻，帮助有需要的游客，保卫我们景区的安全……大家都愿意为景区安全出份力，大家都是很热心的。"杭州市民王女士如是说。戴着"红臂章"，吹着"黄口哨"，这些守护杭州平安的志愿者俨然成了G20的护航者。

Like many other volunteers, Ms. Wang rides her bike to a scenic area to cruise when she has time. "I help the patrol squad patrol, help visitors in need, maintain security in the scenic area… Everyone's willing to contribute to the safety of the park, everyone's ardent." Wearing a red armband and blowing a yellow whistle, these protectors of Hangzhou's safety and security of course became G20 volunteers.

动漫
Cartoon and Animation

邻国日本动漫产业发展成熟，一直令国人难以望其项背。大家都为中国动漫产业捏了把汗，但《秦时明月》的出现改变了中国动漫的前景。这是由杭州的一家信息技术公司所制作的。它的成功之处，除了炫酷的电脑特效，还有融入了许多中国元素的紧凑、玄幻的剧情，在浓郁的中国风中注入时代感，令动漫迷们眼前一亮。

Neighbouring Japan has a well-developed cartoon and animation industry, which means it's a continual effort for Chinese creators to keep up. Many people concern Chinese cartoon and animation industry but the future prospects of it has changed because of *Bright Moon of the Qin Dynasty*, which is made by a Hangzhou-based IT company. It has been successful, not just with impressive computer effects, but also incorporating a number of Chinese elements. The integration of traditional Chinese elements and modernity is a real surprise for Chinese cartoon and animation fans.

互联·创新
Internet and Innovation

摄影：王嫱

移动革命
Mobile Revolution

最近，支付宝继推出"刷脸"支付功能后，又推出了"空付"。杭州人对马云的任何新动作都早已习以为常。如今大街上的水果店和贴膜店都标示着"可用支付宝"。出门不带钱包的人越来越多。这个土生土长的杭州小个子男人正用惊人的速度推动着一场互联网革命。连浙江省政府也效仿阿里集团，着手打造起"政务淘宝"。

Recently, after Alipay rolled out its "face swiping" functionality, it also introduced "KungFu". The people of Hangzhou take anything that Jack Ma does as granted. Fruit shops on the street all have stickers in the window that say "we accept Alipay". More and more people do not carry cash. This short man, a native of Hangzhou, is pushing forward an internet revolution at a startling speed. The Zhejiang provincial government is also following the example of the Alibaba Group, and is setting out to make a "government Taobao".

到处支付宝
Alipay Everywhere

作为阿里帝国的摇篮，杭州无疑是支付宝最普及的城市，衣食住行都可用支付宝交易。北来的游客，看见杭州随便进一家餐馆就能用支付宝结账，吃惊不已。不管e+金融如何博弈，杭州人只知道，银行转账手续费全免、聚餐AA不再尴尬、欠债还钱何须面交——因为杭州有支付宝。

As the cradle of the Alibaba empire, Hangzhou is the city where Alipay is in most widespread use. Food and clothing can be easily bought with Alipay. Visitors from the north of China may be surprised when seeing people in restaurants settling the bill with Alipay. However the e+ financial scheme works out, people in Hangzhou know that Alipay is an option for fee-free bank transfers, splitting the bill without embarrassment, and repaying debts.

微观杭州
HANGZHOU: TRADITION AND MODERN TIMES

刷微信坐地铁
Checking WeChat in the Subway

大多数杭州市民都人手一张市民卡，乘坐各种交通工具很方便。但对于在杭短暂逗留的人来说，尤其碰上旅游旺季，总免不了赶上购票难的戏码。所幸2015年杭州在全国率先推出了利用微信支付购买地铁票的业务，可选择在站内扫码购票，或选择在"杭港地铁友礼会"App上买好票去站内取票。互联网让地球村终成一家。

Most citizens take advantage of the city's transit card to use all kinds of public transportation services. However, for short-term visitors, especially during the peak travel season, facing the queues to buy tickets is an unavoidable hassle. Luckily, in 2015 Hangzhou rolled out a program that allows one to use WeChat to buy tickets for the underground. You can either scan a QR-code in the underground station, or choose to buy tickets through the "Hangzhou Friends of Underground" app, and retrieve your tickets at the station.

最富的区
The Richest District

旅游车行到萧山地带时，喇叭里传来导游小姐的介绍："这是杭州最富的一个区，连续多年被评为'中国十强区'，也是浙江最大的园林基地……"我的印象，这里的农民家家户户都有活干，要么种苗木，要么开家庭小工厂，要么去公司上班，村里没有闲人。勤劳的农民是萧山成为最富的区不可缺少的因素之一。

If you take a tour bus to the Xiaoshan area, the announcer on the loudspeaker will tell you "This is Hangzhou's richest district, and for many years has been in the top 10 richest districts in China. It's also the largest landscaped area in all of Zhejiang…" My impression is that all the ordinary people and farmers had work to do, be it planting trees, or opening a small home factory, or working at a company. Nobody was idle in the village. These farmers are a key factor to the wealth of the district.

地铁也卖萌
Cute Stuff on the Underground

当你带着丝丝困倦踏上新的一天的地铁，杭州地铁一号线的专列车厢定会让你眼前一亮，车窗、车门以及车厢顶部、地面等各种设施都贴满了具有3D效果的元素贴画。走进地铁，仿佛进入了童话世界，让人们带着欢乐出发。世界本来就是我们五彩斑斓的梦乡，带着这样的好心情，开启新的一天。

When you step into the underground, tired on a new day, your mood will be brightened by the special car on Line 1, where the windows, doors, and interior of the car are all decorated with stickers that have 3D effects. It's almost as if you've entered a fairy-tale. Let's happily set out – our world is a dream full of colour and excitement. Start your new day in high spirits!

互联 · 创新
Internet and Innovation

云栖小镇
Cloud Town

除了阿里马云这朵"云",杭城亦是各路祥"云"栖息之地。位于转塘科技经济园的云栖小镇就是一个以云生态为主导的产业小镇。它不是行政意义上的镇,而是一片创新牧场、产业黑土。在当下这个讲大数据的风"云"时代,云栖,力争成为中国首个"富有科技人文特色的云计算产业生态小镇"。

Yunqi Town ("Cloud Town") is a site for cloud activity in Hangzhou. Located in Hangzhou Zhuantang Science, Technology and Economic Park, it's a small village that provides a way of life centering around the cloud concept. It's not a village in the administrative sense, but rather an innovation centre. When talking about the "cloud" concept in big data, Cloud Town is striving to be the first place in innovation and specialisation in China.

摄影:王嬬

出门不带钱
No Need to Carry Cash

支付宝消费早已不是新鲜事,但修鞋摊和小火炉烤地瓜的摊主也可用支付宝,大概也只有在杭州了。到杭五个月,最显著的感触之一便是不出远门不取现金。从高档奢侈品店到小摊小贩,扫一扫二维码,轻松三四秒,避开携现金出门的风险,也省去了找零给零的麻烦。

Alipay is no longer a new thing, but only in Hangzhou do you see people like cobblers and sellers of baked yams also using it. After having been in Hangzhou for five months, the thing that impresses me most is the ability to leave home without carrying cash. From luxury goods outlets to small merchants and hawkers on the street, all you have to do is scan a QR code, and within 3 to 4 seconds, you've avoided the danger of carrying cash, and the hassle of getting change.

微观杭州
HANGZHOU: TRADITION AND MODERN TIMES

大四的 CEO
A Student CEO

司考、考研、考公、毕业论文开题……大四的标哥最近节奏有点紧张,不同于一般专业的毕业生,法律出身的他现已是一家法务咨询公司的 CEO。笔者的朋友圈中,过去一年标哥的定位在全国各地变换着。回顾创办公司的这一年,他说:"真的是奔波了一年。又觉得很幸运,杭州给年轻人的机会很多,优惠政策也很多。"

Taking legal tests, graduate school entrance examinations, public service examinations, writing a thesis... Brother Biao, a 4th year university student, has been a bit stressed lately. Unlike normal graduating students, with a legal background he is already the CEO of a legal consultancy. In the past year, Brother Biao's position was changing all over the country. Reflecting on his first year of starting the company, he said: "It really was a hectic year. Still, though, I feel lucky. Hangzhou gives a lot of opportunities to young people, and a lot of preferential government policies."

可以出售的好空气
Air You Can Sell

正所谓西子湖畔清风逸,龙井虎跑倍清新,杭州有着得天独厚的富氧好空气。毕业于美国约翰霍普金斯大学的刘博士和他的 ECOLIVE 创业团队就把杭城最棒的空气带给了千家万户。无论是汽车、家用还是工业净化,科技感十足的"易可滤"装置皆可全时段、高效提供健康新风,把杭州的清风发往全国各地。

With the cool breeze along the lake and the clear air at the springs, Hangzhou has especially rich resources of good air. Doctor Liu, a graduate of Johns Hopkins University and his Ecolive team bring Hangzhou's best air to thousands of households. In the areas of automotive, home and industrial air purification, they provide clean and fresh air to users anytime and anywhere around the country.

Shutterstock 供稿

互联·创新
Internet and Innovation

主编供稿

创客的野心
Maker's Ambition

无论是尚在校园,还是年过六旬;无论是技术男出身,还是跨界闯入,"创客"这一草根运动正在"云上"野蛮地生长着。在八成参会者为35岁以下的云栖大会上,60岁的老汪无疑是特别的。两鬓泛白的他走上舞台,滔滔不绝介绍起项目来,仿佛自带镁光灯,气场强大。老汪说,创业,任何时候开始都不晚。

Whether you're still in school, or you've been out for years, a tech veteran or someone entering from another field, the "maker" grassroots movement is flourishing "on the cloud". At the Yunqi Computing Conference, where more than 80% of the participants are under 35 years of age, 60-year-old Mr. Wang is undoubtedly special. When the white-haired man steps on stage and introduces his project, he has real energy as the words flow from his mouth. He says that it's never too late to engage in entrepreneurship.

e+ 时代的"萝卜车"
"Radish Cars"

浙江大学研发了一款小清新而又智能化的校园电动车。因以萝卜白和萝卜绿为主色,又被称为"萝卜车"。"萝卜车"没有车门,只有方向盘和踏板。以锂电池供电,连接无线网络,利用手机进行智能控制,实现智能化驾驶。当遇到障碍物时,"萝卜车"就会自动减速和停车,当然了,现在它还不能哪儿都去。

Zhejiang University has developed a small, light, smart electric car for use on campus. As it's mainly green and white, it's been called the "Radish Car". The Radish Car has no doors, just a steering wheel and pedals. It's powered by lithium battery and connects to wireless networks; it uses a smart phone to guide its operation along smart parameters. When it encounters an obstacle, the car will automatically reduce speed. Of course, it's not an all-terrain kind of thing.

微观杭州
HANGZHOU: TRADITION AND MODERN TIMES

支付宝的老家
Alipay's Hometown

杭州是支付宝的老家,"老家"是土话故乡的说法。人有思乡情结,因为故乡给人心灵上的归属感和安全感,我的地盘我做主嘛。到了杭州,才会发现这可真是支付宝的天下!买水果衣物,打车出游,交水电费,凡是用得着钱的地方,支付宝都可以搞定。热心店家还时时提醒你,现在优惠哦。当真是"支付宝在手,杭州任我走"。

Hangzhou is Alipay's hometown. People have strong feelings for their hometowns, because only there can one feel truly safe and at home – on your home turf you call the shots. When I came to Hangzhou, I discovered that this really is the territory of Alipay! Buying fruit and clothing, taking cabs, paying utility bills, pretty much anywhere you'd think to bring cash, you can use Alipay. Shopkeepers also happily remind you there are discounts for using the platform. With Alipay in hand, you can go anywhere in Hangzhou.

旧厂房的昨日今朝
Now and Then at the Old Factory

上世纪中叶,大运河畔拱宸桥边,是杭州最繁忙的工业区。如今,旧瓶装新酒,运河边的这些旧厂房被改造成了博物馆群,免费向民众开放。旧的厂房、仓库式墙壁、高窗、悬挑楼梯,配之以具现代艺术特色的玻璃连廊,是新世纪的创新探索精神和富有时代气息的"工业遗产"的完美邂逅,也体现了一个城市对历史的尊重。

In the middle of the previous century, the fields around the Grand Canal were the busiest industrial area in Hangzhou. Today, like putting new liquor in an old bottle, these old factories have been converted into museums, which are open for free to the public. These old factories, warehouse walls, tall windows, long staircases, and artistic-feeling glass corridors are "remnants of industry" that we've met with in this new century in the course of our search for the essence and vigour of a time passed, and are also a sign of our respect for the history of the city.

摄影:潘益青

互联·创新
Internet and Innovation

摄影：潘益青

古仓新生
New Life for an Old Storehouse

"北南新，南富义"，位于运河杭州段最南端的富义仓，昔日有着"天下粮仓"之称，是国家战略粮食储备仓库，见证了杭州历史上米市、仓储和码头装卸业的繁荣发展。而今，古仓新生，旧粮仓已成为了文化创意园，13幢砖木结构的建筑被打造为传统与时尚结合的开放式创意空间，将"物质粮仓"转变为"精神粮仓"。

"Nanxin in the north, Fuyi in the south." Situated at the southernmost part of the Grand Canal in Hangzhou is the Fuyi Granary, which in times past was known as "the Number one granary". It was a granary used for storage of grain for military use, and is a testament to the development of grain markets, its stores and wharf activity in Hangzhou. Nowadays, the storehouse has new life, as it has been converted into a cultural garden. Thirteen brick and wood buildings have been converted into an open-style innovative space that is a blend of both traditional and modern, turning a concrete storage space into a conceptual one.

"西湖发布"微矩阵
"West Lake Announcements" Micromatrix

联合新浪、腾讯、新华微博和微信，"双微"联动全力打造政务新媒体平台，回应社会热点和群众关切的问题，提升网络舆论的引导能力和为民服务水平，在传递政府声音的同时也倾听百姓的心声，更加立体化地为西湖区老百姓解读最新政策动态，提供最新的乐活资讯。杭州的政务活动真是越来越智慧，越来越亲民了。

Microblogs and WeChat (Sina, Tencent, Xinhua) have joined forces to make a new media platform for the government, allowing it to respond to points of discussion and questions from the populace, enjoy enhanced ability in controlling public opinion online and providing services to civilians, spread government messages and listening to the voices of the people, provide a more approachable medium for citizens of the West Lake District to read about new government policies and regulations, and provide the newest entertainment news. The government of Hangzhou is becoming more smart-enabled, and closer to the people.

**小镇实现
大梦想**

Small Town,
Big Dream

大四的王航是杭州师范大学的学生,在梦想小镇,他已经实习两个月了。下班以后,他没有急着回学校,而是和同事三五成群地坐在台阶上弹琴唱歌:"原来我们是'无经验、无资金、无技术、无场地'的'四无小卒',现在我们是'有梦想、有经验、有资金、有场地'的创客,良禽择木而栖,在这里梦想的实现触手可及。"

Wang Hang is a 4th-year student at Hangzhou Normal University, and has already interned for two months at the Dream Town. After getting off work, he doesn't hurry back to campus, but instead sits on the steps with a few colleagues and plays instruments and sing. "Originally, we had no experience, no money, no skills, and nowhere to be. Now, we have dreams, experience, resources, and somewhere to be as makers. We know which direction we want to go in and how to make what we want to see happen."

摄影:郦文娟

互联·创新
Internet and Innovation

双创小镇
Little Town Combo

"背靠玉皇,面对钱塘,杭城风水,此地为上。"这是莫言对玉皇山南的青睐。如此风水宝地,无疑是运势最佳之处,难怪基金小镇选择在此生息。这个中国版的格林尼治小镇,内外有良好的"金融生态圈",环绕多条"私募金融产业链"。此外,文创产业也渐成气候。"二创"合璧,名副其实的一个精英荟萃之地。

"With the Jade Emperor Mountain at its back, the Qiantang River to the front, this is a great place for Hangzhou scenery." This was written by Mo Yan to describe his view of Jade Emperor Mountain. With such great scenery, it's no wonder that the Fund Town picked this place as its site. It's been called China's Greenwich Village, with a good economic environment both within and without, and is circled by a number of private financial industry chains. Additionally, cultural and creative industries are also taking hold here. These different sectors go well together, and this place is becoming a place where the elite meet.

电博会
Electric Expo

"真的是被'电'到了!"电博会现场,朱同学激动地对身边的同学说。在为期三天的电博会上,各种好玩的高科技产品"争奇斗艳":智能机器人、"Oculus"眼镜、变色玻璃……数世纪前,丝绸之路成为各大洲间繁荣的商贸走廊、文化通道。互联网盛行的今天,"网上丝绸之路"正在跨境电商手上迅速崛起。

"I'm 'shocked', get it!?" says a student surnamed Zhu at the Electric Exposition. This three-day long expo showcases all kinds of high-technology products: smart robots, Oculus 3-D glasses, chameleon glass... A few centuries ago, the Silk Road served as a flourishing corridor of commerce on the continent as well as a channel for culture. In our modern day of a flourishing internet, the "online Silk Road" is contributing to the rapid growth of cross-border digital commerce.

"土"产品也来赶时髦
Products of the Times

使用手机微信功能扫描二维码链接,就可快速得知农作物经销信息;坐在家里点点鼠标,就能进行农作物科技成果定向推广;农田出现病虫害,只需登录APP,社群的农技专家就会给你出谋划策……这是位于萧山的传化集团新推出的"互联网+农业"模式,尝试在最"土"的农业跟最"洋"的互联网之间进行战略破局。

Using the QR-code scanning functionality of the WeChat app, one can quickly gain market information for agricultural products. Sitting at home clicking a mouse, one can promote his achievements of agricultural technology. If your fields suffer an infestation of pests, all you need to do is log into an app, and experts on an agricultural social network can identify your problem and tell you how to deal with it. This is the "Internet+Agriculture" model pushed by the Chuanhua Group in Xiaoshan District, combining the "simplest" field of agriculture with the most "advanced" internet technologies to change the game.

微观杭州
HANGZHOU: TRADITION AND MODERN TIMES

主编供稿

西溪谷
West Creek Valley

美国硅谷,已成为一个时代的标志。依照硅谷的创业模式,杭州西溪一带,一个科技含量十足的西溪谷正以令人瞩目的速度崛起。位于西湖和西溪中间,西溪谷是串联起这两大风景名胜的过渡地带,在承袭了美景的同时,也承袭了这座城市的历史演进以及科技发展。未来,或许我们可以自豪地说:"国际名谷,非惟硅谷。"

Silicon Valley has become a mark of the times. In line with the entrepreneurial model of Silicon Valley, the West Creek area has gained a lot of attention for the speed with which "West Creek Valley" has sprung up. Situated between the West Lake and the West Creek, West Creek Valley connects the two famous scenic areas, and besides inheriting an area of beautiful scenery, it has also inherited the history of the city and its technological and scientific development. In the future, we may be able to say it's not second to Silicon Valley.

跨境电商生鲜产品
Cross-Border Electronic Trade of Fresh Goods

随着国民收入不断增长,海外购物需求量增加,国内电商市场竞争激烈,导致了跨境电商这种新模式的崛起。生鲜这种东西的地域性很强,其特殊性也给它的操作带来了一定的难度。杭州作为全国唯一的跨境电商综合试验区,也不断在为生鲜的跨境电商摸索着道路,未来,也许足不出户一样可以享受美食。

As the income of the Chinese populace continues to increase, the demand for goods from overseas grows, and domestic electronic merchants engage in fierce competition – this has brought about a new model of cross-border e-commerce. Fresh goods have very strong ties to their specific regions of productions, and due to their specific nature, they can be hard to transport. Hangzhou is the only cross-border e-commerce comprehensive test area in China right now, and continually looks for routes to move these fresh goods into China in an e-commerce framework. In the future, we may be able to enjoy fresh food from other countries without setting foot outside.

互联・创新
Internet and Innovation

传感谷
Sensing Valley

想象特斯拉电动汽车的门把手，只有当人靠近时，才会伸出；当车主抱着一大堆物品来到车的后备箱，只要伸出脚在车底晃一晃，后备箱就会打开。这些"神奇"的功能都源于传感技术。传感技术的发展水平是衡量一个国家信息化程度的重要标志，杭州传感谷将成为杭州信息经济"三镇三谷"中的"新经济坐标点"。

The door handle of a Tesla car only pops out when someone comes near; if you are carrying a large amount of stuff to your BMW, just strench your foot and move at the boot of the car and it will open. These "miraculous" functionalities have their origins in sensing technology. The state of a country's sensing technology is a reflection of its overall development in the technology field. Hangzhou's Sensing Valley is the newest of Hangzhou's information-economy focused "Three Towns and Three Valleys".

网购的不平等条约
The Unequal Treaty of Online Shopping

国内网购的第一条不平等条约，大概要数江浙沪包邮了。由于江浙沪的购买力强大，客户群体庞大，加上大部分卖家都在江浙沪及周边，作为淘宝的大本营，杭州有着得天独厚的优势。收货快，更有免邮费送到家的幸福体验。在杭州生活的你是不是也有轻松跷起二郎腿做个懒汉的体验？

The domestic online shopping landscape's first major "unequal treaty" is free shipping for Zhejiang Province. As buyers in Zhejiang and Shanghai have high purchasing Power and form a large consumer group, and many of the sellers are also located in the area, Hangzhou, as the home of Taobao, enjoys a great benefit. Products arrive quickly, and many times come with free shipping. If you want to stay at home with your legs crossed and be lazy, Hangzhou is the place to do it.

淘宝卖茶具，却讲出了人生
Learning Life Lessons While Shopping

"不器"是一家卖茶具的店，注意到这个品牌，起初是因为它的取名——不器，这两个字很美，就像一个人安静地坐在那边，却拥有强大的气场。"不器"追求返璞归真的生活美学，抱着对自然真诚感恩的情感，让人在这个浮华的世界获得舒心。几年光景，淘宝将这个杭州本土品牌发展到了更广阔的市场。

"Not just a vessel" is the name of a teaware shop on Taobao. I noticed the name because it sounded very nice, just like one sits alone next to a table, quietly but overwhelmingly. It's an encouragement of returning to a demure and true aesthetic lifestyle, including a feeling of gratitude for nature, giving you a sense of calm in this world of ostentation. In the course of just a few years, Taobao developed this simple local brand to a much wider market.

创意良渚基地
Creative Liangzhu Base

许多人都知道杭州西北面有一片中国文明的发祥地——良渚，它位于余杭区良渚镇。良渚文化是我们的先民给后人留下的宝贵遗产。在这片土地上，不久的将来会用一种创意文化的方式，进行一场远古与现代的对话。创意良渚基地主要突出玉文化元素，重点发展文化生态旅游等产业，将带动良渚镇及周边区域的和谐发展。

Many people know that the northwest of Hangzhou is home to one of the earliest prehistoric cultures of China – the Liangzhu culture. Its site is in Liangzhu Village in Yuhang District. Liangzhu culture contributed many cultural treasures to China. On this piece of land, soon there a new form of creative culture will be used to construct a dialogue between the ancient and modern. The Creative Liangzhu Base will promote elements of Jade culture, focusing on developing cultural, ecological and tourist industries, driving the harmonious development of Liangzhu Village and surrounding areas.

"潘多拉"盒子
Pandora's Box

一听"潘多拉"盒子，大家会以为是装满疾病和苦难的盒子。实际则是一种新兴产品——生态种植的体验性消费。它由杭州创辉农业科技有限公司推出，一个白色的盒子约莫小型洗衣机的大小，内部采用了德国LED植物光照系统、以色列灌溉系统和智能的温湿度控制系统，可以无土栽培各种蔬菜和花卉，真是一个魔盒。

When one hears "Pandora's box", everyone thinks of a container full of disease and difficulty. Actually, this is a new kind of ecological experience consumption. A product of Hangzhou Chuanghui Agricultural Technology Company, a white box about the size of a washing machine is fitted inside with a German-manufactured LED plant growing system, an Israeli irrigation system and a smart controller that regulates humidity and temperature. You can grow vegetables and flowers without even using soil – it's truly a nifty thing.

创意者的先驱
A Creative Pioneer

杭州不仅是古都还是一座创意城市。Loft 49就开创了创意的先河。一所废弃的工厂被一个年轻人"点燃了"创意。一栋栋老房子里住着一个个设计者，随处可见的涂鸦，各种新奇的设计，还有那可爱的小宠物。这里像是施了魔法的新天地，年轻的魔法师们正用他们的魔法棒点亮我们的未来。

Hangzhou isn't just an ancient city, but also one of innovation. Loft 49 has taken a lead in innovation. An abandoned factory has been transformed by a young person into a centre for creation. Designers living in old houses make drawings left and right of all kinds of new designs. There are also cute little pets. It's like magic has transformed the area into a new space in which young wizards create wonders for our future.

淘宝孕育出的"网红经济"
Taobao's "Web Celebrity Economy"

杭州的淘宝女装店主小怡上新的一批1000多件商品在十几分钟内就被顾客"抢光",短短几天时间,她便完成了普通实体店一年的销量。这个漂亮的女生原本是个设计系毕业的大学生,利用自己的微博人气,赚到了自己人生的第一桶金。这都得益于淘宝平台的开放性,给了90后的年轻人开拓了更为广阔的创业平台。

Female Taobao store owner Xiaoyi puts a batch of 1,000 articles of clothing up on the store to see them snatched up by customers in a dozen minutes or so. In just a few days, she sells more clothing than a brick-and-mortar store does in a year. This beautiful girl graduated with a degree in clothing design, and uses her popularity on microblogs to earn a very handsome living. Her model benefits from the openness of the Taobao platform, which has given post-90s a great platform to innovate upon.

浙大科技园
Zhejiang University Technology Park

浙大建筑工程学院的大四学生辽宁小伙姜浩,是浙大科技园的孵化项目"水稻淀粉胶囊"的创始人之一,项目正进入研发的关键阶段。而他的四人团队成员,都和浙大有着千丝万缕的联系。浙大科技园有别于其他园区,能充分利用浙大的科研、师资等优势,学长、导师组团队做科研。这是创业的好地方。

Jiang Hao, a native of Liaoning Province and a 4th-year student at Zhejiang University's School of Architecture, is one of the creators of the "rice starch capsule" developed at the incubator in Zhejiang University's Technology Park. The research is entering a key phase. His four-member team is in contact with all kinds of individuals at Zhejiang University. What's different about the Technology Park from other areas is that it has full access to the research, professors and resources of the university. It's a great place for innovation.

摄影:卿文娟

微观杭州
HANGZHOU: TRADITION AND MODERN TIMES

让汉服走向世界

Han Chinese Clothing: from China to the World

孙彩领是上世纪三四十年代浙江台州有名的裁缝。如今,她的外孙女陈朝红在杭州成立了善智古润服装公司,生产的汉服还穿到了联合国秘书长潘基文身上。公司从经营时尚女装发展到为顾客定制汉服,最终进入国际市场。可以说,以中国元素打造国际品牌,是许多杭州本土服饰企业的崭新理想。

During the 1930's and 1940's, Sun Cailing was a well-known tailor in Taizhou City of Zhejiang Province.Today, Chen Chaohong, her granddaughter, has established the Shanzhi Gurun Clothing Company in Hangzhou. Even the UN Secretary-General Ban Ki-moon wears Hanfu (Han Chinese clothing) produced by the company. At the beginning, the company dealt with ladies fashion, then transferred to custom Hanfu for customers and entered the international market eventually. It can be said that using the Chinese element to build an international brand is now a new ideal of many Hangzhou local clothing enterprises.

善智古润供稿

公交全员 WiFi

WiFi on the Bus

中国人多,有热闹的好,但也苦了上下班高峰期的市民,曾有人吐槽"我只是路过而已,一大波人硬是把我拥上了车",特殊时段的乘坐公交之苦可想而知。杭州公交集团响应民声于 2015 年年底全面安装了公交车载 WiFi,如此时刻,有手机为伴,刷刷微信,看看股票,车中的烦躁焦急也化为虚无,"智慧城市"名不虚传。

Chinese people are numerous, and enjoy lively atmosphere, but having to put up with the rush hour before and after work, some people have complained, "I was just walking along, and then I was pushed onto a bus by a wave of people." At these times riding the bus can be quite tiring. Hangzhou Public Transit Group responded to the cries of the people, and at the end of the year in 2015 rolled out free WiFi in all buses. At this time, if you have a phone in hand, you can check WeChat, follow stock prices, and watch your worries fall away. The "smart city" name is not undeserved.

互联·创新
Internet and Innovation

摄影：杜红英

西溪创意产业园
West Creek Creative Industry Park

西溪湿地的静谧和源于自然的灵气，对于无污染的IT产业，无疑具有强大吸引力。在春暖花开、万象更新之际，园区内功能齐全的精美建筑，正期待着国内外名家大师的鉴赏与进驻。园区依托对西溪文化的挖掘，以西溪艺术村落等为重点，吸引文化艺术界人士入驻，主要发展文化休闲旅游和文学艺术产业。

The peace and quietness of the West Creek Wetlands originates in its natural atmosphere. For the non-polluting IT industry, it definitely has a strong attraction. The park is welcoming big players both domestic and international with beautifully constructed buildings with replete facilities. The park brings to the forefront the cultural history of the West Creek; with the artistic villages of the West Creek being focal points to attract more people in the cultural and arts sectors to the park. The development is mainly focused on culture, leisure, tourism, literature, art, and other related industries.

微观杭州
HANGZHOU: TRADITION AND MODERN TIMES

I-hangzhou
I-hangzhou

"I-hangzhou",是 2013 年杭州政府启动的向公众免费开放 WiFi 计划,也是全国首例,目的在于让更多的杭州人在智慧城市畅享"无线"的快乐生活,至今全杭已有 3000 多个站点,当真是"杭州有阳光的地方,就有免费 WiFi"。

I-hangzhou is a free citywide WiFi scheme started by the city government in 2013, and is the first example of such a scheme in China. Its objective is to bring more people in Hangzhou in contact with a the smart city concept, and let them enjoy a wireless-based life of enjoyment. There are currently more than 3,000 access points in Hangzhou, in accordance with the goal "wherever the sun shines there will be WiFi in Hangzhou".

杭州国际动漫节
CICAF

"五一"劳动节期间刚好赶上杭州动漫节,和众多市民一样来到表演者巡游的路旁观看。最吸引大家眼球的是今年最新加入彩车队伍的"魅力机器人",站在车头的 3 米多高的黄色变形金刚一出场就引来许多"刚粉儿"的欢呼。我并不算一个合格的动漫迷,但是看了这次游行,也被这些走到现实中的动漫形象打动了。

I managed to catch the China International Cartoon and Animation Festival during the May 1st Labor Day holiday. I went there along with many people from the city to see the parade. The most interesting thing this year was the "charming robot". A yellow "transformer" almost 3 metres high was encircled by cheering fans of the Transformers franchise. I'm not a full-on fan of cartoon and animation, but the parade and the "transformer" in real life really pumped me up.

摄影:俞燕君

古城·寻踪
Ancient City and Traces

微观杭州
HANGZHOU: TRADITION AND MODERN TIMES

**胡雪岩故居
——破败后的辉煌**

Hu Xueyan's Old Residence

听闻我的母亲说起，胡雪岩故居在上世纪 90 年代已破败不堪。那里成为杭州普通民众居住的地方，正巧母亲小时候就住在里面。随她走在高墙外的元宝街，经过早已干涸的水井，一幕一幕都记录着她年幼时的回忆。故居后经政府修复，如今不但是杭城人们的回忆，更是具有极高的历史文化和建筑艺术价值的建筑。

My mother told me that in the 1990s, Hu Xueyan's old house was in ruins. It had become a place where normal people in Hangzhou live, and my mother just happened to live there when she was a child. As I walked with her along the high-walled Yuanbao Street, passed a dried-up well, saw all kinds of things she remembered from her childhood. After the government renovated the area, now the area is a site of not just the memories of Hangzhou people, but also a place of great cultural and architectural value.

主编供稿

古城·寻踪
Ancient City and Traces

摄影：南大雄

最后一片消失的绿野
The Last Green Area

黄龙洞村因黄龙洞而得名，有良田千亩。上世纪80年代初，这里还是绿油油的稻田，白鹭嬉戏飞翔，是城区仅有的一片绿野，令人想到"稻花香里说丰年，听取蛙声一片"的田园风光。随着城镇化建设，村庄消失了，在此地建造了黄龙体育中心，周边也都建起了居民楼。昔日风光不再，只留在了美好的记忆中。

Yellow Dragon Cave Village gets its name, not surprisingly, from the Yellow Dragon Cave. It has a large amount of good land. In the 1980s, the fields were lush and green, and egrets would fly in the air. It was the only place in the urban area with green fields, and provided a nice pastoral escape from the surroundings. As the process of urbanisation continued, the village disappeared, the Yellow Dragon Athletic Centre was built, and the surrounding area was built up with residential buildings. The likeness of the past is gone, and all that remain are beautiful memories.

余杭双塔
Yuhang Twin Towers

余杭双塔分列于余杭镇东南的安乐山和苕溪北岸，为省级文物保护单位。其中安乐塔建于五代，为吴越王子钱镠纪念于此病愈而建，别名天宝塔、雌宝塔；舒公塔乃明代县令舒兆嘉为镇苕溪水患而建，又名地宝塔、雄宝塔。"宝塔镇河妖"，两座高大伟岸的白塔隔溪遥对，镇锁着苕溪这条自古桀骜的蛟龙，堪称古镇一绝。

The Yuhang Twin Towers are in the southeast of Yuhang Village, one on Anle Peak, and the other on the north coast of Shao Creek. They are provincial-level protected cultural locations. The Anle Tower was built in the Five Dynasties to commemorate the Wuyue Prince recovering here from a serious disease. It's also called the Tianbao Tower, or the Cibao Tower. The Shugong Tower was built during the Ming Dynasty under orders of the magistrate Shu Zhaojia, and is also called the Dibao Tower, or the Xiongbao Tower. The two white towers face each other across the creek, like two tameless flood dragons that have sat there for ages.

微观杭州
HANGZHOU: TRADITION AND MODERN TIMES

夜游河坊街
Hefang Street at Night

夜游河坊街，感受到了这南宋老街的别样风情。和白天比，晚上这里似乎更热闹了。华灯璀璨，游人如织，和周围古色古香的建筑融为一体，好像一幅别具一格的风俗画。在这里，尝一口"老杭帮"桂花糕，喝杯"红枣雪梨"，再逛一逛各种特色民俗小店，一天的疲惫顿时消失得无影无踪。

Visiting Hefang Street at night, one feels the elegance of the Southern Song Dynasty. Compared to the daytime, it's much busier. Colourfully decorated lanterns gleam, travellers walk about, and the collected old buildings form a scene not unlike a painting. Here, one can try some authentic Hangzhou-style osmanthus cake, drink a cup of sweet jujube soup, and visit all kinds of local specialty shops. In this way, you will forget any feelings of exhaustion you may have from the day.

西溪别韵
Rhythm of the West Creek

提起杭州，多数人最先想到的定是西子湖，殊不知，另有一处并非在西子湖之下——西溪湿地。它位于杭州的西部，是国内唯一的集城市湿地、农耕湿地和文化湿地为一体的次生湿地。有专家将它的美提炼为"野、雅、幽、静"四个字。据说南宋高宗曾有在西溪建立都城皇宫的念头，因而便有了"西溪且留下"的美谈。

When one mentions Hangzhou, the thing that most people think of first is the West Lake, but there is another nice area – the West Creek Wetlands. It's located in the west of Hangzhou, and is the only wetland area inside a city in China. It has both agricultural and cultural significance. Experts say that its beauty lies in its fields, elegance, and quietness. It's said that the Gaozong Emperor of the Southern Song Dynasty wished to build his palace here, but decided against it, preferring to preserve the beautiful area.

摄影：杜红英

古城·寻踪
Ancient City and Traces

摄影：李选

钱塘江为何又叫"之江"
The Name of Qiantang River

在秦汉时期，杭州叫钱塘，流经钱塘的江，就叫钱塘江。钱塘江为什么又叫之江呢？因为从富春江下来，流经富阳到六和塔这里，曲曲折折浩浩荡荡往东奔向大海，形状就像汉字的"之"。"之"上面的一点，表示的又是什么呢？就是西湖。在玉皇山山顶俯瞰钱塘江和西湖，就可以清楚看到"之"字形了。

In the time of the Qin and Han dynasties, Hangzhou was known as Qiantang, and the river flowing through it was known as the Qiantang River. Why is it sometimes referred to as "'s river"? This is because the Fuchun River flows through Fuyang to the Pagoda of Six Harmonies, and winds its way to the sea, taking the form of the Chinese character *zhi*, which is shaped like "'s". What does apostrophe symbolise? The West Lake. When one looks down upon the river from Jade Emperor Mountain, the shape is clear.

飞来峰
Feilai Peak

灵隐古刹前的那座山，叫武林山麓，是杭州的名胜古迹，我国南方古代古窟艺术重要之地。"飞来峰"传说是从印度飞来的，周围古树参天，泉水潺潺，将自然山水与佛教名胜自然融合。飞来峰并不是一座大山峰，但内部别有洞天，每个山洞的石壁上，都雕刻有逼真的佛像与神仙，令人惊叹这一鬼斧神工。

The mountain before Lingyin Temple is called Wulin Mountain, and is a famous location in Hangzhou, as well as a culturally significant location on a national scale. "Feilai Peak" is said in legends to have flown over from India. The surrounding trees reach towards the sky, and the spring water murmurs as it flows slowly, making for a beautiful fusion of Buddhist history and natural scenery. Feilai Peak isn't a large mountain, but it has a number of fascinating places – caves. On the wall of each cave, there are realistic carvings of Buddhas and sages, the workmanship of which is remarkable.

微观杭州
HANGZHOU: TRADITION AND MODERN TIMES

青芝坞
Qingzhiwu

青芝坞有两个"好听":一条很好听的路,玉古路,它就在这条路上;一个很好听的村,玉泉村,它属于这个村。它的地利也好,左拥林木繁盛的植物园,右傍世界名校浙江大学,这儿是年轻的背包客喜欢驻足下的地方,也是杭州年轻老饕们喜欢聚餐的地方。

Qingzhiwu has two nice-sounding places: first, Yugu Road ("Old Jade Road"), second is Yuquan Village ("Jade Spring Village"). There are also nice geographical features: a botanical garden to the left, and to the right, the world-famous Zhejiang University. This is a place that young backpackers like to walk through, and the old people of Hangzhou like to come to meet and eat.

西山游步
Walking about the West Mountains

西山是西湖西边群山的泛称。西山游步道建于2011年,全长108公里,是杭州最长,也是全国范围内最长的一条山体游步道。它将散落在西山的自然人文景观串联起来。有了这条集运动和游览功能于一体的路线,越来越多的杭州人乐得把西湖让给外地游客,主动上山"游击",还因此诞生了不少夜爬的爱好者。

"West Mountains" is a collective term for the mountains around the West Lake. The West Mountains Walking Path was built in 2011, and is 108 kilometres long. It's the longest walking path in not just Hangzhou but all of China. It connects the various natural scenic locations in the Western Mountain region all together. It's good for enjoying sites as well as exercising, and as more of the Hangzhou locals leave the West Lake to tourists, they turn to this path, which has created a number of fans of night-time hiking.

摄影:施麟麒

古城・寻踪
Ancient City and Traces

枫林咽泉
Fenglinyan Spring

枫林咽泉是一口位于富阳新登的间歇泉。此泉从一巨岩涌出，泉口有一小潭。泉流以十五分钟为周期忽减忽增，最大时会泻成一个小瀑布，潭水也会随之升降，溢满而复浅，循环无穷。新登县志说，泉水如人喝水，喝一口停一下。水来时，石下"咕咕"作响，如水下咽喉，故称咽泉。乡民以之为圣泉，又唤"噎水灵官"。

Fenglinyan Spring ("Maple Forest Choking Spring") is a geyser located in Xindeng, Fuyang District. It flows out of a giant rock, and there is a small pool where water collects in front of it. It erupts on an approximately 15-minute cycle, and with larger eruptions a small waterfall forms. The level of the pool also fluctuates in an endless cycle. According to the Chronicals of Xindeng County, the spring is like a person drinking water – it drinks a bit, then rests for a bit. When the water comes, there is a sound from the rocks that sounds a bit like a person choking, which gives the spring its name. The people of the village think that it is sacred.

满陇桂无语
Manjuelong Osmanthus

桂花在杭州成"桂花雨"，满觉陇无疑是最有名的，有"满陇桂雨"一说。十月秋风将起未起之时，还未到周末，那里就从早到晚都是闹嚷嚷的赏桂人，人气旺得把满树的金桂、银桂、丹桂都压无语了。在香气甜不腻的桂树下，人们喝着、吃着、玩着，享受着人间天堂的惬意，把吴刚都羡慕死了呢。

The osmanthus in Hangzhou sometimes form an "osmanthus flower rain", Manjuelong is the best place to appreciate this. In October when the winds rise, even before the weekend arrives, the scene is full of people observing the flowers, with gold, silver and red osmanthus all around. People drink, eat and enjoy themselves among the sweet smell of the blossoms as if it were heaven on earth.

三台山
Santai Mountain

三台山之美只有杭州人才能知晓。景区内的先贤堂、黄公望故居、于谦祠、武状元坊等著名文化景观，为杭州增添了深沉、厚重的历史感。景区茶楼近水依山，幽中藏雅，飞檐翘角，亭阁宛然；闲暇时分，亲朋好友相聚三台山，或品茗对弈，或追古怀昔，一餐农家饭，三杯清泉茶，其中境界非外乡人可知。

Only the people of Hangzhou know the true beauty of Santai Mountain. The Hall of the Wise Men, the former residence of Huang Gongwang, the Yuqian Shrine, the Wuzhuangyuan Memorial Archway in the scenic area make you feel Hangzhou is a profundand historical city. The teahouse within the scenic area abuts both water and mountains, and is calm and refined with beautiful upturned eaves. When one has time one may go with a group of friends to Santai Mountain, try some tea, observe historical locations, or eat a meal. Only the locals know the taste of having a cup of tea made with fresh spring water here.

微观杭州
HANGZHOU: TRADITION AND MODERN TIMES

徒步林径幽
Walking a Quiet Path

徒步，感受杭州树林幽径之乐。"铩铛岭上览山水，栖霞岭上传英名，梅灵古道见灵山，云栖竹径最清凉，九溪烟树连山水，凤篁萧爽接龙井，麦岭古道通南北，韬光幽径观江潮，慈云遗风显神韵，九里云松达天竺"——是杭城公认的十条最美徒步路线。柳暗复花明，峰回又路转。如此徒步，如何不妙？

Walking the small paths and roads of Hangzhou is a pleasant activity. "Admiring the scenery from Langdang Peak, the view from Qixia Peak, looking at Spirit Mountain from Plum Spirit Old Road, enjoying the cool of the Bamboo-lined Path at Yunqi, Nine Creeks in Misty Forest, path from Fenghuang Peak to Dragon Well, Mailing Old Road, looking at the river from Taoguang Path, the Ciyun Peak, path from Hongchun Bridge to the Temple of Soul"–these are all terms for and descriptions of famous walks that can be taken in Hangzhou. Leaves, flowers, paths and peaks await you – how could you pass something like this up?

摄影：潘益青

古城·寻踪
Ancient City and Traces

信义坊
Xinyifang

信义坊位于城北经济文化中心卖鱼桥,与京杭大运河毗邻。沿余杭塘河两岸是一条长长的步行街,三座别具特色的古桥连接两岸,形成"街中有河,河中有街"的独特景观。这里是年轻人休闲、娱乐的好去处,沿街酒吧、海鲜店多不胜数,异域风情十足的泰国餐厅、巴西烤肉、韩国料理更令人垂涎忘返。

Xinyifang is located at Maiyu Bridge in the economic and cultural centre of North City, and is adjacent to the Beijing-Hangzhou Grand Canal. There is a long walking street along both sides of the Yuhangtang River, and three old bridges connect the two banks. It's a road with a river in the middle, and a river with a road in the middle. This is a good place for young people to relax and amuse themselves. There are bars and seafood restaurants everywhere, as well as foreign food like Thai cuisine, Brazilian barbecue, and Korean dishes.

摄影:徐聘

小河直街
Xiaohezhi Street

小河直街位于城北运河、小河、余杭塘河三河交汇之处。下店上寝式的清末民居,古老的木质建筑,狭仄幽深的民巷,历经风霜的百年埠头,时间仿佛在这里永远停止。酱园、米铺、布庄、孵房、酒庄,步入小河直街,刹那间有种时空穿越的感觉。空闲时分,独坐茶楼,品味历史是何等的幸福!

Xiaohezhi Street is located along the canal in the north of the city where the canal, Little River, and Yuhangtang River meet. There are mixed-use buildings here from the end of the Qing Dynasty, with stores on the ground floor and residence above, built in the old style from wood. One feels that time has stopped when walking the narrow alleys between the weather-worn buildings. Walking among the small shops selling soy sauce, pickles, cloth, eggs and liquor, it's almost as if one has travelled back in time. If one has free time, it's nice to visit a teahouse alone and experience a bit of history.

微观杭州
HANGZHOU: TRADITION AND MODERN TIMES

秋意
Autumn Feelings

最喜欢杭州的秋天。没有春天的绵绵细雨，没有夏天的闷黏酷热，没有冬天的湿冷晦暗，杭州的秋天宛如一个童话。阳光煦暖，天高气爽，满城的桂花香，油画般的湖光山色，我等拙言，杨万里道出了我的心声："梧叶新黄柿叶红，更兼乌桕与丹枫。只言山色秋萧索，绣出西湖三四峰。"只是心境大不一样。

I most like the autumn in Hangzhou. Free from the annoyances of rain in the spring and heat in the summer, or the wet cold of the winter, the autumn here is like a fairy-tale. The sunlight is warm and soft, the sky looks great, the fragrance of osmanthus blossoms is everywhere – it's like being in a painting. I feel like I'm in the poem *Mountains in Autumn* by famous Southern Song Dynasty patriot and poet Yang Wanli.

主编供稿

"小西湖"华家池
Huajia Pond

走在浙大华家池校区，竟然发现池中有一个像西湖"三潭印月"那样的石塔。"那是小三潭印月啊，还有小平湖秋月、小孤山、小苏堤呢，"同学笑着说。这才知道华家池有"小西湖"之美名。甚至有人说这是比西湖更美的所在。的确，这里面积没西湖大，但风景同样宜人，绿化、小路、湖边的长椅，都比西湖精致美观。

When walking the Huajia Pond campus of Zhejiang University, I discovered that there's a stone tower like the one of "Three Pools Mirroring the Moon" in the West Lake. "It's a miniature version of it. There are also miniature versions of Calm Lake Pavilion under the Autumn Moon, Mount Gu and Su Causeway." says one of my classmates, laughing. Apparently, the Huajia Pond is also called the "mini West Lake". Some people say it's even nicer than the West Lake. In fact, while it's not as large, it looks just as nice. The greenery, paths, and benches near the lake are even better than those at the West Lake.

古城·寻踪
Ancient City and Traces

宋江村的来历
The History of Songjiang Village

西湖区有个宋江村。传说当年施耐庵写《水浒传》的时候，才思枯竭，离家游历，后被杭州美景吸引，就在杭州西溪河良渚买下一座二层楼的土木房，楼下开茶楼，南来北往的商贩和当地百姓都爱到此喝茶聊天。施耐庵因有了这些丰富的资料而写成《水浒传》，此村也就被称为宋江村了。

In the West Lake District, there is a place called Songjiang Village. Legend says that When Shi Nai'an was writing *Water Margin*, he ran into writer's block, and left home to travel. He was attracted by the beauty of Hangzhou, and bought a two-storey wooden house in Liangzhu in the West Creek area. He opened a teahouse on the first storey, and it became popular with both travelling merchants and the local population. The stories he told allowed him to write *Water Margin*, and the village was named Songjiang Village.

吴山广场
Mount Wu Square

宋朝苏轼《卜算子》："蜀客到江南，长忆吴山好。"来杭州旅游的人，几乎都要到吴山广场走一趟。一则这里是国家5A级景区，再则这里景点多且免费。尤其是紧邻吴山广场的河坊街，是杭州唯一保持古城历史风貌的老街。走在青石板铺就的路上，听着"店小二"们的吆喝声，真有种穿越到南宋古城的感觉呢！

In a poem of Song Dynasty poet Su Shi, he remarks that if one visits the Jiangnan area, Mount Wu is not to be missed. Those who come to Hangzhou almost always visit the Mount Wu Square. As 5A-level national scenic area, Mount Wu has a number of scenic spots that can be visited without having to buy any ticket. A great option is Hefang Street at Mount Wu Square, where the old architecture has been preserved throughout the street. Walking along the stone street, you may hear people calling out from shops, hawking their wares – it feels like you've travelled back to the Song Dynasty!

摄影：夏利亚

微观杭州
HANGZHOU: TRADITION AND MODERN TIMES

赏雨好去处
Rain View

到杭州游玩，最容易碰到雨天。"赏雨"最著名的地方是望湖楼，苏东坡《望湖楼醉书》言："黑云翻墨未遮山，白雨跳珠乱入船；卷地风来忽吹散，望湖楼下水入天。"描绘的就是瑰丽多彩的西湖雨景。望湖楼回廊曲折，避雨的时候可以凭栏小憩，还可欣赏雨景。此外，白堤、吴山、曲院风荷等也是赏雨的好去处。

When you come to Hangzhou, you're likely to get rained on. The most famous place to enjoy the rain is Lake-House (Wanghulou). Su Dongpo wrote about it in his *Treatise on Views of the Lake*: "Dark clouds obscure view of the mountain, and white pearls of rain bounce upon the boats. The wind blows over as one takes in the view of the vast lake." He is talking, of course, about the famous West Lake in rain. The covered corridor that leads to the building is a twisting and winding one. One can take a rest against a column here when staying dry on a rainy day, and look out at the rainy scene and appreciate. Additionally, there are also the White Causeway, Mount Wu, and Quyuanfenghe, which are all nice places to appreciate a rain view.

摄影：夏利亚

古杭州城门
The City Gates of Old Hangzhou

古时，杭州有十大城门，每座城门外演绎着各色的世俗风情，且看这杭曲小调：百官（武林）门外鱼担儿，坝子（艮山）门外丝篮儿，正阳（凤山）门外跑马儿，螺蛳（清泰）门外盐担儿，草桥（望江）门外菜担儿，候潮门外酒坛儿，（清波）门外柴担儿，涌金门外划船儿，钱塘门外香篮儿，太平（庆春）门外粪担儿。

In ancient times, the city of Hangzhou had ten gates, and outside of each of them had its own special scene outside: fish outside the Wulin Gate, cocoons outside the Genshan Gate, horses outside the Fengshan gate, salt outside the Qingtai Gate, vegetables outside the Wangjiang Gate, liquor outside the Houchao Gate, firewood outside the Qingbo Gate, paddleboats outside the Yongjin Gate, incense outside the Qiantang Gate and fertiliser outside the Qingchun Gate.

古城・寻踪
Ancient City and Traces

吴山天风
Wind on Mount Wu

三面云山一面城，在杭州，山并不稀罕，不过吴山是唯一一座位于老城区的山，它和杭州百姓的生活息息相关，融合在市民的生活中。至今，山脚下、半山腰还生活着杭州人家，是百姓们饭后散步聊天的好去处。人们喜欢到山上聚聚，观风看云拉家常。登城隍阁远眺，江、湖、山、城尽收眼底，美不胜收。

Three mountains and one city – in Hangzhou, mountains aren't a rarity, but Mount Wu is the only one situated in the old city area. It has a close relationship with the people of Hangzhou, and is a part of the lives of the city residents. Today, at the foot of the mountain, as well as its mid-reaches, there are people living. They walk the mountain after eating, chatting as they go. People like to meet up on the mountain, looking at the clouds as they talk about their daily affairs. Looking out at the scene from the Chenghuang Pavilion, one can see rivers, lakes, mountains, and the city all at once – a truly beautiful sight.

西湘记
Twin Lakes

世人皆知西湖，却有许多人不知道杭州还有湘湖。她坐落在钱塘江南岸，与西湖隔江相望，并称为"西湘"。湘湖碧波万顷，风景秀丽，更因出土了距今近八千年的独木舟而出名，陶行知创办的湘湖师范学校也在旁边。深厚的文化底蕴和优美的自然风光，使得西湘成为杭州的双明珠。

Everyone knows about the West Lake in Hangzhou, but not many know about the Xiang Lake, also in the city. It sits on the south side of the Qiantang River, and provides a counterpoint to the West Lake. Together they are known as the "West and Xiang Lakes". The water of the lake is clear, and the scenery is excellent. It's famous for the wooden boat unearthed here almost 8,000 years ago. Tao Xingzhi founded the Xiang Lake Normal Academy next to the lake. The lake is a place with rich cultural history and excellent natural scenery, and together with the West Lake, is one of a pair of beautiful pearls.

摄影：梅莹

微观杭州
HANGZHOU: TRADITION AND MODERN TIMES

摄影：梅莹

桥的故事
Story of the Bridges

杭州是典型的江南水乡，大大小小有10000多座桥。钱塘江上已经建成了7座大桥跨大江南北。运河及市区内河都有桥连接各区域。西湖和公园里也桥梁众多，其中有上千年的古桥，有现代的，也有在建的。每一座桥都承载着一段历史，向人们讲述着自己的故事。它们见证了历史，目睹了现在，跨越着未来。

Hangzhou is a typical city with water of the Jiangnan area. In total, there are more than 10,000 bridges in the city. There have already been built 7 large-scale bridges that cross the Qiantang River. The Grand Canal and the urban area all have bridges connecting various districts to each other. The West Lake and the parks also have a large number of bridges. Among them, there are some that are centuries or even a millennium old, as well as modern bridges, and new ones still under construction. Each bridge has its own history, and they tell their stories to people. They have been witnesses of the history, look over the present, and will see the future.

秋雪庵
The Hut of Autumn Snow

秋雪庵得名和出名与两位明代文化名人有关。庵原叫大圣庵，庵周水隅，弥望芦花，花时如雪。陈继儒取唐人"秋雪濛钓船"命为"秋雪庵"，庵得名；张岱写 "一片芦花，明月映之，白如积雪"，庵出名。现在庵堂平时清净，但每年霜降后十天，各地词人都来此会聚，吟词雅集，闹热一场。庵也顺势成词人圣地了。

The Hut of Autumn Snow gets its name from two Ming-dynasty personages. It was originally called the Great Saint Hut. It is surrounded by water and reed catkins. In bloom season, they are flying all around like a snowstorm. Ming Dynasty poet and painter Chen Jiru borrowed name of the hut from a verse of Tang Dyansty, and Zhang Dai wrote a poem describing it that made it famous. The hut is now usually quiet, but for the "frost descent" period of the lunar calendar, poets come from all over to read poems, which makes it a lively and holy place for them.

古城·寻踪
Ancient City and Traces

三墩
San Dun Town

三墩镇位于杭州的西北部,古称兰里,据传春秋战国时期,荀子到过三墩,并亲手沿河栽种兰花,为民间做过好事,故有此称。三墩是个水乡古镇,因境内有文星墩、灯彩墩、水月墩三个较大的水上土墩而得名三墩。

San Dun Town is located in the northwest of Hangzhou, and was originally called Orchid Village. It's said that in the Spring and Autumn and Warring States Period(770BC-221BC), Xunzi, a great thinker, planted orchids here with his own hands, which gave rise to the original name. San Dun Town is an ancient town upon the water; within its borders are three towns, namely Wenxing Dun, Dengcai Dun, and Shuiyue Dun.

越剧首演地
Site of the First Yue Opera

参观蒋村陈万元故宅,发现这里竟是越剧的首演地。说是当年陈氏祖父家中殷实,五十大寿,邀来嵊县艺人马潮水等人做寿,觉得听唱书不过瘾,就劝马潮水上台演《珍珠塔》。午饭后,演员们身穿戏服在简陋的舞台上演出了《方卿别母》《九松亭》等,首次将唱书形式变成了戏曲形式演出。越剧就这样诞生了。

The former residence of Chen Wanyuan is the site of the first performance of Yue Opera. His family was well off, and for his father's 50th birthday, they invited Ma Chaoshui and other performers from Sheng Country of Shaoxing to put on performances. They asked Ma Chaoshui to perform *Pearl Tower* as they were bored with the normal form of storytelling with accompaniment after lunch, the performers adorned simple costumes and performed *Fang Qing Parts with His Mother*, *Pavilion of the Nine Pines* and other plays, making it the first time the original style of storytelling was transformed into a costumed performance. This is how Yue Opera, otherwise known as Shaoxing Opera, was born.

摄影:梅莹

微观杭州
HANGZHOU: TRADITION AND MODERN TIMES

"塘栖"的由来
The Origin of "Tangqi"

《卓氏家乘》唐栖考有言:"唐栖者,唐隐士所栖也。"此隐士姓唐名珏,宋末元初人,世居绍兴攒宫宋六陵旁。因痛恨元僧杨琏真珈盗六陵、弃帝骸,深夜邀乡里壮士,移六帝骨骸于兰亭附近。事后,他为避其祸,匿名陷居于唐栖的三分村,村人敬重他的义行,就将其居住之地命名为"唐栖",也即今天的"塘栖"。

Tangqi is described in an old text as "The place where the hermit surnamed Tang lives". This man, Tang Jue, resided in Shaoxing near the imperial burial site in Cuangong, Shaoxing at the start of the Song Dynasty. He hated a Yuan Dynasty monk for robbing the tomb of the emperor, and thus one night hired some strong men to move the bones of the emperor to the Orchid Pavillion. Afterwards, to avoid misfortune, he moved to Sanfen Village in Tangqi and lived there in anonymity. The villagers respected his heroism, and changed the name of the place where they lived to "Tangqi", or meaning "Tang's Residence".

夏日避暑地
A Place to Avoid the Summer Heat

一般人说起杭州,总会先想到西湖。其实,杭州本地人更喜欢去一些城周围的自然区,如西山国家森林公园。这里有长长的游步道方便游客进入公园,也有比较原始的石头台阶供登山爱好者攀爬。公园森林覆盖率很高,进口处就有重重竹林。空气清新凉爽,堪称大自然的天然氧吧。炎炎夏日,这里更是一个避暑胜地。

When you mention Hangzhou, what most people will think of first is the West Lake. In fact, Hangzhou people prefer to go to other scenic areas around the city, such as the West Mountains National Forest Park. There are long pathways within where visitors can take walks on primitive stone steps. It's an ideal destination for hiking enthusiasts. The forest coverage rate within the park is quite high, and trees will surround you wherever you go. The air is clean and cool, like a natural oxygen bar. It's a great place to avoid the summer heat.

盛夏的老宅子
An Old House in Midsummer

夏天的天很蓝,地上随时能摊个鸡蛋,老杭州还是喜欢以前的老宅子。邻里间支张麻将桌,微微扇着竹扇子,阳光只有在天井下那么一小块,麻将子都是冰凉凉的。祖宗在堂前的阴影里排排站看着你,越发阴凉。不时听到"祖宗保佑"的喊声,却也常常摸不到和牌的那一张。

The summer sky is blue and the ground very hot, but the old people of Hangzhou still like the old houses. Set up a mah-jong table, fan yourself with a bamboo fan – the sun only comes in through the skylight. The mah-jong tiles are still as cold as ice. Your ancestors watch over you, and you feel cool. Sometimes, you hear someone call out "ancestors, bless me!" as they play the game.

古城·寻踪
Ancient City and Traces

御街
Imperial Street

历史的车轮滚滚向前，留下的轨迹令后世后代回味无穷。南宋御街，一个光听名字仿佛就能穿越回南宋都城的古街，涌现出无尽的古味。脚踏在曾被千万马车疾驰而过的石板路，手抚着曾被万千将士镇守的城墙，纵使今日现代商业之繁华，也依旧掩盖不了昨日古镇之熙攘，而不变的还有古今百姓共同的愿望：国泰民安。

As the cart of history rolls forward, the tracks that it leaves behind become rich history for future generations. The Southern Song Imperial Street is full of history even its name. When you step upon the stone road you are walking on a thoroughfare over which so many thousands of horses have galloped, when you feel with your hand touching the old wall, you're touching something on which countless soldiers have stood watch. It's a modern commercial centre now, but the current hustle and bustle can't drown out the avenue's boisterous past. One thing that hasn't changed since ancient times is the common wish of the people for a prosperous and peaceful country.

主编供稿

半山的来历
History of the Banshan Mountain

城北横亘着一条山脉，主峰叫皋亭山。在半山腰，建有一座倪姓女子的祭祀庙，一度香火旺盛。主峰森林覆盖，灌木丛生，人们到了半山腰，也就留步不前，很少有人登顶。人们习惯叫它半山，寺庙也叫成了半山庙，后来整个山都叫半山了。富阳也有一个半山村，在一条山脉主峰的半山腰。半山应该就是半山腰的简称吧。

A range of mountains passes through the north of the city, with the chief peak being called Gaoting Mountain. Halfway up the mountain, there is a sacrificial temple for a girl surnamed Ni where incense burn brightly. The forest cover on the main peak is thick, and shrubs grow densely. Ascending to the top is a difficult task because of this, and few people accomplish it. People referred to the temple on the mountain as the Banshan Temple, and then the whole mountain came to be called Banshan(mid-level) Mountain. Fuyang also has a Banshan Village, which is in the mid-levels of the main peak of another range of mountains.

摄影：潘益青

一块朝内挂的匾
An Inward-facing Sign

在胡庆余堂内，很多匾额都是朝外挂的，唯独一块"戒欺"的匾额是挂在营业厅后，面对经理室、账房间，专门挂给员工看。匾书："凡百贸易均着不得欺字，药业关系性命尤为万不可欺。"这种道德上的自觉，秉承了传统文化中最基本的德行准则。"戒欺"是胡庆余堂的一种店规、一种理念，更是一种道德、一种文化。

Inside Hu Qingyu Tang, there are many signs that face outside, but only one that faces inside. It has a simple message: "Don't cheat". It faces the supervisor and accountant's offices, and is there for the employees to see. It reminds the accountants to not cheat on the books, and the other employees to not cheat the customers. This kind of moral self-awareness is one of the fundamental moral principles in traditional culture. "Don't cheat" is part of the rules of the shop, a concept, and more than that, a moral code and a kind of culture.

古城·寻踪
Ancient City and Traces

贴沙河
Tiesha River

从公元861年开始，贴沙河就泄钱塘江潮水，护卫杭州城。经过一千多年的变迁，今天的贴沙河，南起候潮门板桥，北至艮山闸，沿着河道跑一圈，要跑四个1500米还不止。民国时清泰门自来水厂建成，贴沙河的水成了杭州人嘴里喝的水，现在不需要护城了，贴沙河边处处绿树环绕，成为附近居民休闲的地方。

The Tiesha River has carried excess water from the Qiantang River since the year 861, and has protected the city. After more than a thousand years, the current river runs from the Houchao Gate to the Genshan Gate. To run around the entire river, it would be a jog of more than 6 kilometres. During the Republican Period the Qingtai Gate water station was built, and the Tiesha River became a source of drinking water for the people of Hangzhou. In the modern era, it's not needed to protect the city, and green plants are all around it – it has become a place for rest and relaxation.

人家尽枕河
Living Near the River

京杭大运河到达杭州拱宸桥南，分出了一条百米小河。在这里沿河而建的民居，青瓦黛顶，层层叠叠，绵延不断，这就是"人家尽枕河"的小河直街。小街很安静，行走在宽窄只有两三米的白墙黑瓦，没有车马的喧闹，没有人声的鼎沸，时光好像退回几十年，淳朴杭州小巷人家的生活状态，慢慢地还原了，展开了。

South of the Gongchen Bridge, the Beijing-Hangzhou Grand Canal has a small, 100-metre long river that splits off from it. The houses built upon it have green tiles and black roofs, with multiple storeys, and are packed together one after another, as everyone wants to live close to the river. The small streets are very quiet, and when you walk along the narrow road, only 2 or 3 metres wide, among the white walls and black roofs, you won't hear the sound of carts or cars, nor anyone shouting. It's like you've gone back a few decades. A simple life in Hangzhou is slowly being restored.

摄影：朱琦

微观杭州
HANGZHOU: TRADITION AND MODERN TIMES

历史的杭州
Historical Hangzhou

我喜欢有历史的城市，因为历史的年轮承载着城市的文化。折服于北京紫禁城"九天阊阖开宫殿"的威严雄伟，惊叹于西安兵马俑"岂曰无衣，与子同仇"的豪情壮志，沉醉于杭州西湖"淡妆浓抹总相宜"的钟灵毓秀。这三句诗，道出了我最喜爱的三座城市。在杭城的日子，我将开创属于自己的故事。

I like cities with history, because history is the record of the culture of a place. Beijing has the Forbidden City, Xi'an the Terracotta Warriors, and Hangzhou, the West Lake. These are my three favourites, all described in poems and historical records. The days I live in Hangzhou now will become the stories I tell later on.

方回春堂的金字招牌
Fang Huichun Tang's Golden Sign

免费保健凉茶，免费发放香袋、腊八粥，免费熬药加工，免费赠阅《祝您健康》养生手册，遵循"扶危济困""许可赚钱、不许卖假"的古训，善待顾客、善待客商、善待员工，这些理念应该是杭城三百余年老字号国医国药馆方回春堂传承至今的立身之本和金字招牌吧。国医国药的博大精深在这里延续，福泽百姓。

Free healthy cold tea, free incense bags and congee, free processing of medicines, free health publications. The store operates on the principles of "Help those in need. It's ok to earn money, but not to sell fake goods. Treat customers, clients and workers well." These are the golden rules of Fang Huichun Tang, a provider of Chinese traditional medicine that has been around for more than three centuries. The traditions continue here for the benefit of the people.

江南私家名园郭庄
Guo's Villa

郭庄作为一家沿西湖而筑的私家园林，可谓把借西湖湖山绝美之景做到了极致。不仅使自己成为西湖中一小景，更使西湖成了自家最大景。立于园内"乘风邀月"轩，则六桥烟柳，湖光山色尽收眼底；登假山顶上之"赏心悦目"亭，则居高临下，四围山色，环湖胜景，饱览无余。秋夜里于亭中吟饮赏月，真乃神仙之乐。

Guo's Villa is a private garden along the bank of the West Lake, and can be said to be one of the nicest spots on the lake. It's a small piece of scenery on the lake, and from inside the entire scenery of the lake is the view that it enjoys. Within, there is a "wind and moon corridor", the famous "six smoky willows", and a great view of the lake and mountains. One may climb a rockery to the "Pavilion of Wonderful Views" to enjoy a panoramic view of rocks and water. It's a great place to enjoy a drink on an autumn night.

古城·寻踪
Ancient City and Traces

坚守只为那份信念
Holding to Faith

狭小的门面，一架"吱嘎"作响的老旧木制弹棉花机，满屋飞扬的尘絮，隔板上翻好的棉花被，墙上挂着刚过世第三代店主潘文彪老人的遗像。这家百年老店"潘永泰棉花店"还能守住这门濒临灭绝的弹棉花手工技艺吗？"赚多少不要紧，最重要的是能守住这个行业"，潘老女儿决心继续坚守杭城最后的棉花店。

Behind a narrow door, a wooden cotton gin kicks into gear, and sends cotton dust flying around the room. On the partition is a cotton quilt, and hung upon the wall is an image of recently deceased third-generation shop owner Pan Wenbiao. Can this hundred-year-old shop, Pan Yongtai's Cotton, hold out in the area of handcrafted cotton processing when the field is almost on the brink of extinction? "Don't worry about how much we earn, what's important is that we keep going," says Pan's daughter about her conviction to keep on running Hangzhou's last cotton store of this kind.

有"腔调"的富义仓
Fuyi Granary

京杭大运河畔霞湾巷8号的富义仓清代曾有"天下粮仓"美称，是杭州粮食集中地和南粮北运的中转站。时代变迁中陆续做过军用仓库、军属和造船厂职工宿舍，还在十年前遭遇一场毁灭性火灾。所幸在2007年修复中由"物质粮仓"转为"精神粮仓"，成为杭州人口中有"腔调"的文化创意园区，焕发了新的时代光彩。

At No. 8, Xiawan Lane near the Beijing-Hangzhou Grand Canal there is an important granary that had the nickname of "No. 1 Granary" during the Qing Dynasty – it's a storehouse for grain and a transfer station on the north-south corridor for grain transit. Over time, it's served as a military storehouse and a dormitory for the military and ship makers. Ten years ago it experienced a large fire. Luckily, in 2007 it was transformed from a material storehouse to a "spiritual storehouse", and became a creative industry park in the preservation of Hangzhou culture.

摄影：徐骋

微观杭州
HANGZHOU: TRADITION AND MODERN TIMES

江墅铁路遗址公园
Jiangshu Railway Park

站在拱宸桥头看京杭大运河中繁忙穿梭来往的船只，你一定想不到这古桥畔曾有过蒸汽机火车的轰鸣声吧？而当你走过宽阔笔直的绍兴路时，你也一定不知道脚下踩的就是浙江省首条铁路——江墅铁路的路基吧。是的，如果你想寻那曾经的老站房、老铁轨、老火车头，江墅铁路遗址公园应该会勾起你的旧日怀想。

Standing at the Gongchen Bridge looking out at the busy array of boats on the Beijing-Hangzhou Grand Canal, you may not necessarily know that trains once passed over this bridge. When you walk over Shaoxing Road, you probably wouldn't guess that under your feet is the site of Zhejiang's first railroad – the Jiangshu Railway. If you look for it, you'll see that old stations, tracks, and trains can all be found at the Jiangshu Railway Park. It's a good place to go for a dose of nostalgia.

一所大学一座城
University and City

2016年1月9日，300位老杭大师生从各地赶往木马剧场举行跨年聚会，当屏幕上出现老杭大熟悉的点点滴滴，当见证母校40年沧桑、受人尊敬的余式厚老师朗诵起叶芝的诗歌《当你老了》时，全场不禁泪崩。每个有尊严的城市都应该有一所自己的大学，对于杭州这座充满人文情怀的城市，失去杭州大学则成了永远的痛。

On January 9, 2016, 300 students and professors of Hangzhou University went to the Trojan House for a year-end party, after seeing the familiar scenes of the university on the screen, showing 40 years of development of the university, and professor Yu Shihou read William Butler Yeats' poem *When You're Old*, everyone had tears in their eyes. Every respectable city should have its own university. For a city so full of culture and feeling, losing Hangzhou University is a topic that will forever be painful.

浙江大学之江校区　摄影：陈心远

古城·寻踪
Ancient City and Traces

"头顶天，脚踏边"
Tianzhang Hat and Bianfumao Shoes

"头顶天，脚踏边"是早前杭州的一句俗语，意为头上要戴"天章"帽，脚下要穿"边福茂"鞋。就说这"边福茂"鞋庄吧，硬是不简单，连毛主席、周总理都在这里定制过布鞋呢。边氏制鞋技术上总结出"宽蹬一字平，穷腰富后跟"的十字经验，用料考究、工艺精细、讲究信誉，难怪历经170年仍长盛不衰了。

A traditional saying among the people of Hangzhou is that you should wear a Tianzhang brand hat, and Bianfumao brand shoes. These are shoes that have been custom ordered by the likes of Mao Zedong and Zhou Enlai. The materials used are of top-quality, the workmanship is fine – it's no wonder these famous shoes have been around for 170 years.

寂寞的"饾版"技艺
A Lonely Printing Technology

黄小健住在杭州市区一个民国时期的老建筑里，他是"饾版"印刷技艺唯一的传人，家里很简朴，到处都是饾版印刷的工具和作品。他把所有的时间和热情都倾注在研究饾版印刷的工艺里，花鸟虫鱼在他的刻笔下栩栩如生，文化古籍在他的刀锋下行云流水。只可惜这门精美绝伦的"饾版拱花"技艺，至今还没找到传人。

Huang Xiaojian lives in a house from the Republican Era in Hangzhou, and is the last practitioner of the "pile printing" technique. His house is simple, and everywhere there are tools for and products of this printing process. He spends all his time and energy on researching this printing technique, all kinds of designs of flowers, birds, insects and fish flowing forth from his pen. Printing plates of ancient books in the old style flow from his knife. It's a shame that he hasn't found a successor to continue his craft.

"欧Ⅲ公园"背后的城市记忆
Memories of the City

研发出欧Ⅲ标准柴油机新品的杭州汽车发动机厂，曾是很多50后、60后老杭州人的青春骄傲，是70后、80后的儿时记忆，可惜如今人们只能到位于京杭大运河拱墅段最南端的"欧Ⅲ公园"旁的工厂旧址去缅怀了。旧城改造中杭城许多显赫一时的大厂陆续外迁，曾经辉煌的历史成为了城市背后的记忆。

Hangzhou Automotive Factory was the site of the development of diesel engines meeting Euro-3 standard, and is a proud memory for those born in the '50s and '60s. For those born in the '70s and '80s, it's a childhood memory. It's a pity that one can only go to reminisce now at the site of the former factory, located at the Gongshu section of the Beijing-Hangzhou Grand Canal. As the city modernised, many old factories successively moved out of the city, and their glimmering histories became mere memories in the background of the city.

微观杭州
HANGZHOU: TRADITION AND MODERN TIMES

摄影：孙宏茂

良渚博物院
Liangzhu Museum

初见良渚博物院，四个粗犷的长方建筑跃入眼帘，杂乱而无序地散落在青山绿水间。我一度以为这佳作只是大自然的鬼斧神工。后来才了解到，它的设计理念便是"一把玉锥散落地面"。黄洞石砌成的建筑玉质般浑然一体，与周围环境构成一幅和谐相融的自然之景。置身其中，仿佛同时拥抱着自然与人文，让人流连忘返。

When I first saw the Liangzhu Museum, a collection of roughly-constructed rectangular buildings strewn randomly upon some hills, I thought it must be some kind of bizarre work of nature. Later on, it was constructed in line with the concept of jade awls scattered around the ground. The buildings made of yellow travertine glimmer like jade, and merge nicely with the surrounding landscapes. It seemingly blends human culture and nature, and makes one want to stay for a while.

杭州话"儿"字童谣
Children's Rhymes

一群小伢儿在大街上蹦蹦跳跳，欢呼雀跃，嘴里不时说着："小丫儿，搞搞儿，搞了不好闹家儿；大丫儿，搞搞儿，搞了不好生丫儿；老头儿，搞搞儿，搞了不好翘辫儿。""杭州小伢儿，头上戴帽儿，坐的小凳儿，吃饭用筷儿，喝汤用镖儿，吃好撒子儿。"这带"儿"字的童谣，大抵只有我们杭州小伢儿说得多哩。

A group of children jump around on the street, playing happily, and singing a rhyme: "Little girl, do it well, if you don't, you'll have trouble at home. Big girl, do it well, if you don't, you'll have a little girl. Old man, do it well. If you don't you'll die." "Hangzhou kids, put your hats on, sit on your stools, eat your rice, drink your soup…" These unique rhymes can only be said correctly by the children of Hangzhou.

古城・寻踪
Ancient City and Traces

南宋官窑博物馆
Southern Song Official Kiln Museum

周杰伦一曲《青花瓷》，尽现"青花瓷"的"素眉勾勒、屏层鸟绘，色白花青"，让人们对其泛起浓浓向往。南宋官窑博物馆倒是一个欣赏青花瓷的好去处。从六朝浙江青瓷到明、清时期的青花瓷，一件件传世精品勾勒出瓷器文化的发展脉络，更体现了中华文化的深厚底蕴。这官窑博物馆，是千百年的时代缩影。

This museum is a nice place to go to appreciate this specific kind of porcelain. There are specimens from the time of the Six Dynasties up to the Ming and Qing dynasties, and looking at them you can trace the path of the development of porcelain culture in China, and gain a feeling for the richness of Chinese culture. This museum presents a condensed picture of centuries of history.

朝晖枫叶
Maples at Dawn

秋风起，枫叶红，正是赏枫之时。杭州枫叶处处，灵隐路、杨公堤、西溪湿地、满陇桂雨……皆是名声在外的枫叶观赏佳地。但对于老杭州而言，身处闹市之区的朝晖公园才是人们最热衷的赏枫之地。不是什么大红大紫的风景名胜，也不在西湖一带，但也正因为如此，最亲民，最可人，秋天到了，不妨去那儿走一走吧。

When the autumn wind blows, and the maple leaves turn red, the time has come to admire them. Maple leaves are everywhere in Hangzhou, from Lingyin Road, to Yang Gong Causeway, to the West Creek Wetlands, to Manjuelong. These are all great places to admire the famous maple leaves, but for local people, Zhaohui Park in the middle of the city was one of the best places to admire these trees in the past. It's not some amazing scenic vista, nor is it in the West Lake area, but because of these reasons, it's intimate. When fall comes, you should head on over and check it out.

摄影：俞燕君

微观杭州
HANGZHOU: TRADITION AND MODERN TIMES

宋城
Song City

好友来杭,行程紧张,一时不知去哪里玩好。着急之下请教当地司机,司机说:"来了杭州,不去宋城等于没来。"一早前去,看了"宋城千古情",然后又根据各个景点的时间安排看了几个精彩的节目,一天竟然紧张地过去了。好友感慨万千,一个月后,又带了一帮人专门去宋城游玩。司机大哥之言不虚啊!

One of my friends came to visit, but was on a tight schedule. I didn't know where to take around here. I asked the driver, and he said: "Man, when you come to Hangzhou, you gotta hit up the Song City. If you don't, it's like, you haven't even been to Hangzhou!" We went and saw the "Song City of Eternal Love". We worked out a schedule so that we could visit all the exciting places that we wanted to. The day went by quickly. My friend had a great time, and came back with a group of friends specifically to go to the Song City – the driver had a good recommendation after all!

主编供稿

胡庆余堂老师傅
The Old Man at Hu Qingyu Tang

吴山北麓,笔者一路闻着草药味儿找到了这家国字号老药店——胡庆余堂。66岁的丁光明师傅做了40多年的传统手工泛丸,说起自己的手艺,丁师傅总是很带劲,但更多时候,这样的工作是寂寞的,考验着人的耐力和执着。"中药的手工制作手艺就是一份财富,即使现代机器再先进,也不能完全替代,总要有人坚持下去。"

At the northern base of Mount Wu, I followed the smell of herbs to find an old medicine shop – Hu Qingyu Tang. The 66-year old Ding Guangming has worked making traditional medicine for more than 40 years. He's always energetic when talking about his craft, but at many times, this work is lonely, and tests one's endurance and persistence. "The craft of hand-made Chinese medicine is a rich one. Although some processes can now be performed by machines, these machines can't do everything – we still need the human component, so we need to keep at it."

舌尖·记忆
Taste and Memories

微观杭州
HANGZHOU: TRADITION AND MODERN TIMES

**奎元馆的
两碗面**

Two Kinds of Noodles at the Kuiyuan Hall

论起面条，北方人不免有一种优越感。面、汤、料中，面无疑是灵魂。北方人恰在塑造灵魂上得心应手，而江南的面条多数采用机器挂面，缺乏灵气。不过，奎元馆不仅使用"大竹杠人工坐研"的霸气方法做面，配料也考究。镇店之面"片儿川"和"爆鳝面"，笋和鳝都是江南美味。这两碗面成了杭州美食的招牌。

When talking about noodles, northerners definitely feel that this is their territory. In a bowl of noodles, soup, and flavourings, the noodles themselves are of course the soul. Northerners put their greatest efforts into crafting these noodles by hand, whereas in the Jiangnan region most use machines to form them, making them lack "soul". However, the Kuiyuan Restaurant not only uses the powerful technique of a skilled noodle crafter equipped with a large bamboo pole, the flavourings are also excellent. The local noodle dishes "river of slices" and "exploding eel noodles" use flavourings such as bamboo shoots and eel, which are local flavours. These two have become the signature noodles of Hangzhou.

摄影：施鳞麒

**乌米饭
非黑米饭**

Crow Rice, Not Black Rice

每年农历四月，母亲总会从山上采回一些乌树叶，捣碎后与白糯米一起浸泡过夜，然后煮成紫黑发亮、清香扑鼻的乌米饭，拌上一点糖，全家每人来一碗。据说这是一种纪念古德孙膑和佛子目犍连的文化食品，吃了还可以祛风解毒、防蚊叮咬。常遇外地人问：为什么不直接用黑米做？我一般不着急解释，而是先请他尝一口。

During the fourth month of the lunar year, my mother would always pick some leaves of vaccinium on the mountain, and after grinding them up, mix them with white glutinous rice and soak them over night, boiling the rice the next day until it turns black and glossy. This fragrant "vaccinium rice", mixed with a bit of sugar, made a tasty bowl for everyone in the family. It's said that this cultural dish is a way of remembering Sun Bin and the Buddha Maudaglyayana. It's supposed to remove toxins from the body and keep mosquitoes away. People from other places ask me frequently: Why not just use black rice? I don't hurry to explain, I just let them taste a little first.

舌尖・记忆
Taste and Memories

主编供稿

胖子烧饼

Fatty's Baked Cakes

文三路浙大西溪校区边的胖子烧饼店异常火爆。92年，应师傅经商失败，独自一人来到杭州，开始了艰辛的烧饼之路。皇天不负有心人，几经探索，应师傅独创的胖子烧饼在杭城打开了局面。有时，排队等饼的人群有数十米长。现在的应师傅在杭州买了个200多万的房子，安心静气做起老板。

Fatty's Baked Cake shop on Wensan Road near the West Creek Campus of Zhejiang University is unusually popular. In 1992, his former business failed, Mr. Ying came to Hangzhou alone, and started the difficult path of making baked cakes. Heaven, however, rewards those who are persistent, and Mr. Ying came to open his baked shop in Hangzhou. Sometimes, the queue of people waiting to buy cakes is dozens of metres long. Mr. Ying has purchased a 2-million Yuan house in Hangzhou, and enjoys a peaceful life of running his shop.

微观杭州
HANGZHOU: TRADITION AND MODERN TIMES

咸豆浆怎么了
Salty Soy Milk

初到北京求学时，有一次去早餐摊儿点了咸豆浆，却被摊主一声呛："咸豆浆怎么能喝？"我方才意识到北方人只喝甜豆浆和淡豆浆的。喜欢甜食的杭州人，却从小喝惯了咸豆浆：热油条剪碎，配以酱醋及各种调料，紫菜若干，再将纯白的豆浆飞流入碗，加上一客热气腾腾的杭州小笼包，想想也是美味吧？

When I first came to Beijing to study, I went for breakfast once and ordered a salty soy milk, but the booth owner asked me: "How could you want to drink salty soy milk?" This is when I discovered that in the north they only drink sweet and mild soy milk. The people of Hangzhou like to eat sweets, but from a young age I have been used to drinking salty soy milk: cut up a bland Chinese fritter, add some vinegar and other spices, such as dried pickles, and then pour some pure white soy milk into the bowl, and eat it with a hot Hangzhou steamed bun – doesn't that sound nice?

猫耳朵
Cat Ears

杭州有一道名为"猫耳朵"的小吃，实则是一道面点，因形似猫耳得名，是杭州百年老店"知味观"的招牌菜之一。它之所以能成为杭州名食，还得归功于热衷微服出巡的乾隆皇帝。一次下江南到杭州之时，天公不作美，躲避舟中数时，饥饿之际船夫的孙女将面捻成猫耳状，为皇帝做了这道让其赞不绝口的"猫耳朵"。

Hangzhou has a famous "Cat Ears" snack, which is a kind of bread-based snack that gets its name because it resembles the ear of a cat. It's one of the specialties of the old and famous Zhiweiguan in Hangzhou. It can be said to be one of Hangzhou's famous food, and even has the honour of being purchased by the Qianlong Emperor of the Qing Dynasty during a plainclothes patrol. One time during a visit to Hangzhou when the emperor was on a boat in bad weather, the granddaughter of a boatmaster twisted bread into the shape of a cat's ear, causing the emperor to remark upon it.

摄影：陈海芳

舌尖·记忆
Taste and Memories

摄影：王建华

龙井虾仁
Longjing Shrimp

相传清朝皇帝乾隆下江南，到杭州时正逢清明时节，御厨正准备烹制"白玉虾仁"，闻着皇帝赐饮的明前龙井散发出的清香，突发奇想，将茶叶连汁洒入炒虾仁的锅中，于是有了这道美味。"龙井虾仁"中虾仁玉白，食之极为鲜嫩，龙井芽叶碧绿，清香，食后清口开胃，回味无穷。

It's said that when the Qianlong Emperor went to the Jiangnan area, it happened to be the Tomb-Sweeping Holiday. The imperial chef prepared a dish of "white jade shrimp". When he was to inquire as to what the emperor wished to drink, he suddenly had the idea to put the tea leaves into the pot in which he was frying the shrimp, and the result was even better-tasting. The shrimp used in the dish are jade-white and tender; the tea leaves are deep green and lightly fragrant. The dish is refreshing and quite enjoyable.

青梅滋味
The Taste of Green Plum

西溪有个青梅园，留下了杭州人历来喜种青梅爱吃青梅的美好记忆。曾在杭州住过的李清照写过一首关于青梅的词，"见客入来，袜刬金钗溜。和羞走，倚门回首，却把青梅嗅"，描述了纯情女子见男子登门来访羞涩忸怩的场景。如今姑娘们是没有这样的激动和慌乱了，只是青梅酸酸甜甜的滋味仍是杭州姑娘的最爱。

The West Creek area has two green plum gardens, which are a reminder of how throughout history the people of Hangzhou have liked to eat green plums. Li Qingzhao, who used to live in Hangzhou, even wrote a poem about green plums: "A guest rushed in, in such a hurry that she forgot to put slippers on, and her golden hairpin fell out. Embarrassed, she turned to run away, but stopped at the door, and turned her head back to smell the fragrance of the green plums once again." Girls in modern times might not be so clumsy or shy, but the sweet and sour taste of these plums is still greatly beloved by the girls of Hangzhou.

微观杭州
HANGZHOU: TRADITION AND MODERN TIMES

小笼包
Small Steamed Buns

北宋时,开封灌汤包享誉中原。南宋定都杭州,灌汤包随之南下,在精细的杭州人手里,再次大放溢彩。杭州小笼包滚水渌粉,皮薄馅靓,肥瘦适宜,汤汁肥厚;咬上一口,满口流香;与上海小笼包、无锡小笼包并称江南小笼三绝。在很多老杭州眼中,早餐没有小笼包,白天工作都浑身没劲。

During the Northern Song Dynasty, the soup-filled dumplings of Kaifeng were quite famous. During the time of the Southern Song Dynasty, the capital was moved to Hangzhou, and these soup-filled dumplings migrated south. In the delicate hands of the people of Hangzhou, they grew even better. The small steamed buns of Hangzhou have thin skin, plenty of moisture, and a good ratio of fat to lean meat. Take a bite, and your mouth will be filled with flavour. Along with those of Shanghai and Wuxi, the small steamed buns of Hangzhou are one of the three best in the Jiangnan area. For some people of Hangzhou, a breakfast without Hangzhou steamed buns means no energy to work for the rest of the day.

小钵头甜酒酿
Jars of Sweet Liquor

"小钵头甜酒酿来的,毫稍来买。"夏秋的傍晚,杭城一些老小区,总会响起这样的叫卖声。于是,大伯大妈们就会出门买上一小钵这正宗土法酿制、香香糯糯、有着醉人甜香的甜酒酿。"老底子要凭粮票才好买嘞,要屋里厢有产妇才会舍得去买来吃哦,个毛生活真当是越来越好的,"大妈的一口杭州话也是甜甜糯糯。

"Sweet liquor in a little jar, come and get some." At dusk on summer or autumn nights in some old parts of Hangzhou, there will always be bustle of hawkers like this. Old people will come out to buy a small jar of this authentically distilled liquor, thick with the fragrance of sticky rice and an intoxicating sweetness. "I used to buy this stuff with my food tickets. I'd only spend them on actual food if there was a woman pregnant in the family. Ah, life just gets better and better," says an old woman in Hangzhou dialect, the sound of her voice sweet like the liquor.

摄影:程永艳

舌尖·记忆
Taste and Memories

摄影：朱琦

金黄脆嫩油墩儿
Golden, Crispy, Oily Cakes

油墩儿是很多杭州人钟爱的路边摊美食。那金灿灿、圆墩墩、在油锅里被炸得吱吱作响、冒着油光的样子着实可爱，让人看了立马就垂涎欲滴。买上一个爽脆萝卜丝拌雪菜馅儿的油墩儿，吹着热气狠狠地咬上一大口，哇，世上山珍海味统统都不是它的对手。唉，啥也不说了，赶紧出门下楼巷口买油墩儿解馋去啰！

Oily cakes are a snack sold in roadside booths that are much beloved by the people of Hangzhou. They are golden in colour, round, and crackle vigorously when they are fried in a pot of oil. They shine with the oil that they are absolutely full of, and make one drool when looking upon them. Buy one stuffed with carrots and crispy vegetables, blow on it to cool it off, and experience some amazing flavour. Ah, there's no need to say more; let's head out, go downstairs and get some right now!

宝宝的荷花糕
Lotus Cake for Baby

荷花糕因在方形的米粉糕上印有荷花图案而得名，是杭州本地宝宝的传统辅食，养育了一代又一代杭州人。它易消化，耐饥，营养丰富，口感好。买来时是潮湿的，可以晒干或冷冻保存。宝宝要吃时，放在凉开水里浸半小时，上锅蒸约20分钟，出锅后，拿筷子朝同一方向搅拌至均匀。还可加入果汁、鸡汤、鱼汤等配料。

The square rice cake is decorated with a lotus flower on top, and this is from where it gets its name. It's a traditional snack for babies in Hangzhou, and has raised generation after generation of Hangzhou people. It's good for digestion and staves off hunger, nutritious, and tastes nice. They're bought wet and can be dried in the sun or frozen. When you want to feed your baby, place it in cold boiled water for half an hour, and then steam it for 20 minutes. Afterwards, take chopsticks and mix it up until it's even. You can also add fruit juice, chicken soup, fish soup, or other ingredients.

微观杭州
HANGZHOU: TRADITION AND MODERN TIMES

吴山酥油饼
Crispy Oil Cakes on Mount Wu

吴山酥油饼因其美味被称"吴山第一点",至今已有七八百年历史。据说苏东坡任杭州知州时,某日冒雨游吴山,见众人争购油饼,也买下几只品尝,觉其一层层,一丝丝,又油又酥,如身上所着蓑衣,便随口为其取名"蓑衣饼"。从此"蓑衣饼"生意兴隆,声名远扬。因"蓑衣饼"与"酥油饼"谐音,后改称"酥油饼"。

The crispy oil cakes sold of Mount Wu have been called the best thing about the place, and have seven or eight centuries of history. It's said that when Su Dongpo was in charge of Hangzhou, on a rainy day he went to Mount Wu, and saw people flocking to buy these oily cakes. He bought a few to try, and thought the multi-layered, delicate cakes resembled the palm-woven rain cloak he was wearing, and thus called them "rain cloak cakes". Afterwards, they became famous far and wide. As the pronunciation of "rain cloak" is similar to "crispy oil" in Chinese, they later became known as "crispy oil cakes".

一品南乳肉
Top-tier Southern Roasted Pork

南乳肉以五花条肉调以红腐乳卤汁焖制而成,色泽鲜艳,肉酥而不腻。传说南宋时元兵大举南侵,当权宰相贾似道独揽朝政,置国家危亡于不顾,朝野对他怨声载道,恨之入骨。于是百姓将他的一品官衔名移至家乡菜南乳肉上,用以表达对他寝皮食肉的心头之恨。从此,"一品南乳肉"就成为地道杭城名肴。

The top-tier "southern roasted pork" is made from fatty meat that is braised with fermented red bean curd. It is bright in colour, the meat is crisp and not oily. It's said that when Mongolian soldiers pushed southwards during the Southern Song Dynasty, then the prime minister Jia Sidao arrogated the court. Both the court and common people complained loudly, and hatred boiled in their hands. They applied his "top-tier" title to their local specialty, the "southern roasted pork", to display the extent of their hatred of him. After this, "top-tier southern roasted pork" was thus called.

灵隐寺的腊八粥
Laba Congee at Lingyin Temple

"火升起,锅上灶,料下锅,粥香四溢。腊月初八好去处,灵隐寺里喝好粥。"这仿佛已经成为杭州人约定俗成的习惯了。小小一碗粥,选料、剥壳、搅拌、翻勺、放凉、装盒,点点滴滴,满满福气和情意。更遑论灵隐寺腊八节风俗现已成功入选第六批杭州市非物质文化遗产,浓浓的人文情怀,扑面而来。

The fire rises, the pot is placed on, the ingredients are placed within and the congee is realised. On the eighth day of the 12th lunar month, there's great congee at Lingyin Temple. This has practically become an established custom in Hangzhou. To make a small bowl of congee, one picks ingredients, shucks rice, mixes it, turns the spoon, lets it cool, and then puts it in the box. The congee of the temple has already been listed as an intangible cultural heritage asset.

舌尖·记忆
Taste and Memories

"甘其食"包子
"Ganqishi" Steamed Buns

甘其食包子在杭州餐饮业可真是个奇迹。从 2009 年创立至今，几百家连锁店在杭城遍地开花，日卖 40 多万只包子，据说一年已经做到了三个亿。甘其食包子皮薄馅多汁多，还带点杭州人喜欢的甜味。品名取意于老子对百姓食仪的理解，意为要百姓吃的好。有这样的经营理念，难怪他们的事业会蒸蒸日上了。

Ganqishi steamed buns are a culinary peculiarity in Hangzhou. From 2009 to now, several hundred of this chain of shops have opened around the city, selling more than 400,000 buns a day, with annual avenue of about 0.3 billion Yuan each year. They have thin skin and lots of filling and juice inside, and have a bit of the sweet flavour that Hangzhou people like. The "gan" in Ganqishi means to provide good food for the people, as the word means "slightly sweet" in Chinese. With such an understanding of their market, it's no wonder they've done so well.

葱包烩儿香
Fragrant Onion Rolls

下班回家最爱在小区门口买上一副大妈的葱包烩儿来吃。大妈的制作工具特别霸气，是用电熨斗来做压板的，因此她的葱包烩儿特别脆香。只见大妈用薄薄的春饼包裹住油条，放上几根小葱，拿起电熨斗霸气的一压，葱包烩儿顿时"滋滋"作响，香气四溢。然后再涂上独门秘制甜辣酱，咬上一口，哇，真乃人间第一美味也。

I love eating the fried onion rolls that a woman sells outside my compound when I get home after work. She really has her own way of doing things – she uses an electric iron to cook the rolls as she presses them flat, and for this reason they're especially crispy and fragrant. She wraps a spring cake around a fritter, and then sprinkles some onions on top, wraps it up, presses the iron down upon it and with a sizzling sound, fragrance flies outward. She then paints them with her own special spicy sauce. Your mind will be blown by the flavour when you take a bite.

摄影：徐骋

微观杭州
HANGZHOU: TRADITION AND MODERN TIMES

摄影：施麟麒

独当一面的
片儿川
Pian Er Chuan Noodle

杭州是南宋国都，受中原饮食影响，面食也相当流行。街头巷尾，各种面馆数不胜数。但不管来自全国各地的面条们多么来势汹汹，杭城总有一碗面够格站出来大喝一声：这是我的地盘！这就是片儿川，选用笋、雪菜、肉片做浇头，鲜香爽口，百吃不厌。因笋和肉都切成片状，加上杭州方言的"儿"化音，故得此名。

Hangzhou was the capital of the Southern Song Dynasty and its cuisine was influenced by the culture of the Central Plains Region, where noodles are popular. In the streets, lanes and alleyways, all kinds of noodle shops are everywhere. However, no matter how popular certain noodle dishes may be, Hangzhou has a noodle dish that can claim Hangzhou as its own territory. This is the "Pian Er Chuan". It's made with bamboo shoots, crispy vegetables and meat slices. It smells and tastes great, and is liked by everyone.

西湖莼菜汤
Water-shield Soup of the West Lake

朋友来杭，指名想吃"西湖莼菜汤"，说是十年前来杭一游，一道"西湖莼菜汤"让她一直朝思暮想。于是，赶紧带她去楼外楼点上一大碗配以鸡丝、火腿，碧翠鲜醇，清洌爽口的西湖莼菜汤解馋，然后再去商店买上二十袋莼菜汤料准备让她带回。想想乾隆每次游江南都必尝莼菜汤，朋友对此汤如此钟爱也情有可原。

When a friend came to Hangzhou, she said that she wanted to eat the "water shield (brasenia schreberi) soup of the West Lake". She said that she'd been to Hangzhou 10 years before, and the soup had left a lasting impression in her mind. Thus, I took her to Louwailou and ordered a big bowl of water-shield soup with chicken and ham, clear and fresh with amazing flavour. Afterwards we both went to a market and I bought more than 20 bags of water-shield soup mix for her to take with her. Think about how the Qianlong Emperor had this soup every time he came to the Jiangnan area; it's understandable that my friend's so obsessed with it.

舌尖·记忆
Taste and Memories

东坡肉
Dongpo Meat

苏东坡曾任杭州通判和知府，主持疏浚西湖，用淤泥修建了堤坝。感民工辛苦，杀了几只猪，用大锅红烧，犒赏民工吃肉。肉味道鲜美，大家叫它东坡肉。他性格豪放得罪了不少官员，遭到贬谪。百姓为纪念他，就把修的堤叫苏堤，把一条街叫东坡巷，把一条路叫学仕路。

When Su Dongpo was in charge of Hangzhou, he dredged and deepened the West Lake and used the excavated mud to build the Su Causeway. To thank the labourers for their effort, he slaughtered a few pigs and braised them in soy sauce in a large pot, then presenting them to the labourers to eat. The flavour of the meat was excellent, and everyone called it "Dongpo meat". His forthright and bold character angered a number of other officials. He subsequently was relegated of his duties. In order to remember him, people called the causeway he had built the Su Causeway, a street in the city Dongpo Lane, and a road Scholar Road.

湖畔居喝茶
Drinking Tea in a Lakeside House

杭州茶楼有熙熙攘攘热闹的，也有安安静静清雅的，最清雅的恐非湖畔居莫属。窗外，一平如镜的西湖水，衬着依稀的山；窗内，一壶龙井，二三知己，卸了面具，话话家常。半日的清闲，又岂止抵十年的尘梦呢？

There are teahouses in Hangzhou that are boisterous and noisy, and those that are quiet and calm. The most quiet and delicate of these is the Lakeside House. Outside the window, there is the scenery of the water of the West Lake, so still as to reflect like a mirror, with the faint image of mountains in the background. Within, friends sit together and talk. What a great place to pass the time and catch up with those you care for!

摄影：梅莹

微观杭州
HANGZHOU: TRADITION AND MODERN TIMES

摄影：俞燕君

吃馆子和懒得烧
Eating Out, Too Lazy

以前杭州人外面吃饭，叫"吃馆子"，馆子就几家：杭州酒家、楼外楼、山外山，一年里也难得有一两回吃；现在外面吃饭叫"懒得烧"。每到周末或假日，杭帮的外婆家、绿茶、老头儿油爆虾，进驻的衢州兔头、千岛湖鱼头、东阳土菜、舟山小海鲜……都坐满了懒得烧的小两口、老两口、三代同聚的十几口。

People in Hangzhou used to rarely eat out, and there were few famous restaurants in the city: the Hangzhou Restaurant, Louwailou, Shanwaishan; in a year people would go maybe once or twice. Now, people call eating out "being too lazy", i.e. too lazy to cook. Every weekend and holiday, there are Hangzhou cuisines: Grandma's House, Green Tea, Old Guy Shrimp. There are also cuisines from elsewhere in China: Quzhou Rabbit Head, Thousand Island Lake Fish Head, Dongyang Local, Zhoushan Seafood, and the like. Pairs of young people, pairs of old people, groups of a dozen or more classmates all flock to these places.

撤不去的茶食
Chinese Pastry

凡南方城市，无论闽粤、湘川还是江浙、皖赣，朋友一聚，三两知己，喝茶总是常规选项，杭州也无例外。不过杭州的茶楼茶馆多和他地有别，喝茶为虚，自助的各式小点零食为实。两人对坐是一席，三五人围坐也是一席，席上浅碟浅碗满满，说说笑笑，热热闹闹地吃，吃完即取，席上是永远撤不去的茶食。

All southern cities, be they in the provinces like Guangdong, Fujian, Hunan, or Sichuan, or even Zhejiang, Anhui, or Jiangxi, when friends get together, or people gather, tea will be present. Hangzhou is of course no exception. However, Hangzhou's teahouses are special, different from elsewhere. There are all kinds of snacks one may help oneself to. Two people sit at one table, but a group of three to five also sit at the same small table. The table will be full of small cups, plates, bowls and the like. People sit, chat, laugh and have a good time while eating, fetching more as soon as they finish – the table will never be empty of Chinese pastries and snacks.

舌尖 · 记忆
Taste and Memories

知味观点心
Zhiweiguan Dim Sum

"欲知我味、观料便知。"知味观杭帮点心传统制作技艺完全依靠手工操作，工序技艺繁琐而精致，有和、揉、压、搓、摁、挤、切、卷、包、折、雕等几十道工序。可归纳为煮、炸、蒸、煎、烤、煨、烫等制作方式，其在点心上做字做花、画龙画凤，集多种工艺于一身，具有独特的手工艺价值。

"If you want to know how it tastes, look at the ingredients". The dim sum at Zhiweiguan is made by hand, according to traditional techniques. The processes are both complicated and precise. Mixing, kneading, pressing, rubbing, squeezing, cutting, rolling, wrapping, folding and carving are all performed manually. Different items are boiled, fried, steamed, baked, and roasted all with precision. The flowers, dragons and phoenixes drawn on the food are all done so with great artistic which makes the edibles have special artistic value.

东坞山豆腐皮
Mount Dongwu Bean Curd Skin

东坞山豆腐皮有悠久的历史。杭州有佛国之称，离杭州只有数十里的东坞山村的水是向西流的，这稀有的地理风貌，引得高僧驻足。古时，村里有九庵十三寺，终年香火不断，香客成群，加上众多的僧尼，需大量的素斋，豆腐皮成了僧尼及香客的主要素肴。千百年来，东坞山豆腐皮的技艺一直代代相传，盛传不衰。

The bean curd skin of Mount Dongwu has a long history. Hangzhou has been called the "Buddhist kingdom", and less than 10 km away at Mount Dongwu the water flows west, which is geographically rare. It became a place where accomplished monks lived. In ancient times, in the village there was 9 nunneries and 13 temples, where incense burned all year round. Many guests and many monks and nuns meant there was a need for a large amount of vegetarian food, and bean curd skin became the main food for both residents and visitors. After more than a millennium, the technique of making the bean curd skin still persists.

红糖麻花
Brown Sugar and Dough-Twists

西溪湿地公园的河渚街上，有家卖土特产的店，这里每天挤满了游客，想买他家特产，天天座无虚席。其中，最受欢迎当属红糖麻花了。油炸后的麻花，呈现出自然生态的金黄色，伴着一层"红糖衣"，带有一股焦香味儿。每拿一根都能拔出长长的红糖丝，嚼起来香脆可口。游客们都以之作为伴手礼，高兴地捎回家去。

On the Hezhu Street in the West Creek Wetlands Park, there a store selling local products. Every day it's full of customers looking to purchase what's available. The most popular item is dough-twists with brown sugar. After being fried in oil, they turn golden yellow, and are given a coat of brown sugar. They have a caramelised taste. Every single one is covered in strings of crispy sugar. They are crispy and tasty. You will also see people purchasing them as gifts, happily carrying them home.

微观杭州
HANGZHOU: TRADITION AND MODERN TIMES

芡实糕
Foxnut Cake

杨先生店里的芡实糕非常畅销，那是一种很有特色的地方糕点。芡实糕最早是西塘古镇的居民制作的，他们选用七八月份新鲜的芡实，去壳晾干，研粉，和着糯米粉、白糖一起做成芡实糕，蒸熟即可。待芡实糕冷却后，便可切成方块形食用了。这种古老的糕点做法代代相传，卖出去的不只是糕点，更是那浓浓的乡味儿。

The foxnut cake in Mr. Yang's shop sells very well, because it's a special cake, specific to the locality. Foxnut cake first originated in the Xitang Old Town, where it was made by local residents. They would take foxnuts (the seeds of Gordon Euryale, *Eurale ferox Salisb*) picked in July and August, dry them in the sun, grind them up as glutinous rice powder, and add sugar to make cakes that they then steamed. After the cakes cooled off, they are cut into squares and eaten. This old method of making the cake has been passed down through the generations. What's on sale in the shop isn't just cake, but a slice of local flavour.

老头儿油爆虾
Old Man Fried Shrimp

在杭州的"角落美食"中，"老头儿油爆虾"人气最高。以前，在老头儿饭店吃饭，店里的招牌菜早被食客们倒背如流了，自然就用不上什么菜单了。近些年，"老头儿"自己已经很少在江湖上露面，倒是他的后辈们开出了好些分店，依旧延续着天天排长龙的神话。不夸张地说，老头儿家可真是黏住食客们的胃了。

Talking about "corners restaurant" in Hangzhou, "Old Man Fried Shrimp" is quite popular. In this restaurant run by an old man, the specialty dish is so popular that there's no real need for a menu. In recent years, the old man himself rarely makes an appearance, as his descendants have opened a number of branches, and continue to do excellent business. It's not an exaggeration to say that people are obsessed with the old man's restaurant.

康康饭店
Kangkang Restaurant

邻居王先生一家不做晚饭，下馆子了，不用说，肯定又去康康饭店了。老杭州们都还有印象，1982年开在小车桥附近的小饭馆，各式各样的酱货吸引了大批食客，那就是康康饭店的前身。这些年来，他家的菜式新款不多，老菜式倒是越做越经典，依旧是那几道招牌：酱鸭、酱肉、酱鲫鱼、八宝酱丁、煎带鱼、杭州卷鸡……

My neighbour family doesn't make dinner at home today – I know where they go. It's always Kangkang restaurant. The old people of Hangzhou all remember when the small restaurant opened next to Xiaoche Bridge in 1982. All kinds of soy-sauce flavoured dishes attracted a large amount of customers – that was the Kangkang of those years. In recent years, few new dishes have been rolled out, but the old dishes are more classic than ever. The classics never die: soy sauce duck, soy sauce pork, soy sauce carp, chopped vegetables and meat with soy sauce, fried cutlass fish, Hangzhou chicken rolls…

舌尖·记忆
Taste and Memories

主编供稿

楼外楼
Louwailou

"西湖醋鱼何处美,独数杭州楼外楼。"杭州人有种习俗,凡有宾客,必到楼外楼品尝杭菜风味。楼外楼,创建于清道光二十八年(1848年),是一家具有150多年悠久历史的老店,有"江南第一楼"的美誉。它坐落于风景优美的孤山之麓,像一颗明珠镶嵌在山光水色之中,熠熠生辉。

The people of Hangzhou frequently say that that Louwailou is the place to go for West Lake Fish – when guests come from out of town, it's customary to bring them there. The restaurant was established in 1848, and with over 150 years of history, it's one with quite a long history. It's sometimes called the most famous restaurant in the Jiangnan area. It's situated in a scenic location, at the foot of Mount Gu, and it shines like a pearl inlaid into the face of the mountain.

城东美食小街
East Town Food Street

城东双菱路是一条美食街。光是奶茶店就有好几家,最老资格的晓麟奶茶,最亲切的阿姨奶茶;烧烤店种类繁多,台湾鸡排,韩国烤肉,本土烤鱿鱼炸豆腐,等等,各种香馋死人;还有各色饼店,安徽来的胖子做的面饼天天长队,而夏记烧饼、永康肉饼、缙云烧饼、栗子酥饼也生意不错,最开心的是二三十块能吃遍全街!

Shuangling Road in the east of the city is a food street. Milk tea shops alone make many appearances. The most "legit" of these is the Xiaolin Milk Tea Shop, the one with the warmest feeling is Auntie's Milk Tea. There are also many barbecue shops: Taiwanese chicken, Korean barbecue, local squid, fried tofu, and many more. There are so many tempting flavours. There are also many kinds of cake shops, a noodle shop run by a fat guy from Anhui that is packed all the time, and Xia Ji's Baked Bread, Yongkang's Meat-stuffed Bread, Jinyun Baked Bread, flaky chestnut cakes… The best thing is that you can fill up on just twenty or thirty Yuan!

微观杭州
HANGZHOU: TRADITION AND MODERN TIMES

蛋黄南瓜
Egg-yolk Pumpkin

不爱吃鸡蛋，亦不爱吃南瓜的我，却独独爱上了蛋黄南瓜。顾名思义，这就是一道由南瓜、咸蛋黄做成的甜品，黄灿灿的。与其说是甜品，其实更像是主菜，既咸又甜，既好吃又顶饱，是每次吃杭帮菜时必点的。初次吃时，因为名字中有蛋黄、南瓜字样，硬生生拒绝了，所幸后来有朋友一再推荐才没有错过。

I don't like egg yolk, and I don't like pumpkin either, but I do like egg-yolk pumpkin. It's a bright yellow sweet made from egg yolk and salted pumpkin. It's classed as a sweet but it looks more like a main dish. Salty and sweet, tasty and filling, I have to get some every time I go to a restaurant that serves Hangzhou cuisine. The first time I tried it, because of the name, I firmly refused when it was offered to me, but my friend insisted. I take his recommendations now.

幸福双
Double Happiness

幸福双是杭州风味小吃，最早由知味观创制，因它一般成双供应，取吉庆之意，故名幸福双。它的制作过程有点像做包子，都是将配好的馅儿放入擀好的皮子里，用手捏拢，然后放到火上蒸。蒸熟的幸福双油润多馅，皮薄绵软，香甜可口，如若复蒸，其味更佳。有机会来杭州一定要品尝，顺便讨个好彩头。

Xingfushuang or "Double Happiness" is a traditional snack in Hangzhou which has been manufactured by Zhiweiguan for quite some time. It's usually sold in pairs and is said to be auspicious, thus the name. The method of making it is similar to a Chinese steamed bun, where prepared filling is put in a shell, and then rolled around before being placed in a steamer. A finished *xingfushuang* is smooth and has quite a lot of filling. The skin is thin and soft, and the flavour is nice and sweet. If it's re-steamed, it will taste even better. If you have the opportunity to visit Hangzhou and try one, maybe your luck will get a boost, too.

西湖醋鱼
West Lake Fish

西湖醋鱼是杭州传统风味名菜，属浙系菜，有"西湖第一珍馐"的美誉。西湖醋鱼又名"叔嫂传珍"，这个名字还有一个典故，说的是嫂嫂为出逃的小叔子烧了一条鱼，做法奇特，有酸有甜，寄意小叔将来发达时勿忘今时辛酸。细想一下，人生其实就像这西湖醋鱼，甜中有酸，酸中有甜，"悲欣交集"方为人生。

The vinegared fish of the West Lake is a traditional and famous dish which belongs to the cuisine of Zhejiang. It's said to be the best thing to eat from the West Lake. It's also called "Legend of Uncle and Aunt" – there is a name behind this story. It's said that when the younger brother of a woman's husband ran off, she prepared an excellent fish, both sour and sweet, and he returned and forgot his worries. Life is a bit like this fish, when you think about it: there's sweet in the sour, and sour in the sweet, as joys and sorrows mix together.

吴越·包融
Wu-Yue and Inclusiveness

摄影：董思申

微观杭州
HANGZHOU: TRADITION AND MODERN TIMES

古荡蚕桑
Sericulture in Gudang

旧时古荡一带土地肥沃，桑树成荫，蚕市利好。村民们以茶、竹易米，或养鱼育蚕，过着自给自足的农耕生活，引来许多文人雅士隐居，留下了诸如"山应犬狺声似豹，桑稀蚕老茧成蛾"等歌颂桑蚕的优美诗句。遗憾的是，城市改造变迁中，如今只有学院路与华星路交汇处那座"古荡蚕桑"雕塑还在诉说着古荡桑蚕兴盛的历史。

In the old days Gudang was a place with good soil and good mulberry trees, which made for good silkworms. The people of the village would raise tea, bamboo to exchange for rice, or fish and silkworms to support themselves. Many men of letters were attracted there to live as hermits, and many wrote poems about the scenery and sericulture there. Sadly, as the city has been transformed, all that remains of sericulture in Gudang is a sculpture at the intersection of Xueyuan Road and Huaxing Road.

细十番
Xishifan

楼塔细十番属民间弦乐，演奏综合运用十余种弦乐器，具有独特的地域风格。相传由明朝御医楼英返乡后与一帮琴友创制并流传民间。楼英用"工尺"记谱了《一条枪》《望庄台》等曲谱，上世纪80年代李麟、楼峰又分别转写简谱、五线谱。经过六百年的传承发展，细十番目前已列入国家非遗名录，楼塔镇则成为"中国民间文化艺术之乡"。

Xishifan is a kind of musical ensemble of stringed instruments that is popular among the people. It has its own unique local style. It's said that it was created by imperial physician Lou Ying, and after he returned to his hometown, it was popularised by him and a group of musicians. Lou Ying used the notes of the traditional Chinese musical scale to make songs such as *One Gun and Platform Overlooking the Village*. In the 1980's, Li Lin and Lou Feng rewrote these songs in the simplified Chinese musical scale and Western-style musical notation. With its history of more than six hundred years of development, *Xishifan* has already been listed as a national intangible cultural heritage, and Louta Town has become known as an "artistic and cultural town of all China".

摄影：楼正寿

吴越·包融
Wu-Yue and Inclusiveness

摄影：王嫱

越剧
Shaoxing Opera

越剧是杭州的主要地方戏曲，七十年前流行在嵊州一带，后广为传播。杭州人爱唱越剧，黄龙洞、西湖边是越剧票友们常去的地方。秋日爬完山，游好湖，在亭边小憩，听一曲《梁山伯与祝英台》或《西厢记》，心绪随那婉转悠扬的唱腔千回百转，真是人生一大乐事。

Shaoxing Opera is the most popular performance form in Hangzhou, with more than a 70-year history in the Shengzhou area. It has spread over a larger area now. The people of Hangzhou enjoy these plays, and the Yellow Dragon Cave and West Lake both see a large number of fans enjoying performances. On an autumn day after you've finished hiking, walking along the lakes and resting in the small pavilions, you can listen to *Butterfly Lovers* (*Liang Shanbo and Zhu Yingtai*) or *Tale of the Western Chamber*, and your spirit will be carried through the twists and turns of the beautiful music and voices – this is one of the great enjoyments in life.

滚灯
Rolling Lamps

余杭滚灯是国家非遗项目，距今有800多年历史。发源地翁梅临钱塘北岸，古代盐业兴旺，海盗频频入侵，当地民众以滚灯竞技比武，以示实力强大，令海盗不敢侵犯。民间视滚灯为吉祥之物、强体之宝、娱乐之器，每逢元宵或庙会必参与表演。它有九套二十七个表演动作，融技巧、力量于一体，集体育、舞蹈、杂技于一身。

The rolling lamps of Yuhang District are a national intangible cultural heritage, and have more than 800 years of history. They originated in Wengmei, on the north bank of the Qiantang River. In ancient times when the salt industry was strong, pirates frequently made incursions, so the local residents held athletic competitions with the rolling lamps as a demonstration of military skills. The impressive display caused pirates to not dare to attack them. People view lamps as a sign of prosperity and strength, as well as objects for entertainment, and decorations for the Lantern Festival and temple fairs. A full performance involves 9 sets and 27 actions to be displayed, combining technique and might into one for a performance that involves athletics, dance and juggling.

微观杭州
HANGZHOU: TRADITION AND MODERN TIMES

不能买饭的饭馆
A Restaurant that Doesn't Sell Rice

黄焖鸡米饭大家都听说过吧,那"黄焖鸡米面"呢?杭州西斗门路上,饭馆的牌子都把"饭"改成"面"了,什么隆江猪脚面、石锅拌面……真是有趣极了。仔细打听,才知道这一片都是居民住宅区,原本的饭馆因为油烟太大影响到附近居民了,经环保部门考察后被整改,于是就有了改名后的各类"面"馆。

Everyone's heard of yellow braised chicken and steamed rice, but what about yellow braised chicken and noodles? On Xidoumen Road in Hangzhou, there's a restaurant that has replaced well-known rice dishes with noodles: Longjiang Pork Trotter Noodles, Korean Bibim-noodles, you name it. I looked into this, and it turns out that as it's located in a residential area, the people living there complained about the noise, oil, and smoke of all the rice being fried, and the environmental protection department paid a visit. The menu was altered to centre around noodles.

孤山名人
Famous Personages at Mount Gu

人文杭城,仅小小一孤山便已是名人荟萃。北麓放鹤亭,乃梅妻鹤子林和靖之地;西泠桥边,"人以印集,舍以地名",众多金石名家相聚于此,研讨印学;辛亥女杰竞雄安眠于西麓,孙中山亲题"巾帼英雄"四字;慕才一亭,苏小小青冢犹在;俞樾故楼六一泉,文澜书阁楼外楼……真道是"人间蓬莱是孤山,有梅花处好凭栏"。

In the cultured city of Hangzhou, there are many famous people, even just the Mount Gu you can find a lot. At the northern foot of the mountain, there is the Pavilion for Releasing Herons, where the Northern Song Dynasty poet Lin Hejing resided and was known for having "plum trees for wives, and herons for children". Near the Xiling Bridge is the site of the Xiling Society of Seal Arts. Qing-dynasty heroine Qiu Jin was executed at the western foot of the mountain in 1907. The place is also connected with other famous personages and locations: the grave of Su Xiaoxiao, the former residence of Qing-dynasty academic Yu Yue, the Wenlan Library, Louwailou… The Mount Gu, covered in plum trees, is a site of significance.

"别墅型"的民居
"Villa-style" Residences

杭州的民居很统一,整齐。我所说的这类民居并不是花园式商品房,而是在市区周边、高速公路两旁的一幢幢房子,三四层高,斜肩的瓦块顶,一条小楼梯,这基本就是杭州房子的标准式模型,即便郊区的很多房子也都很相似。我的朋友开了个玩笑:"要是咱中国的民居都这个样子,是不是就赶上发达国家了呀。"

The residences of Hangzhou are very uniform and orderly. The residences that I'm talking about aren't garden-style commercial housing, but instead are detached buildings, three or four storeys tall with slanted roofs and a single small staircase, located on the outskirts of cities and lining the sites of expressways. This is the standard format for houses in Hangzhou, and many houses in the suburbs are like this. My friend said jokingly, "If every family in China built a house like this, our growth figures would be off the chart."

微观杭州
HANGZHOU: TRADITION AND MODERN TIMES

摄影：程永艳

水上人家
Life on the Water

在钱塘江通往运河的闸门口，每天都会有运沙船排成长长一列，等着水警开启闸门。一条船上通常就是一户人家。男人驾船，女人负责家务。外人乍一看，这种水上吉普赛人的生活很吸引人。其实一问他们就知道，常年生活在水上，日子有多么艰辛和枯燥。尤其是航行时候遇到暴风雨，更是危险重重。一句话，天道酬勤。

Every day there is a long line of boats waiting for the water police to open the gate from the Qiantang River to the Beijing-Hangzhou Grand Canal. One boat normally represents one family. The man pilots the boat, and the woman takes care of housework. To outsiders, this life of being an "aquatic gypsy" is appealing. However, ask these people and they will tell you that living for years on the water, day in and day out, is difficult and tiring, especially when wind and rain make one's home into a dangerous location. Well, good things come to those who work.

最后的绿皮火车
The Last Green Train

一个拥有洲级大火车站，高铁地铁齐飞的城市，目前竟还保留着一条绿皮火车线路。它是一班往返乔司和南星桥编组站的内部通勤车，偶有乔司菜农和游客搭乘。只有7节车厢，没有空调广播和窗帘，没有装满食品的手推车，每天来往三趟。这辆据说也是全国唯一的通勤火车，现在成了人们怀旧的寄托。

A city with a massive intercontinental rail station and awesome high-speed rail in frastructure, Hangzhou still has one green train line. It's an internal commuter train between Qiao Si and the Nanxing Bridge. It only has 7 cars, and no air conditioning, curtains, or announcements. There are no carts selling refreshments, and it only makes three round trips per day. This is the only commuter train in China, and has now become a symbol of nostalgia.

吴越 · 包融
Wu-Yue and Inclusiveness

民间艺人节
Folk Arts Day

一口叙说千古事，双手对舞百万兵，三根竹能文能武，一片皮呼圣呼贤。声影并茂的皮影戏就是民间传统艺术的杰出代表。而江浙地区向来不乏指尖灵活的民间艺人，在杭州举办的民间艺人节就是巧匠的汇聚，艺术的盛会。民间艺人节是传统艺术的世代传承，也是制造工艺的返璞归真。

A mouth speaks countless stories as two arms greet myriad dancing soldiers. Three sticks of bamboo represent the arts of writing and fighting, and shadow puppets dance about. The art of Shadow Puppetry is one of the best examples of folk performance traditions. The performances in the Zhejiang area aren't just a show of those with quick fingers, but also the intersection of craftsmanship and art. The Folk Arts Day is a longstanding artistic tradition, and connects us with simpler time.

摄影：杜红英

微观杭州
HANGZHOU: TRADITION AND MODERN TIMES

主编供稿

城标起航
Sign of the City

2008年，经过一年多的全球征集活动，杭州城标从两千多件作品中诞生。城标"杭"字巧妙地融合了航船、城郭、建筑、园林、拱桥等诸多要素：整体似航船，暗藏大禹"舍舟登岸"的历史典故，可辨的翘屋角、圆拱门和"三潭印月"，显示了杭州的地域特征，下方带有笔触的笔意，凸现了杭州"五水共导"的城市特征。

In 2008, after a global campaign, the Hangzhou Sign of the City project was launched with more than 2,000 candidate items. The design of this logo draws upon elements such as boats, walls, buildings, gardens, arched bridges and many others. It represents famous historical incidents, such as ancient emperor Da Yu leaving his boats for the land, geographic features such as Three Pools Mirroring the Moon, functional features such as river diversion.

邻居节
Neighbours' Festival

每年十月的杭州邻居节，满城飘扬着代表幸福守望的黄丝带，《邻居之歌》回荡在各个居民社区。敲门日、健康日、互助日、欢聚日、社区烹饪大赛、饺子宴、相亲会……各种主题活动让邻居们乐在其中，而大家也在微笑中由陌生变为熟悉，由冷漠变得真诚。今年的邻居节又要来临，亲，准备好去敲邻居的门了吗？

Neighbours' Festival comes around in October in Hangzhou each year. You will see the entire city filled with yellow streamers symbolising prosperity, and *Song of the Neighbours* will echo throughout the compounds. Door-knocking day, health day, mutual aid day, party day, the community cooking competition, the dumpling banquet and blind date parties... All kinds of themed activities allow those who live close to each other to meet and have fun, and everyone smiles as strangers become acquaintances. When the holiday comes around this year, are you ready to go knock on your neighbour's door?

吴越·包融
Wu-Yue and Inclusiveness

"62"骂人?
Hey "62"

几年前去选车牌号，一眼相中了一组"62……"的号码，当时，工作人员连问两次"确定吗？"让人感觉很奇怪。号码选好后，非常开心。第二天，得知"62"在杭州话中有骂人蠢笨的意思，心情就有点糟糕。大概有一个月左右的时间，只要坐在车上，就到处寻找"难兄难弟"，以此来宽慰自己。现在，当然释怀了。

A few years ago when I was selecting the number plate for my car, the worker at the office asked me twice if I was sure when I selected one that had "62" in it. I found that odd. I was very happy after getting my car plate, but the next day learned that "62" is used in Hangzhou dialect to tell someone he is an idiot. I didn't feel so great after that. For about a month after that, I would look for "fellow sufferers" as I scanned everyone else's car for people that had made the same mistake as I had. I'm over it now, though.

西湖绸伞
Silk Umbrellas of the West Lake

杭州的丝绸很有名，用丝绸做的绸伞也是特产之一。绸伞的骨子是用竹子做的，一丝一竹，江南的味道就出来了。小小的绸伞就是个装饰物，拿来把玩或收藏，顶多遮个阳或拍个照。最好不要拿来给人，因为"伞"和"散"同音，送伞有分离之意，总归不大吉利。

Hangzhou is famous for silk, and the umbrellas made of silk from Hangzhou are one of the local specialities. The frame of a silk umbrella is made from bamboo, with bamboo and silk both being representative of the Jiangnan area. A small silk umbrella is a decorative item that can be used for fun or collection, as well as used to block out the sun or take pictures. It's best not to give these umbrellas as a gift, as the word for "umbrella" in Chinese sounds like "scatter" – presenting one of these umbrellas as a gift carries a message of parting.

摄影：王嫱

微观杭州
HANGZHOU: TRADITION AND MODERN TIMES

用音乐为逝者送行
Seeing the Deceased off with Music

假如你在杭州的郊区听到某户人家在昼夜不停地连续播放一段越剧或一首歌曲的时候，就意味着家中有老者逝去。过去，家中有老者逝去，都会燃放爆竹，请道士和尚到家中诵经，俗称"做道场"。现在不再燃放爆竹，改用音乐为逝者送行，更加文明，应该是一种进步。

If you hear someone playing a Shaoxing Opera or a song continuously, day and night, in Hangzhou, this means that someone in that family has died. In the past, when an old person passed away, people would light firecrackers and ask monk or priests to come by and chant sutras. People no longer set off firecrackers, but use music instead – still a bit of sonic pollution, but progress, considering the alternative.

演奏会
Concert

"终于听得起大师的演奏会了！"凭身份证花60元，买到了"史蒂芬·米克斯自在世界"演奏会惠民票的大学生王璐高兴地说道。话剧、舞台剧、演奏会……曾经，这些高雅艺术的高高在上的价格，让普通民众望而却步。杭州大剧院60元惠民票的推出，真正推动了大众走进大剧院欣赏高雅艺术。

"Now you can finally hear the masters preform!" university student Wang Lu happily exclaims after having bought a ticket to a Stephan Micus performance for just 60 Yuan with her citizen's ID. Dramas, dances, performances. In the past the ticket prices for these fancy events were quite high, which resulted in a high barriel to entry. Now with the 60 Yuan ticket scheme in Hangzhou, the masses are being motivated to appreciate this high culture.

垃圾与文化博物馆
Museum of Rubbish and Culture

北郊天子岭，中国首个垃圾博物馆静静矗立着。馆内展品，"西泠四老"合写的"止于至善"、蔡履平的石头印、张笑荣的古砚砖……都体现了和谐发展的主题。有人这样评价垃圾与文化的结合：用提高审美来遏制人类的贪欲，从而减少垃圾的增长。听起来像天方夜谭，其实恰恰是治本之策，是滋润高雅的精神养分。

At Tianzi Peak in the northern suburbs there is the first rubbish museum in China, which stands there quietly. Within the hall, the "four old guys of Xiling" have written a four-character inscription for the sign, Cai Lüping has contributed a stone stamp, and Zhang Xiaorong has contributed an old ink stone. They are all there with the message of harmonious development. Some people have thus critiqued the Museum of Rubbish and Culture: In order to stimulate the desire of people from things of aesthetic value, we have to start with reducing rubbish. When you hear this odd theory, you might think that it's simply an administrative campaign, but actually it's a program to promote cultivation.

吴越·包融
Wu-Yue and Inclusiveness

鬼节
Spirit's Day

夜幕降临，走到小区的桥头，竟发现桥头、路两边、楼梯口点满了红色的蜡烛。一问才知，今天是阴历七月三十日，是地藏王菩萨的诞辰，杭州人叫"鬼节"。这一天，嫁出的女儿都要回来给娘家送红蜡烛，然后在桥头、家门口插满点燃的红烛，以祭祀鬼神，求得平安。也有人烧香、摆放祭品供奉地藏王菩萨。

As the curtain of night falls upon the stage of the day, I walk to the bridge in my compound and find lighting candles from end of bridges, roadsides to stairways. After asking, I find out that it's the 30th day of the 7th lunar month, the birthday of Ksitigarbha, which the people of Hangzhou call "spirits' day". This day, a daughter who has already married comes back home, and gives her parents candles. Then at the door of the household and end of the bridge, all of which are covered with candles, people pray to the gods for peace. Some people also burn incense and arrange sacrifices for Ksitigarbha.

茶道之源
The Origin of the Tea Ceremony

径山茶宴起源于唐，盛行于宋，传承至今已有千余年，且体制完备、程序规范、意境高远，在我国禅茶文化和礼仪史上享有尊位，影响深广。日本江户时代《类聚名物考》记载："茶宴之起，正元年中，驻前国崇福寺开山南浦绍明，入唐时宋世也，到径山寺谒虚堂，而传其法而皈。"这证明了径山茶宴乃日本茶道之源。

Jingshan tea ceremonies originated in the Tang Dynasty and flourished in the Song, and after more than a thousand of years of history continue to the present day. They have many elements and rules, and a respected position in the tea culture of China, as well as a far-reaching influence. Even Japanese history records the tea ceremony as being born in the Tang Dynasty and flourishing in the Song, proving that the Japanese ceremony has its roots in China.

摄影：施麟麒

微观杭州
HANGZHOU: TRADITION AND MODERN TIMES

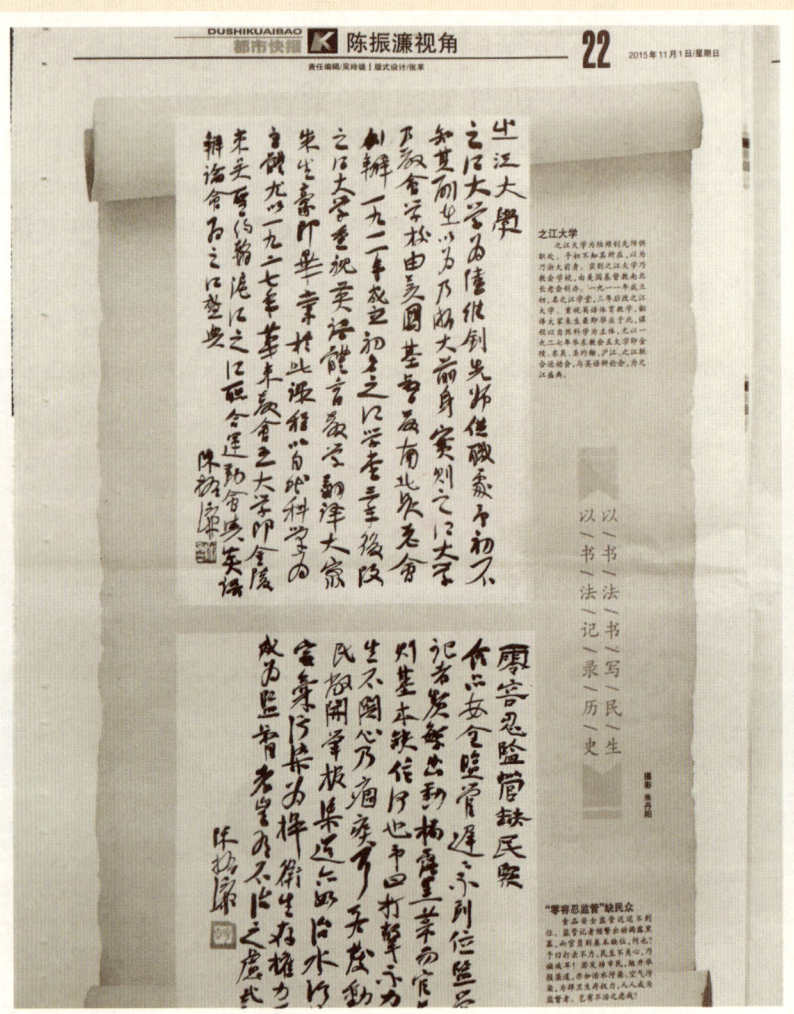

摄影：潘益青

书法新闻
Calligraphy News

翻开周日的《都市快报》，能看到一版别具新意的"书法新闻"。执笔人陈振濂说，在古代，书法本就是记事述史的工具，今天我们把书法提升为艺术，却逐渐丢失了它与生俱来的文化能力，使其成为一种思想贫乏、内容空洞的书写技术大比拼。以书法记录民生、历史是在还原书法本应有的社会功能与存在价值。

If you open up the Sunday edition of *City Express* you can see a new "calligraphy news" section. As calligrapher Chen Zhenlian says, calligraphy was used in earlier times as a tool to record history, yet now we view it as art. Sadly, it has gradually lost most of the cultural functionality that it came into existence with, and become more of an empty form that's simply used for appreciation. Recording our lives and histories with calligraphy can bring societal functionality and value for existence back to the artform.

吴越・包融
Wu-Yue and Inclusiveness

金属球
Metal Balls

杭州市附近的乡间小楼，楼顶上几乎无一例外地顶着三个不锈钢金属球，它们从下往上被一根金属管连起，宛如一根棍子中间串着的大中小三颗糖葫芦，多是不锈钢结构，很是独特惹眼。它们的最初作用是避雷，但现在很多人装这种球只是为了好看，并不接底线，避雷针反而成了引雷针，杭州还发生过因此遭雷击的事呢！

On the tops of buildings in the villages near Hangzhou, practically every one has three metal balls on top, one on top of another with a metal rod going through the centre of each ball. They look like a string of candied cherries on a stick, and are mostly made out of stainless steel – they are a noticeable feature. They were originally used as lightning rods, but as many people thought they looked cool, more and more buildings installed them without connecting a ground wire, making them function as a lightning attractor rather than a lightning arrestor. For this reason, there have been some lightning-related incidents in Hangzhou!

天竺筷
Tianzhu Chopsticks

天竺筷采用杭州天竺山大叶箬竹为原料，保留原始竹青，自然成形，不着油漆，天然环保，筷身烙有西湖风景、诗文花鸟、菩萨佛像、店家字号等图案，独具杭州地域文化特色。天竺筷制作有二十几道工序：其产品从色泽分为红脚筷、白脚筷，从图案可分游客的旅游纪念筷、香客的菩萨寺庙筷、酒楼饭店的字号招牌筷等。

Tianzhu chopsticks are made from the bamboo of Mount Tianzhu in Hangzhou, and maintain their natural green colour. They are naturally formed, unpainted, environmentally friendly, and nice looking. Designs may be burnt into them, such as scenes of the West Lake, poems, flowers, birds, Buddhist figures, and the names of famous old stores. They are a showcase for the unique cultural features of Hangzhou. There are more than 20 steps involved in making them. There are red-footed and white-footed varieties, some with designs that make them attractive as souvenirs for tourists. There are versions made for visitors to Buddhist temples, and some that come with the marks of famous restaurants, and the like.

舒羽的情思
Feelings of Shu Yu

舒羽咖啡馆是杭州文艺小清新的一个新去处，创办于 2011 年。位于拱宸桥头桥西一号，一上桥映入眼帘的是木格花窗红灯笼，仿佛回到了远去的那个年代。"黑色是最彻底的奢华"，这是青年诗人舒羽的诗句，刻在入门的屏风处。我更愿意说，纯粹是一种难能可贵的力量。犹如杭城。

The Shu Yu Café is a new place to go in Hangzhou for an arty time; it was founded in 2011. Situated at the end of the Gongchen bridge, the first thing you'll see when you look upon it from the bridge is windows with intricate woodwork and red lanterns. It feels as if you have stepped into the far past. "The colour black is the most fundamental luxury" is a line from one of the young poet Shu Yu's poems, and is inscribed upon the screen at the entrance. It has a kind of power that inspires admiration, much like the city of Hangzhou itself.

微观杭州
HANGZHOU: TRADITION AND MODERN TIMES

摄影：王杰于

大学校园里的小茶园
A Small Tea Garden on Campus

大学校园里有一两个茶吧很平常，但在大学校园里有茶园就寥寥了，可杭州的浙江科技学院校园里就有这么个挺稀罕的茶园。每到初春，当薄雾还在缓缓的小坡上未散去时，三两个戴草帽的工友就在矮矮茶树丛中忙开了，她们所采之茶是校园里最受追捧的龙井茶。园边还有间茅舍供茶，假日闲暇，约朋友喝几口新茶去。

It's common for there to be a teahouse or two on a university campus, but a tea garden on campus will usually be deserted. However, at Zhejiang University of Science and Technology, there is one of these rare tea gardens. As soon as spring arrives and the mists still gather on the slopes, two or three workers in straw hats go to work on the short tea trees, picking tea that is the most sought after on campus: Longjing tea. Next to the tea garden there is a small cottage that provides tea and a place to relax. On a free day, you can come here with your friends and have some new tea.

水乡婚礼
Wedding in a Water Town

流传在余杭区塘栖、崇贤、五常一带的江南水乡婚礼，带有着浓郁的江南水乡特色，颇为吸引人的眼球。迎娶新娘时除了伴好花轿外，还要租用花船，轿子抬到船上，摇着花船去迎娶新娘。新娘的花轿抬上花船后，要由新娘的兄弟在船头上跺上几脚，谓之"刹浪"。据说，这样跺过之后，一路上就不会有风浪。

Weddings in water towns such as Tangqi, Chongxian and Wuchang in Yuhang District are full of the cultural trappings of the Jiangnan area and are very attractive spectacles. When the bride is retrieved by the groom, there isn't just a floral bridal sedan chair, but also a floral boat upon which the palanquin is placed. After it has been loaded on the boat, the bride's brothers stomp on the boat a few times to "stop the waves". Tradition holds that after this is done, currents and winds will not pose a problem.

吴越·包融
Wu-Yue and Inclusiveness

"到门"何解
"To the Door"

"格个变戏法的变得到门的！"此"到门"取"好"之意。又如家里正在煮饭，孩子吵着开锅吃饭，妈妈会说："再等等，还不到门来。"此时"到门"是指火候没到！如果正在看球赛，有人说："到门的，快射门呀！"这"到门的"就有"机会来了"的意思。你看，杭州话里就"到门"一词，这学问也是够大的。

"Man, that play was to the door!" In this context, "to the door" means great. When cooking dinner at home, your mother may tell you "Hold on, it's not arrived to the door yet" which means the food isn't finished cooking. When watching a ball game, you might hear someone says "To the door, take the shot!" In this case it means "the opportunity is here". "To the door" is a useful phrase in Hangzhou dialect.

浙派古琴
Zhejiang-Style Zither

古琴是中华民族最早的弹弦乐器，是中华传统文化之瑰宝。历史久远，内涵丰富，影响深远。浙派是我国最古老的一个古琴流派，其操琴风格属于吴越系统，指法圆润，节奏紧凑。其创始人是南宋时期著名琴家郭沔，他用自己高超的艺术造诣、对琴乐的独特体会，创作了《潇湘水云》《泛沧浪》《秋鸿》等传世金曲。

The Chinese zither is a classical string instrument used by the peoples of China, and is a cultural treasure. It has a long history, and is well-known and much-liked. The Zhejiang School of zither playing has a style that is part of the Wu-Yue tradition. The plucking style is smooth, and the pace is fast. Its creator is the famous zither player of the Southern Song Dynasty, Guo Mian, who used his skills to bring a unique new form of the art to life. He wrote the pieces *Mist and Clouds over Xiao-Xiang*, *Itineration*, and *Autumn Egret*, among others, all of which are quite famous.

摄影：茅晚菱

微观杭州
HANGZHOU: TRADITION AND MODERN TIMES

当苏轼遇见"苹果"

When Su Shi Met "the Apple"

"水光潋滟晴方好,山色空蒙雨亦奇。欲把西湖比西子,淡妆浓抹总相宜。"这是大诗人苏轼对于西湖极尽赞美的七言绝句。2015年初,这首古诗却气势磅礴地出现在即将开业的西湖苹果店外墙上。浓墨的诗句间,一颗红色"苹果"赫然其中。红与黑、古与今、现代与传统、时尚与古典的碰撞,亦是杭州国际化的一个印证。

"The brimming waves delight the eye on sunny days. The dimming hills give a rare view in rainy haze. The West Lake looks like the fair lady Xi Shi at her best, whether she is richly adorned or plainly dressed." This is an incredibly famous poem by Su Shi. At the start of 2015, when the Apple Store in Hangzhou opened, these lines were written on the storefront. Between the two lines of black text, there was a red apple in the middle. Black and red, old and new, traditional and modern, chic and classical – this is the way things blend together in Hangzhou.

摄影:潘益青

吴越·包融
Wu-Yue and Inclusiveness

耶稣弄堂
Jesus Alley

人们常说基督教堂，在杭州却有个独具特色的耶稣弄堂。耶稣弄堂东起中山北路，西至延安路北段，宋代名叫兴福寺巷，清朝改叫耶稣堂弄。耶稣弄堂的教父司徒雷登本是美国人，却生于此，葬于此，在中国倾注一生，死后选择魂归杭州，这片土地就是他灵魂的归宿。他不仅是耶稣的传教士，也是中美交往的灵魂使者。

When talking about places of worship, Hangzhou has a special "Jesus alley". Extending from Zhongshan North Road in the east to Yan'an North Road in the west, the alley was called Prosperity Temple Alley in the Song Dynasty, and in the Qing Dynasty had its name changed to Jesus Alley. The priest here, John Leighton Stuart, was an American, but he was born and buried here. He was into China his whole life, and elected to have his remains buried here after he died in the United States. He was not just a disseminator of Christianity, but also a link between China and the United States.

杭州话"跑单帮"
"Bill Runners" in Hangzhou

杭州话的"跑单帮"，容易被误认为吃完饭没买单就跑走了。其实，跑单帮是对旧时从事异地贩运工作的小本生意人的称呼。通常这些生意人来往于两地之间，使用自备的交通工具贩运物资，通过差价谋取利润。因旧时的交通没有现在这么发达、方便，人们也多依赖这些生意人进行商品流通。"跑单帮"真是生动形象。

When one hears talk of people who love to "run the bill", it can frequently be misinterpreted as people who love to dine and dash. In fact, a "bill runner" was someone in older times who transported small amounts of cargo from a neighbouring region. They would run between two locales, using their own means of transport, and make profits by exploiting pricing differentials between two markets. As the transport infrastructure in old times was less well developed, many people took advantage of these businesspeople to move goods.

摄影：许敬

微观杭州
HANGZHOU: TRADITION AND MODERN TIMES

"煨灶猫"到"灰灶猫"
Cooked Cat to Ashy Cat

老杭州有人会说"煨灶猫",有人会说"灰灶猫",到底是怎么回事呢?从前家里烧柴灶,冬天猫怕冷了便会趴在灶台上取暖,大家称其为"煨灶猫"。炉灶里不烧柴火,暖气渐渐淡息,这时猫便会钻进灶炉里打滚取暖,出来后满身灰,这便又有了"灰灶猫"。从"煨灶猫"再到"灰灶猫",贴切地比拟人慵懒,提不起精神。

Some people use the term "cooked cat" and some "ashy cat" in Hangzhou, but what do they mean? In older times, cats would climb onto the firewood stove in winter to enjoy its warmth, and people would call them "cooked cats". When the fire would go out, the cat would gradually wedge itself into the burnt-out firewood to absorb the last of the remaining heat, becoming an "ashy cat". Thus, both cooked and ashy cat are terms for someone who is lazy and does not like to move around.

南北相融的酒球会
A Mixture of North and South

对于爱音乐的人来讲,在一个城市,都要有那么一个地标性的 Livehouse,才显得完整。这些年杭州曾经的那些可以演出的场地开了又关,位于万塘路262号的酒球会仍旧坚守着杭州演出要地的位置。酒气和人情味汇聚成了酒球会的江湖气息,基于南方的温情,又掺杂着北方的豪气,不失为杭城一景。

For people who love music, it's essential for every city to have a live house. Places where people can perform in Hangzhou have opened up and closed down over the years, built at 262 Wantang Road there is still the old Wine Club. Here, one can enjoy drink and music in a nice environment, where the warm feelings of South China blend with the elegance of North China for a truly classy scene.

杭州人不会说杭州话
Hangzhou People and Dialect

随着大力推广普通话,出生在杭州的新一代80至00后大多不会说杭州话了。那天老朋友聚会用杭州话聊天,90后的孩子们一句也插不上嘴,只能无趣地在一边低头玩手机。小孩幼时甚至还闹出"杭州人说杭州话,普通人说普通话,我们是普通人,所以我们说普通话"的笑话。杭州人不会说杭州话了,遗憾呢。

As a result of the nationwide push to get people to speak Putonghua, most of the people born after the eighties in Hangzhou can't speak the Hangzhou dialect. When old friends get together, people in their twenties can't join in the conversation, and are left sitting around playing with their phones. As "Putonghua" means "common language", some kids make the joke "Hangzhou people should speak Hangzhou dialect. Common people speak Putonghua. We're common, so we'll speak the common language!" It's a pity that the city is losing its native dialect.

吴越·包融
Wu-Yue and Inclusiveness

湖蟹坐飞机——"悬空八只脚"
"Eight Legs in the Air"

"悬空八只脚"是杭州与上海共用的老方言，说的是这人做事不可靠、不着边际。"八只脚"指的是杭州的八脚大湖蟹，上海人称其为大闸蟹。从前做生意的人都爱聚集上海吃湖蟹，有些商人生意做大了到香港发展，每到吃湖蟹的季节，只好通过飞机把湖蟹运输到香港。湖蟹坐飞机便引出了"悬空八只脚"的说法了。

This is a phrase used in the dialects of both Hangzhou and Shanghai, and is used to mean someone is unreliable. The eight legs refer to the large eight-legged river crab of Hangzhou, which the people of Shanghai call "hairy crab". In the past, businesspeople in Shanghai liked to gather and dine on these crabs, and some merchants managed to expand their business to Hong Kong. When the season rolled around, they would put the crabs on a plane and fly them to Hong Kong. The idea of having crabs fly gave birth to the phrase.

工大向日葵
Sunflowers

看到同学在工大拍的向日葵：阳光肆意地照射着黄灿灿的花和花丛中的少年，这鲜活的画面总让人向往。也捡了个晴好的天气，约上小伙伴来赏花。这里人不少，有像我们一样结伴的一堆堆，也有牵手的一对对，附近的居民也来这里闲坐，爱宠卧在主人脚边陪着。我们也该学学努力向阳的葵花，积极向上，不留阴暗。

It's always a nice scene to see my course mates at the Zhejiang University of Technology taking pictures among the sunflowers as the sunlight spills over the yellow flowers. On a clear day with nice weather, gather a few friends and go to appreciate the flowers. Many people enjoy this, and thus many participate. There are people holding hands, local residents from nearby that come to relax, some with their pets. We should all try to be like the sunflower, making effort to grow upward every day rather than stay in darkness.

杭州话里的"虾"
"Shrimp" in Hangzhou Dialect

北方人骂人的时候，可能会用一个词——"熊"。杭州话中，"虾"与"熊"意思相仿。但是，北方人说人"熊"时，很反感，也是对人的侮辱，说不定两人还会就此来一场唇枪舌剑或大打出手。杭州人说"虾"，却没有那么重的语气，只是被看做取笑。

When people from northern China swear at each other, they may call each other a "bear". In Hangzhou dialect, the word "shrimp" is used in a similar manner. However, whereas the insult of calling someone a bear in the north may lead to a heated argument or physical confrontation, being called a shrimp in Hangzhou isn't so serious, and has more of a playful tone.

微观杭州
HANGZHOU: TRADITION AND MODERN TIMES

摄影：王嫱

中国扇博物馆
China Fan Museum

乘公交到桥西古运河边，走过拱宸桥，穿过一条老街，就到了中国扇博物馆。馆内复古味十足，展品丰富，古今中外，不论材质，各式各样的扇子应有尽有。馆内还有介绍扇子的历史和文人画扇、题扇的故事，以及各种卖扇的小店。倘若你运气好的话，没准还能见着制作扇子的大师，顺便DIY一下。

If you take transit to the west side of the Beijing-Hangzhou Grand Canal and walk to the Gongchen Bridge, you're just one old street away from the China Fan Museum. The architecture gives the place an old feeling inside, where there are many exhibits of fans, both Chinese and foreign, old and modern, in all kinds of styles. There are all kinds of stories introducing historical fans and the things depicted upon them, and all kinds of small fan shops. If you're lucky, you can meet the fanmaster, and try to make a fan yourself.

晓风书屋
Xiaofeng Bookstore

杭州有很多家晓风书屋，分布在市区各处。体育场路的晓风书屋就是最古老的一家，据说已经有十几年的历史了。这里不仅藏书众多，还有咖啡、甜点、复古沙发，在这里看书就是一种享受。还设有别具特色的儿童图书区，里面除了孩子喜欢的书籍，还有一定数量的玩具，可以让孩子边娱乐边读书。可谓是成人和孩子的好去处。

Hangzhou has branches of the Xiaofeng Bookstore distributed all over the city. The oldest one is the branch on Tiyuchang Road, which was founded more than 10 years ago. There aren't just books here, but also coffee, sweets, and old sofas for one to enjoy. There is also a special section for children's books which also has toys for their entertainment. It's a great place for people of all ages to visit.

吴越 · 包融
Wu-Yue and Inclusiveness

晕车也值得
Bus of Love

你听说过公交车让人吗？杭州的公交车可真是有爱。看到行人要过马路，司机总会停下来，并招手示意行人先走。每当这个时候，我都特别愿意做那个行人，哈哈，安全且自由，谁不爱呢？反倒是苦了坐在车上的乘客，走走停停，头晕得厉害。不过生活在这样一个有爱的城市，见证这么多的礼让与感动，晕车也值得呢！

Have you heard of the "bus of love"? Hangzhou's buses really are full of love. When pedestrians are crossing the street, the driver will stop and wave them along. I love it whenever I see this – safety and freedom, who doesn't want that? Now, this may cause a little bit of extra discomfort for the bus riders, also tired, stopping and going, but isn't it worth it to risk a little bit of bussickness for an extra helping of thoughtfulness?

腊八粥
Laba Rice Porridge

杭州人有个老习俗：年年腊八节，都要喝上一碗灵隐寺的腊八粥，福气满满地过新年。发放腊八粥是杭州千年古刹灵隐寺持续多年的传统，现在灵隐寺不再寺内送粥，而将寺外施粥对象转向福利院、老人院等。就在今年1月8日，灵隐寺腊八节风俗，成功入选第六批杭州市非物质文化遗产。这碗腊八粥更有文化意味了。

The people of Hangzhou have a custom: if you drink a bowl of rice porridge on the day of the Laba Rice Porridge Festival at Lingyin Temple, you'll have a year full of prosperity. Giving out the porridge at the temple is a tradition with more than a millennium of history in Hangzhou. The temple doesn't give out porridge on its ground anymore, but instead sends porridge to charitable venues and old peoples' homes. On the day of the festival this year, this custom was included in the six round of things to be listed as intangible cultural heritages of Hangzhou. The bowls are full of culture.

中国伞博物馆
China Umbrella Museum

来到伞的天堂，有种恍如隔世的错觉。精致的工艺，独特的文化，动人的故事，一把把伞宛如一幅幅画。馆内虚拟的雨景，巷子里撑着伞的姑娘，这不正是戴望舒的《雨巷》吗？特色的互动区，正在讲解着老祖宗制伞的过程，年轻的姑娘们忙着拍照，倒是家长和孩子认真地听着这门古老的手艺的讲解。

When you come to this heaven of umbrellas, you'll feel as if you've stepped into another world. Fine craftsmanship, moving stories, and umbrellas painted like beautiful paintings are what are on display here. Walking with an umbrella under the virtual rain backdrop of the museum, a girl appears like the one in Dai Wangshu's poem *Rainy Lane*. At a special interactive area, as a docent talks about the traditions and history of these umbrellas, young girls busy themselves with taking pictures on their phones, but parents and children listen intently to the explanation of the craft.

微观杭州
HANGZHOU: TRADITION AND MODERN TIMES

杭剧
Hangzhou Opera

杭剧是杭州的汉族地方戏曲剧种，一度流行于杭州、嘉兴、湖州一带水乡和苏南等地。起源于杭州曲艺宣卷，在杭、沪、甬一带广为流传，抗日战争以前尤为兴旺。杭剧《银瓶》《李慧娘》等均影响巨大，田汉曾这样评论杭剧："与北昆相比，各有所长。"

Hangzhou Opera is one of the forms of traditional opera popular among the Han people. It has enjoyed popularity in Hangzhou, Jiaxing, Huzhou and other similar areas. It has its origins in the local folk art form Xuanjuan, which was popular in Hangzhou, Shanghai and Ningbo, especially more so prior to the invasion of the Japanese. The plays *Silver Bottle* and *Li Huiniang* are quite popular, and Tian Han once commented on it as at the same level as northern Kunqu Opera.

印世界
Seal Arts

坐落在西湖边孤山南麓、西泠桥畔的西泠印社，是中国研究金石篆刻的一个百年学术团体，有"天下第一名社"之称，收藏了历代印玺，堪称"印世界"。小小印章在方寸之间给人们带来了无穷的艺术享受。徜徉于这3000多年的文化海洋中，说不定你也会邂逅到那枚属于自己的"印"章。

Situated on the southern foot of Mount Gu, Xiling Society of Seal Arts, next to the Xiling Bridge, is an academic group dedicated to metal and stone seals that has more than a century of history, and has been known at times as the "No. 1 Society of Seal Arts in China". As it has a massive collection of historical seals, it's also known as "seal world". Rows of small seals one after another give one a very artistic feeling. Wandering in this sea of 3,000 years of culture, you might just meet the seal that you were destined for.

摄影：孙宏茂

吴越 · 包融
Wu-Yue and Inclusiveness

用"闹"发嗲
You Must Be Joking

杭州女孩发嗲，喜欢"闹"。这里"闹"倒不是"闹腾""无理取闹"的意思，而是用"闹"发嗲，比如："帅哥，你表噶闹！（帅哥，你不要这么闹！）""好不好啦？好地闹！（好不好啦？好的啦！）""帮帮忙闹！（帮帮忙吧！）""女孩子和我讲话，带个闹字，我是没有办法拒绝的。"杭州小伙子实在地说道。

When girls in Hangzhou speak coquettishly, they like to talk about "joking". For example, girls will say "Come on, don't joke around!" or "Are you ready? You must be joking" or "Help me, you joker!" A local boy says honestly: "When I hear girls use this word, I'm powerless to refuse."

商人重利亦重情
Money and Emotion

刚来杭州，一个人出去吃饭，茶足饭饱之后，一摸口袋，完了，出来换了一身衣服，钱包在之前的衣服里……怎么办？只好硬着头皮跟老板解释了，"不好意思，出门忘带钱包了，能不能下次给你？"准备好无情的嘲讽和怀疑的质问了。"好的，没问题。"根本不相信自己的耳朵，匆匆返回宿舍拿了钱就往店里跑。

When I first got to Hangzhou, I went out to eat alone, and after I finished, reaching for my pocket, I realised that I'd left my wallet in my old clothes after changing. What to do? I had no choice but to tell the boss: "I'm sorry, but I left my wallet at home. May I pay you next time." I'd already braced myself for the inquisition, so I was pretty shocked when the boss told me: "Sure, no problem." I ran back to my door, fetched my wallet, and hurried back to the restaurant to pay.

数数童谣
Counting Rhymes

小伢儿在家学数数："一只鸡，二会飞，三个铜板买来滴，四川带来滴，五颜六色滴，骆驼背来滴，七高八低滴，爸爸买来滴，酒里浸过滴，实在没有滴，骗骗伢儿滴。"小孩儿上学之前，家里人会把老一辈留传下来的童谣教给孩子，亲情通过朗朗上口的童谣沟通传递，一代接一代，吟唱的是歌，传承的是满满的爱。

A little child learns numeracy at home: "One chicken, two fliers, only cost three coppers. They're from Sichuan ('four rivers'), different faces and colours, five or six, they came on a camel, about seven or eight feet high. Daddy bought them, and soaked them in liquor (*jiu*, sounds like 'nine')… but actually he didn't, he tricked me…" Before children attend school their family will teach them these kinds of traditional rhymes so that they can get a head start on their education and have fun at the same time.

微观杭州
HANGZHOU: TRADITION AND MODERN TIMES

深山静寺
Quiet Temple Deep in the Mountains

骑车不觉到了一处幽静山林，此处应有一座庙，想到这，黄墙红瓦的一座寺庙就跳入眼帘，比起那些闻名遐迩的古刹，身居山林的你也稍显低了。下车悄悄走进寺门，空无一人，但地上一尘不染，一切都井然有序，望而生畏，庙堂上的佛像也只是静静看着远方，我虽不是教徒，但在那一刻，我不自觉地双手合十，默默祈祷。

While riding my bike I come unexpectedly to a quiet forest. There should be a temple around here, I think, as a temple with yellow walls and red bricks pops into my field of view, even more low-key than those fabled old temples or hermit residences that you may think of. I get off the bike and walk quietly through the gate. It's empty, with nobody around, but there's no dust at all on the ground. Everything is orderly, and I'm a bit unsettled. The Buddhist statues look quietly off into the distance. I'm not a Buddhist, but at that moment I unconsciously put my hands together in a gesture of prayer.

摄影：董思聪

扫叶人
Leafraker

站在寺庙的台阶上，突然看到一个人在树下扫落叶：蓝天为背景，绿树为衬托，一片青草地上阳光正好，手持扫把，悠悠然。莫名地被这幅画面打动了，心情变得平和。突然就想自己是否可以接他的班？可又笑自己如何能知他的想法，我所看到的是一份"闲"，他心里体会到的会不会是一份"累"？矛盾并行，珍惜当下。

Standing on the steps of a temple, I suddenly noticed someone was sweeping leaves under the trees: with a blue sky as a background, and the green of trees as contrast, standing under the sun with a broom in hand, he swept slowly. I was somehow moved by this scene, and my mood became calm. I thought, could I take his place for a while? I knew that there was no way I could do it like he did, and that what seems like a leisure activity to me might be tiresome to him. In the face of these contradictions one must cherish the present.

佛国·诗话
Buddhas and Stories

摄影：孙宏茂

佛都
Buddhist Capital

"南朝四百八十寺，多少楼台烟雨中"说的是江南，在我眼中这说的是西湖。仿佛看见了杭州佛教开山鼻祖——印度高僧慧理踏着烟雨而来。他在杭州的武林山下，即现在的北高峰一带，建造了首座寺庙。杭州的佛教史从此拉开了序幕。杭州之所以为佛都，不仅因为这里曾佛事盛行，更是由于现在杭州存在的寺庙有百余所。

"Of the 480 temples built by the Southern Dynasties, many towers and terraces still remain erect in the misty rain" – this is a description of the Jiangnan area, specifically a view of the West Lake in my eyes. The history of Buddhism in Hangzhou began when a high-ranking monk from India came to the area and saw the scenery, and built the first temple on the Beigao Peak under Mount Wulin. Hangzhou isn't just called the Buddhist Capital because of the actions of monks long ago, but because of the more than one hundred temples that are within the city.

幽谷之中寻法华
Searching for the Fahua Temple in the Quiet Valleys

法华山的法华寺是东晋昙翼法师创建的，这座掩映在幽谷中的寺庙，经过历史的洗礼，几经兴衰，千年历史使它越发肃穆和厚重。爬北高峰的游人往往会进来烧炷香，拜个佛；而那些专门上山的善男信女则是无比虔诚，他们会带上香烛和祭品。有时还可以看到一群结着红头绳的人，一起朝着寺里走去。

The Fahua Temple on Mount Fahua was founded by the monk Shi Tanyi. It's a temple located in a quiet valley, with a history of more than a thousand years. It has had its ups and downs, but it remains today as a solemn and respected place. People who climb Beigao Peak will smell the fragrance of burning incense when they enter the temple to pay their respects. The pious and devout men and women who make the journey specifically to visit the temple will bring fragrant candles and offerings. Sometimes you will see groups of people with red ribbons in their hair walking to the temple together.

**江南名石
"绉云峰"**

The Peak of Creased Clouds

作为"江南三大名石"之一的"绉云峰",上部看上去就像个将军。前人说它"形同云立,纹比波摇",极尽绉、瘦、透之奇妙。数百年间它经历奇特,饱经沧桑,数易其主。清吴六奇不忘查继佐帮助,知恩图报;清道光年间蔡文广千两重金买下,不放自家后花园,却置之福严禅院任人观赏,真乃此奇石的最大知己!

"The Peak of Creased Clouds" is one of three most famous rocks in the Jiangnan area. The top of the rock looks like a military general. It's been described as having "the shape of a cloud, and the creased patterns of rippling waves". It's admired for many of its facets, and has a long history. In the Qing Dynasty, Wu Liuqi bought this stone to thank Zha Jizuo for his assistance. Later, it was bought by Cai Wenguang. Rather than placing in his own garden, he chose to put it in Fuyan Temple for all to enjoy.

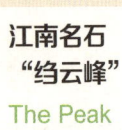

主编供稿

佛国·诗话
Buddhas and Stories

活佛济公
Living Buddha Ji Gong

济公是南宋得道高僧，浙江天台县永宁村人，后人尊称为活佛。他衣衫褴褛，初在灵隐寺出家，后住净慈寺，嗜好酒肉，举止似痴若狂，撰有《镌峰语录》。他扶危济困、除暴安良、彰善罚恶等种种美德，在人们的心中留下了独特而美好的印象。他的名言"酒肉穿肠过，佛祖心中留"更是家喻户晓。

Duke Ji was a righteous monk of the Southern Song Dynasty, a native of Tiantai County, Yongning Village. He has been called a living Buddha. His clothes were ragged and his appearance crazed. After he first left home to be at Lingyin Temple, he later moved to Jingci Temple. He loved liguor and meat, and described such delights in *Chronicles of Juan Peak*. He aided the poor and those in danger, helped with disaster relief, punished the evil and performed all kinds of good deed, leaving a beautiful impression in the hearts of the people. One of his sayings is famous: "Liquor and meat pass through me, but the teachings of the Buddha remain within me."

主编供稿

禅意图书馆
Zen Library

如果你行经天竺路，可能会发现一个低调的图书馆——杭州图书馆佛学分馆。图书馆为密林所蔽，一般游客不易察觉，相遇要看缘分。建筑风格古色古香，馆内藏有丰富的佛教典籍并免费提供茶水。每周都有书法班及讲经活动。盛夏来访尤其惬意：一杯凉茶一卷经，半日如梭而过，累了还能去法喜寺享用一顿素斋。

If you're passing by Tianzhu Road, you might find there is a very low-key library there – the Hangzhou Library's Buddhist Library Branch. The library is hidden by dense forest and won't be discovered by the average passers-by – you need fate to find it. The architectural style is ancient, and the library is full of classical Buddhist texts. Free tea is provided. There are Chinese calligraphy training and preaching activities on a weekly basis. The memories of a visit on a midsummer's day are nice: a cup of cold tea and a Buddhist scripture accompany one as half a day flies away, and when tired, one can retreat to the Faxi Temple for a vegetarian meal.

微观杭州
HANGZHOU: TRADITION AND MODERN TIMES

阿弥陀佛的生日
The Birthday of the Amitabha

阿弥陀佛本是极乐世界的无量寿佛，但中国佛教徒却以农历十一月十七为其生日。这其实是唐代杭州净土宗大德释延寿之诞。高僧生前立倡"禅净双修"并身体力行，为众钦服。晚年居净慈寺，以日诵弥陀圣号十万声等百八件佛事为常课，勤施鬼神食，买放生命，所行功德皆以回向净土，时人疑为弥陀下生。

The Amita Buddha, or Amitabha is the Amitayus, or Buddha of Immeasurable Life, of Sukhavati, the world of life after death, but in China is said to have a birthday on the 17th day of the 11th lunar month. This is actually the birthday of an important monk from the Tang dynasty, Shi Yanshou. He was devout, practiced multiple disciplines and dedicated himself to serving the masses. In his later years, he lived at the Jingci Temple, He was dedicated in his provision of food to spirits and buddhas, and cared not for his own material existence. People of the time suspected that he was an incarnation of the Amita Buddha.

灵隐寺
Lingyin Temple

怪石瘦骨嶙峋，群山跌宕起伏。飞来峰上腾云驾雾，缥缈似九天仙境。都说杭州灵隐寺拜佛最为灵验，终日香火旺盛。我虔诚地匍匐在灵隐寺的大雄宝殿，沐浴佛光于梵唱。我看到了前世因果轮回，我领悟到了人生应多行善良。这里是仙灵汇聚的杭州，这里有为信仰执着追寻的原想。

Mountains rise up bold and unconstrained, the forms of odd rocks and jagged cliffs everywhere. At the Feilai Peak, clouds roll and mists come and go, and the entire scene takes upon a surreal feel. It's said that Lingyin Temple, where the incense always burn, is the best place for one to worship the Buddha in Hangzhou. Hard full of piety, I advance towards the main shrine hall of the temple on all fours as I am bathed in the chanting of the monks. I see the progress of the cycle of karma and reincarnation and realise our obligation to do good deeds in life. This is a meeting place for souls and spirits in Hangzhou, a place where believers can go to be one with their thoughts.

摄影：董思聪

佛国·诗话
Buddhas and Stories

弘一与叔同
Master Hongyi

知道虎跑寺，是因为弘一法师。当年大师在此出家，了断红尘俗念，从此青灯古佛，再无凡尘牵念。槛内人弘一，槛外人叔同，就此别过，恍若来生。他将过去的自己关在了门外，也将叶子关在了心门外。如果叶子事先知道故事的结局，是否还会不顾一切陪这个男人远渡重洋？爱从来都不在乎公平。

You probably know the Tiger Spring Temple because of the Master Hongyi, Li Shutong. When he left his family home, he gave up the petty thoughts of the mundane world, and turned his focus to Buddhist matters, and thus Shutong became Hongyi. He forsook his former self, and together with his female companion. If she'd know how the story was to end, she probably wouldn't have accompanied him on his travel. Love, however, rarely concerns itself with fairness.

三生石
Sansheng Stone

在三天竺后的茶园竟看到传说中的"三生石"，石上篆书"三生石"，石后刻《唐圆泽和尚三生石迹》。传说，唐李源与僧圆泽结伴峨眉山游玩，在河边遇一怀孕三年的孕妇，圆泽说他注定要做此妇之子，当晚圆寂，孕妇顺利产子。他和李源约定13年后三生石见。13年后，李源如约前来，但圆泽说他尘缘未了，高歌离去。

There is a legendary "Sansheng Stone" in the tea garden behind Santianzhu, which has just that name inscribed upon it. Behind, it is inscribed with the words "The monk Yuanze of Tang Dynasty and Sansheng Stone". Legend states that Li Yuan and the monk Yuanze visited Mount Emei together, and met a woman who had been pregnant for three years by the river. Yuanze said that he had decided to be the son of this woman, and passed away that night. The woman gave birth successfully. He said that he would meet Li Yuan thirteen years later at the Sansheng Stone. Thirteen years later, Li Yuan came as promised, but Yuanze said that he had already prepared to ascend to the next realm, and took off with a song.

飞来峰下弥勒佛
Maitreya beneath Feilai Peak

弥勒佛是众多佛像中最为人所知的，他慈颜善目，笑口常开，半卧半躺，露着个大肚子。"大肚能容，容天下难容之事；笑口常开，笑世间可笑之人。"代表了佛教宽宏大量、慈悲为怀的宗旨。进入灵隐寺大门，你就可以看到飞来峰岩壁上刻满了佛像，而弥勒佛最显目。他的造型，启迪人们如何为人处世。

Maitreya is the Buddha best known to the common people. His appearance is a kind one, mouth open laughing, half-reclining to reveal his large stomach. "A large stomach can contain, contain all the troubles on earth. A laughing mouth can laugh at all the silly people in our realm." This represents the great compassion of the Buddha. When you enter the gate of Lingyin Temple, you can see the stones of Feilai Peak carved with all kinds of Buddhist statues, Maitreya being the most prominent. His appearance will make you think of your obligation to conduct yourself in society in an enlightened manner.

微观杭州
HANGZHOU: TRADITION AND MODERN TIMES

月下白云庵
White Cloud Pagoda under the Moonlight

深秋晨雾的西湖之畔，是被金色笼罩的。我们来到雷峰塔侧，小步穿过翠芳园枫林，走上白云庵石阶，迎面一股清泉在庵檐前凌空垂下，像水帘，像飞瀑。寺后一径通幽，棋枰琴榻，位置得宜。左祀月下老人，一手执"婚书"，一手牵"红绳"，慈颜善目，笑容可掬，无数善男信女虔诚的跪拜，似在祈求有情人终成眷属。

Deep in autumn the morning mists gather around the West Lake – the sun shines and turns them all gold. When I arrive at the Leifeng Pagoda, I walk with small steps through the jade garden and maple forest, up the stone steps of the White Cloud pagoda to be greeted with a scene of clear spring water cascading down like a waterfall. It's very quiet behind the temple, with only the faint sounds of people playing at checkers, or maybe some music in the distance. There is the man in the moon, with a marriage contract in one hand and a red cord in the other. Many devout men and women have worshipped in front of him, with his expression mild and disarming, and smile clearly visible. The popular tale of the man in the moon and his marriage has inspired many people to come here and ask for assistance in emotional matters.

来一场身体的修行
Physical Self-Cultivation

杭州的法云安缦，这个号称全球最顶级的酒店，全国开了两家，一家在北京颐和园，另一家就在杭州法云村。这里的客房是原来的法云古村遗留下来的，法云古村据说起源于唐朝，凹凸不平的青石板路，满满的历史感。历史悠久的古村，安缦里佛味很浓，服务人员着装也都是麻布粗服，宾客大多都为静心休心而来。

The Aman is an ultra-high-end hotel of which there are only two in China – one at the Summer Palace in Beijing, and the other at Fayun Village in Hangzhou. The rooms are original architecture from the old village, which are said to date from the Tang Dynasty. The uneven stone roads are full of history. In this village with such a long history, the air inside the Aman is full of Buddhist atmosphere. The staff wear rough linen clothing, and most of the guests are here for rest and relaxation.

杭州寺庙
The Temples of Hangzhou

著名作家郁达夫曾说，杭州的特产有两样，一是夏天的蚊子，一是庙里的和尚。夏天的蚊子在我看来并无特别，庙里的和尚也还未见深意，杭州寺庙之多却触人心神。单说西湖附近，就有灵隐寺、净慈禅寺、法镜寺、法华寺、法喜寺、理安寺、云栖寺等。

Famous author Yu Dafu once said that Hangzhou has two special things: one the mosquitoes in summer, the other the monks in the temples. To me, the mosquitoes in summer aren't really that special at all, and I don't have a deeply ingrained opinion about the monks in the temples, but I can say that the temples in Hangzhou are quite impressive. Just near the West Lake, we have Lingyin Temple, the Jingci Zen Temple, the Fajing Temple, Fahua Temple, Faxi Temple, Li'an Temple, and Yunqi Temple, to name a few.

摄影：许敬

微观杭州
HANGZHOU: TRADITION AND MODERN TIMES

山门在寺外的仙林寺
A Separate Temple and Gate

仙林寺遗址在杭州下城区。据说唐太宗幼时拜仙林和尚为师父，称帝之后，仙林和尚向他要一座建在杭州的大寺院养老，他就派尉迟恭监造。寺造好后，尉迟恭回京，和尚因嫌寺小一路赶到海宁县，要求建一个五里开外的山门，尉迟恭便把山门建在了海宁。这样，就有了这么一个主体在杭州、山门却在海宁的寺院。

The Xianlin Temple is located in Xiacheng District in Hangzhou. It's said that when the Taizong Emperor of the Tang Dynasty visited as a child, he took one of the monks there as a master, and after his ascension, the monk Xianlin asked him to build a monastery in Hangzhou to spend the rest of his life. So the emperor sent Yuchi Gong to oversee its construction. When it was complete, Yuchi Gong returned to the capital city. The monk thought it was too small, and went to Haining County, where he asked for a gate to be built. Yuchi Gong had the gate built in Haining – this is why there is a temple in Hangzhou that has its gate in Haining.

伊斯兰教的杭州圣地
Hangzhou as an Islamic Site

凤凰寺之前不叫凤凰寺，因整修后其整体布局似凤凰而改名为凤凰寺。它是中西建筑风格融合的产物，最大特色是用砖砌结构的无梁顶代替梁架，外观却又是宋代八角形的攒尖顶，有江南独特的秀气和质朴。殿内存有大量以阿拉伯文、波斯文书写的经文，还有宋代的文物古迹，是中西文化交流的历史见证。

The Phoenix Temple wasn't so called before – it gained this name after a major reconstruction gave it a shape that resembled the shape of a phoenix. The architecture is a fusion of Chinese and Western styles, with the most distinctive feature being that the tile roof is built in a beamless construction, rather than one with traditional rafters. From the outside it looks like a Song Dynasty-style octagonal peaked roof, an example of the particular architecture of the Jiangnan area. On the inside, there are a number of Arabic and Persian inscriptions, as well as traces of literary culture from the Song Dynasty – it's a concrete exhibit of east-west cultural exchange.

天竺三寺
The Three Temples of Tianzhu

来到杭州，如果你是虔诚的香客，不必非去灵隐寺。闻名杭城的灵隐，香客是那么多，佛祖怎么顾得过来那么多的心愿呢。天竺三寺中的法喜、法镜、法净寺，它们就在灵隐边上，比起喧闹的灵隐，这里是真正的佛门清净之地。在佛祖面前你可以尽情诉求，因为，他的面前只有你。

If you come to Hangzhou as a pious supplicant, you don't necessarily have to visit Lingyin Temple – there are so many people there, how could the Buddha respond to all their prayers? The three temples of Tianzhu: Faxi, Fajing and Fa-jing are just next to Lingyin Temple, and are much quieter, purer places compared to the crowded clamour of Lingyin Temple. The Buddha can do his best to answer your prayers there, as you are the only one before him.

佛国·诗话
Buddhas and Stories

灵隐寺里寻佛缘
Looking for the Buddha at Lingyin Temple

灵隐寺久负盛名，外来游客一下火车，就有人坐上七路车来到灵隐寺，其中不乏头扎红头绳的烧香客。可见灵隐寺在人们心目中的地位。去那里的人主要有两种目的：一去祈福，二为观光。灵隐的千年古刹和奇峰异石为这座古寺增添色彩。很多人来到灵隐或许只为逃离尘世，寻找心中的慰藉。

Lingyin Temple has long been famous. When visitors got off the train, some would take bus No. 7 to the temple, where many of them were believers with red ribbons in their hair. Seeing this, you know that the position of the temple was in their heart. Most of the people there had two objectives: to pray, and to see the sights. The thousand-year-old structures and amazing mountain scenery make the temple a great place to visit. Some people come here to escape the troubles of the mundane world, and search for a bit of comfort.

摄影：董思聪

微观杭州
HANGZHOU: TRADITION AND MODERN TIMES

摄影：董思聪

灵隐之隐
The Retreat of Lingyin Temple

灵隐寺所处之地确实如名所说，隐没在一片山林翠绿之中。和好友一路爬山上来走走停停，看景拍照，也算乐在其中。游玩到中午，吃一碗这里的素斋面，竟然觉得比平时吃的面都要好吃一些，很有味道。看着各路来拜佛的人，觉得心境澄明。少一些奢求，多一些淡然，那些所谓的贪嗔痴念扰乱的心，也会舒服一些吧。

The name of Lingyin Temple, or the Temple of Soul's Retreat is definitely not undeserved, as it's a retreat among lush forests of green trees and leaves. You can take a day off with a friend to climb the mountain, look at the scenery, and take pictures – in this way, you see how enjoyable it is. After entertaining yourselves to noon or so, you can enjoy a bowl of vegetarian noodles that really blow your mind. You can look at all the worshippers and adherents coming and feel a sense of mental clarity. Let go a bit of that luxury, the modernity, and just relax, be natural. Forget the silly concerns of the world and just enjoy comfort.

上天竺的斋饭
Eating at Upper Tianzhu

从灵隐寺沿一条石板路一路往上，走过下天竺、中天竺，就到了上天竺。和一般寺庙的建制不同，一进门供着的并不是释迦牟尼，而是观世音菩萨。观音殿后面的才是大雄宝殿。到吃饭时间，庙里还有斋饭供应。做斋饭的多是自愿来庙里帮忙的信徒，他们烧得敬业，虽是豆腐白菜、毛豆茄子的大锅菜，吃来依旧可口。

Walking upwards along a road at Lingyin Temple, you will pass Lower Tianzhu and then Middle Tianzhu before arriving at Upper Tianzhu. The structure of the temple is different from a normal one – when you enter you will be greeted not by a statue of Shakyamuni, bur rather one of Avalokitesvara. Behind the hall of Avalokitesvara is the main shrine hall. When the time to eat comes, the temple places out the food that monks have traditionally had to beg for. This food is voluntary provided by Buddhism adherents. Although it's a simple mix-up of tofu, cabbage, beans, and aubergine, it's a decent-tasting meal.

佛国 · 诗话
Buddhas and Stories

腊八节
Laba Porridge Festival

腊八指的是阴历十二月初八，据说是释迦牟尼成佛的日子。作为"东南佛国"的杭州，信佛者众多，对腊八就特别重视，寺庙更是如此。除了腊八前一天举行放生活动外，腊八当日还会把供佛后的腊八粥送到福利院、敬老院和医院等处，践行布施，传播佛法的温暖和爱。若你有幸，这天在西湖边还能领到腊八粥呢！

The Laba Porridge Festival is on the eighth day of the 12th lunar month, and is said to be the birthday of Shakyamuni. Hangzhou, as "Asia's Buddhist capital", has many adherents, and they take the festival seriously. Aside from the religiously significant releasing of captive animals to the wild on the day before, the porridge presented as offerings to the Buddha is then later presented to charitable organisations, old people's homes, hospitals and the like. This is a practical realisation of the warmth and the love of the adherents of the faith. If you're lucky, maybe on this day you'll get a bowl of porridge at the West Lake!

灵隐寺里韦陀像
Vedda at Lingyin Temple

老同学来杭，第一站西湖，第二站就是灵隐寺。刚进入天王殿，搞雕塑的老同学就盯上了弥勒佛背面的韦陀菩萨。该雕像高二米多，金盔黄甲，很是威武。老同学白了我一眼说："它的珍贵处在于整个雕像以香樟木雕成，没用一个钉子，能一块块卸下重装，距今有七百多年历史呢！"

When an old course mate of mine came to Hangzhou, I took him first to the West Lake, and then to Lingyin Temple. When we entered the gate of the Hall of Heavenly Kings, my course mate, a sculptor, looked upon the statue of Vedda behind that of Maitreya. This statue must have been two metres tall, gold and armour everywhere – it really looked mighty. My course mate told me: "What's most amazing about this is that it's made entirely of camphor wood, with no nails! You can take it apart and put it back together again! It's more than seven hundred years old…"

菩萨过生
Bodhisattvha's Birthday

今天大街小巷的墙角、树下摆上了蜡烛，夜幕降临，烛光悦动，似火光铺成的地毯，走在中间，不免毛骨悚然。房东阿姨告诉我说今天是地藏王菩萨的生日，我们在给他过生日。原来是生日蜡烛，吓死宝宝了。在杭州、温州一代都有纪念地藏王的习俗，在这样一个快节奏下的杭州也不失民间风俗啊。

Today I walk down the small streets and alleys of Hangzhou, as the curtain of night falls. Candlelight plays off the walls, forming a kind of carpet. I walk, frightened, through this scene when suddenly my landlady informs me that today is Ksitigarbha's birthday, and that we are celebrating it. These were birthday candles after all! It freaked me out. In Hangzhou and Wenzhou, it's common to celebrate the birthday of Ksitigarbha, and the traditional custom is maintained even against the backdrop of faster-paced modern life.

微观杭州
HANGZHOU: TRADITION AND MODERN TIMES

呼猿洞的来历
The Origins of Calling Monkey Cave

呼猿洞在灵隐寺飞来峰的西面。传说某天知府到灵隐游玩，看见和尚在和猴子下棋。一时技痒，便与和尚对弈。和尚故意输棋给他，他却奚落和尚。和尚推荐猴子与其对弈，知府只输不赢，恼羞成怒，要差役殴打猴子，猴子逃入石洞，只有和尚呼它才会出来。后和尚去世，猴子再没出来。后人称此洞为"呼猿洞"。

Calling Monkey Cave is to the west of the Feilai Peak of Lingyin Temple. Legend says that one day the governor came to the temple, and saw a monk playing chess with a monkey. The governor asked to play with the monk. The monk made a losing move on purpose, but the governor treated him coldly. The monk then recommended the governor to play with the monkey and he didn't win even once. He was angered, and flew into a rage, calling upon people to beat the monkey. The monkey ran into a cave, and would only come out when the monk called. When the monk died, the monkey no longer came out. Thus, the cave is called "Calling Monkey Cave".

观音道场 上天竺
Avalokitesvara at Upper Tianzhu

初到杭州，师弟不去灵隐寺，径直带我和师妹到绿林深处的上天竺寺。"为什么不去灵隐呢？"师妹嘟囔道。"这里可不比灵隐寺差，南宋时被朝廷评为教寺五山之首。农历二月初二开始到端午结束的天竺香市，聚八方来客。中国三个著名的拜观音道场，这里是其一，历史上以观音灵验、香火兴旺闻名大江南北呢！"

When arriving at Hangzhou, my male disciple didn't go to Lingyin Temple, instead taking me and my female disciple deep into the green forest where Upper Tianzhu Temple is. "Why didn't we just go to Lingyin Temple?" My female disciple mumbled. "This is much better. During the time of the Southern Song Dynasty, this was named as the first of the five most important temples by the court. From the second day of the second lunar month until the Dragon Boat Festival, people came from all around. Among the three most famous places to worship Avalokitesvara, this is one of them! Can't you see how great it is?"

校园里的寺庙
Temple on Campus

师弟带我到他供职的浙江科技学院走走，这里湖水清澈，白鹭闲游，群山环绕，环境清幽，真有人间仙境之感。感叹之间，师弟在林木掩映处停下，顺眼看去，赫然见一黄墙，上书"南无阿弥陀佛"。啊，学校里竟然有寺庙！学校所在原来是森林公园，寺是公园的一部分。森林公园成了学校，寺僧自然也离开了。

A younger friend of mine takes me to the campus of the Zhejiang University of Science and Technology where he works. There are clear waters, flying egrets, encircling mountains, and a calm environment which really makes one feel as if one is in a special space. I'm surprised as he stops in a small grove. I look and see a yellow wall, and the words "Namo Amitabha". There's a temple on campus! This campus was originally a forest park, so the temple must have been a part of it. When the park became a university campus, the monks left, but the buildings remained.

佛国 · 诗话
Buddhas and Stories

东南佛国
The Buddhism Kingdom of Southeast China

"上有天堂，下有苏杭"，杭州向来以风景优美闻名于世，中外游客来杭，差不多都要去灵隐寺逛逛，却少有人知杭州还有"东南佛国"之称。有此美称是因杭州佛教兴盛、名僧代出、宝刹众多。杜牧《江南春》中"南朝四百八十寺，多少楼台烟雨中"，说的就是杭州众多的寺院在烟雨中静观历史的沉静之美。

"Up there is heaven, but down here we have Suzhou and Hangzhou." Hangzhou has always been famous for its scenery, attracting visitors from both around China and broad, most of whom will visit Lingyin Temple, but few of whom know about the fame of Hangzhou as the "Buddhism Kingdom of southeast China". It has this name as it's a place where Buddhism has flourished in the past. Many famous monks have come from Hangzhou, and there are many temples. In Tang Dynasty poet Du Mu's *Spring in Jiangnan Area*, there is even a famous phrase that describes the view from the West Lake as "Of the 480 temples built by the Southern Dynasties, many towers and terraces still remain erect in the misty rain".

吴越寺塔
Temples and Towers of Wuyue

吴越时期杭州佛教禅学兴盛。灵隐寺建于东晋，由印度高僧慧理创建。六和塔建于宋开宝年间，由延寿禅师主持建造。宝石塔据传为钱弘俶而建，初称应天塔，后改保俶塔。南屏山上有座黄妃塔，后改称雷峰塔，因凄美动人的白蛇传说闻名中外。"吴越国寺塔之盛，为南方诸国之首。"

During the Wuyue period, the Zen school of Buddhism flourished. Lingyin Temple was built in the Eastern Jin Dynasty (317-420) by the high-level Indian monk Hui Li. The Pagoda of Six Harmonies was built during the reign of the Kaibao Emperor of the Song Dynasty, and was constructed by Master Yanshou. The Baoshi Tower is said to have been built by Qian Hongchu, and was originally named the Yingtian Tower, later having its name changed to Baochu Tower. Upon Mount Nanping there is the Huang Fei Tower, which later became famously known as the Leifeng Pagoda because of the the classic love story of the Lady of the White Snake. Hangzhou has most temples and towers in the south of China.

摄影：陈心远

摄影：许敬

时尚·潮涌

Fashion and Waves

文史书店
Wenshi Bookshop

杭州书林文史书店的环境优雅别致，与文史之名契合的仿古装修，檀香缕缕、琴声袅袅的阅读环境迎合了这一品味。这里的书籍主要选择文学、历史类中的精品图书，以精取胜。除新书更新外，经常会将一些经典但不再版的库存图书上架，带给淘书人无限的惊喜。

The environment of the Wenshi Bookshop in Hangzhou is elegant, blending in faux-classical elements in the architecture. The smell of incense and sounds of music float through the air. Most of the books are selections of the best volumes on literature and history, but there are also out-of-print books that the bookstore keeps stock of and puts out in stages, giving excellent surprises to bookseekers.

找不到教室的大学
A University with Hard-to-Find Classrooms

初探中国美院象山校区，青山绿水，白鹭满山。由质朴而谦逊的本色墙所组成的教学楼犹如潘神的迷宫。那里的同学说很多次上课都找不到自己的教室，永远不知道下一个转角会遇见什么，或许遇见同样迷路的同学，也或许会遇见 Ta。

When you first come to the Xiangshan Campus of the Chinese Academy of Fine Arts you will see green mountains, blue water, and white egrets all around. The modest-looking buildings form a kind of labyrinth there. I've heard that students often have problems finding classrooms. You never know what's around the next corner – maybe another lost classmate, maybe the love of your life.

摄影：杨慧丽

时尚·潮涌
Fashion and Waves

人情味
A Human Touch

爱上一座城,不仅因为它的美,更因为那里的人情冷暖。从公交车私家车主动让路人的那一刻起,我就深感杭州是一个有人情味的城市。路上司机大哥侃侃而谈,嘴里说出的杭州是令他骄傲的,是令我安心的。杭州图书馆是允许流浪汉入馆的,一个如此注重精神建设、尊重个人权利的城市,实不愧对"人间天堂"的美称。

One falls in love with a city not just because it is beautiful, but because it has nice people. Seeing buses and cars stop to give way to pedestrians, I think about what a nice place Hangzhou is. The taxi drivers talk frankly about how they're proud of Hangzhou and feel safe there. The Hangzhou library allows vagrants in. A city that has such nice infrastructure and respect for people truly deserves the name "heaven on earth".

摄影:余优留

微观杭州
HANGZHOU: TRADITION AND MODERN TIMES

星级公厕
Star-Rated Toilet

地铁站出来，穿过幽径来到一处建筑前。抬头看，五颗星后面的英文 TOILET 证明这的确是厕所。进去，除了男女的分别，还有母婴、老人专用的房间。公共洗手的地方，华灯高悬，典雅的木质镜框、窗户、门，还有那袅袅檀烟，恍若进入一所豪宅。杭州的公厕，不但是全国率先实行免费的，而且不乏高大上之作啊。

Coming out of the subway, you head down a quiet alley to find yourself in front of a building. You can find a sign with five stars and the English word TOILET written upon it, which confirms you're in the right place. Aside from men's and women's areas, there is one for mothers with infants, and one for the elderly. There are nice lamps and wood-framed mirrors, doors and windows in the hand-washing area, as well as the floating scent of camphor-tree incense. Being in this toilet is like being in a mansion. Not only are the public toilets in Hangzhou the first free ones in the country, they are quite nice.

此地免费
This Place Is Free

朋友说前两日因为找不着聚会场所，问了跳广场舞的大妈，大妈以为她是来旅游的，热心地给她指路，还不忘提醒，西湖边上的景点都是免费的！朋友说虽然大妈的提醒对她来说是多余的，却油然而生一种身为杭州人的自豪。2003 年起，杭州市政府开放了西湖沿线的全部景点，西湖景点从此以开放姿态迎接八方来客。

My friend told me that for the past two days, she couldn't find a place to get together with friends, so she asked one of the old ladies dancing in the square, who mistook her for a tourist and gave her great directions, and reminded her that all the scenic spots on the West Lake are open for free! My friend said that even though the old woman talked a bit much, it made her proud of being from Hangzhou. In 2003, the Hangzhou city government opened all scenic spots for free around the West Lake to welcome visitors from all over.

摄影：施麟麒

时尚·潮涌
Fashion and Waves

摄影：许敬

新式环卫工
New-Style Sanitation Workers

杭州的地面总很干净，却从没看到提着撮斗、拿着笤帚的环卫工。一天，在公交站等车，一辆电动车在旁边停下，一人用夹子夹起地上的垃圾放进车后面的箱子里，然后慢慢离去。看去，箱子上写着"打造最清洁示范路"字样。原来杭州的环卫工配有专门的电动车，他们是骑车打扫的，怪不得总看不到呢。

The streets in Hangzhou are very clean, but you never see sanitation workers with a dustpan or broom. One day, when I was waiting for the bus, I saw someone on an e-bike stop and use a grabber to pick up some waste, and then throw it in a bin on the end of the bike, then drive off. I saw a slogan on the bin: "Make our clean streets a model." Apparently the Hangzhou sanitation workers have been equipped with e-bikes which they use to do their cleaning – no wonder you never see them.

防空洞的华丽变身
A Beautiful Transformation

炎炎夏日，家住众安桥的陈大妈总会约上亲朋好友一起去宝麓山庄的防空洞纳凉，"我们年年都来的，在这里喝茶聊天，蛮好。"开放市内经过特别装修的11处老防空洞供市民免费避暑纳凉，是杭州市变闲置为有用的一大创举，至今已有13年。洞内不仅有纳凉用的椅子、桌子和水，还有电视、网络、民间艺人表演……

On scorching summer day, old Ms. Chen, who lives at Zhong'an Bridge, takes her friends and family to the air-defence basement at Baolu Mountain. "We come here every year, drink tea and chat." The city has opened 11 air-defence bsements across the city, transforming them into nice underground spaces where people can cool off, a big step in the development "chill" culture. It's been 13 years now, and there aren't just chairs and tables, but also water, TVs, internet, and folk art performances.

微观杭州
HANGZHOU: TRADITION AND MODERN TIMES

摄影：夏利亚

爱心熊猫
Loving Panda

正感叹那些八九成新的衣服扔掉可惜时，小区路上几步一个、肚子上写着"旧衣回收"的爱心熊猫吸引了我的眼球。原来旧衣服等都可放进熊猫的大嘴里，社区人员会把八成新以上的旧衣慈善捐赠，余下的加工制造成布篷、地毯等新产品返回社区，由社区支配。这真是旧衣物的好去处，回去整理旧衣物"喂"熊猫咯！

Just as I was remarking that it was a pity to throw away clothes that are still practically new, I saw a panda with "recycle used clothes" written upon its stomach just a few steps down one of the pathways in my community. You can put your clothes in its mouth, and community workers will donate those that are new enough to charity, and turn the others into awnings, rugs and other items that can be returned to the community. This is a great place to put your old clothing – just "feed" it to the panda.

时尚·潮涌
Fashion and Waves

流动书柜
Mobile Bookcase

在杭州的旅游景点,西湖边,广场上,钱塘江畔,你时不时会在一棵大树底下发现一个书柜。这让游玩的人在坐下来休息时,可以随手拿到一本书看看。你也可以把你自己的书放进书柜供其他游人看,也可以把你喜欢的书换回家慢慢看。这真是一座充满文化味和温馨感的城市。

At tourist spots in Hangzhou, along the West Lake, in the plazas, the Qiantang River, sometimes you will find there is a bookcase under a large tree. These are put there so that visitors can come there to relax. You can take any book you like to read. You can also put books you like there for other people to read, and you can take a book you like home to enjoy. Does that not sound like a very nice scene? This is a city that truly is full of culture and warmth.

YHA 国际青年旅舍
Youth Hostels

这里不是经济型酒店,不提供酒店式服务;这里的床铺如学校寝室的上下铺;这里你可以偶遇来自世界各地的行者……这里,就是YHA国际青年旅舍。在杭城,"明堂、吴山驿、岚水、柳湖小筑、青庭、荷方、岭上、江南驿、风荷"是她的代名词,或与西子湖相伴,或毗邻南山路梧桐大道,真可谓"一步一景一桃源"。

These aren't budget hotels, nor do they have hotel-like service. These places have bunk beds like in a university dorm; you can meet travellers from all over the world. These are youth hostels, and there are many in Hangzhou, with names like Mingtang, Lanshui, Qingting, Hefang, etc. Meaning things like "bright garden", "mist over mountain peaks", "celadon court", "lotus place" and the like, walking between them is like reading a poem.

摄影:潘益青

微观杭州
HANGZHOU: TRADITION AND MODERN TIMES

摄影：梅莹

自行车，城市新风景线
Bikes and Scenery

走在杭州街头，不难发现路边整齐停放的公共自行车。在全球最佳16个地区公共自行车系统中，杭州与武汉入围前三。无论在数量、使用率，还是便捷程度、费用上都具优势。站点密集分布，每天约25万次使用率，市民游客都能使用。红绿灯旁自行车专用道和遮阳棚的设置，是不是也很贴心呢。

When you walk around Hangzhou you'll find stands of public bikes parked everywhere. In the ranking of the 16 top cities in the world with public bike rental schemes, Hangzhou and Wuhan are both in the top three. Whether it's in terms of total scale, usage rate, convenience or low fees, Hangzhou's scheme is at the forefront. There are rental points everywhere, and people take more than 250,000 rides a day. Both city residents and visitors can use them, and with bike lanes and coverings to provide protection from the sun, it really is a nicely-designed scheme.

浪漫公交
Romantic Bus

七夕到来，全市K155路公交车的电子显示屏全部变为"KISS"。每对上车的情侣都会获得一份甜蜜小礼物。开通于1989年的"K155"路，因编码酷似"KISS"，激发了无数人的浪漫遐想，也为此赢得了"杭州最浪漫公交车"称号。2006年起，"K155"路曾停运7年，2013年再次上线，不但恢复了编码，行车路线也基本一致。

When Chinese Valentine's Day (the 7th evening of the 7th month in lunar calendar) comes, all buses on line K155 change their sign to "KISS". Couples boarding the bus together are given a sweet little gift. With service starting in 1989, the graphical similarity of the name of the line to "kiss" drove people nuts, and everyone started calling it Hangzhou's "most romantic bus line". In 2006, line K155 ceased operations for seven years until it was brought back in 2013 with a different designator, although the route is more or less the same.

时尚·潮涌
Fashion and Waves

杭州姑娘的旗袍
Qipao of Hangzhou Girls

外婆是住在西湖边的杭州姑娘。记得小时候住外婆家,外婆总喜欢穿一身旗袍。那娉婷的莲步,踩踏在我的眼底,步步成诗。如今见的最多的画面是外婆在月下一脸幸福的样子,不时将针在发间擦拭缝补衣裳,偶尔也拿出放在衣柜最上格的旗袍,抚摸着,端详着。那样的旗袍,在衣柜里,就把人间烟火锁得牢牢的。

My grandmother is a "Hangzhou girl" who lives by the West Lake. I remember staying at hers when I was a child – she liked to always wear a qipao. I watched as she took her delicate, beautiful steps in front of me. Now I see my grandmother by the moonlight, full of joy. Occasionally she'll crack out her needle and mend some old clothing, and sometimes she'll take her qipao down from the top shelf and feel it as she admires it. That kind of qipao that she has in the closet really is dynamite.

"彩虹"隧道
"Rainbow" Tunnel

从杭州去富阳玩,开的是彩虹快速路,进入隧道的时候我对孩子说:"这是彩虹隧道哦。"孩子问:"隧道里有彩虹吗?""是啊!"当然并不是真正的彩虹,而是在防撞墙的内侧有着"赤橙黄绿青蓝紫"的色带,这是彩虹隧道采用的灯光构建设计,把轮廓标与照明灯相结合,既美观,又实用。

Going from Hangzhou to Fuyang, taking the Rainbow Express, we entered a tunnel, at which point I told my son we were entering the "Rainbow Tunnel". He asked if there would be a rainbow in the tunnel, and I replied in the affirmative. There isn't a real optical rainbow in the tunnel, of course, but there is a rainbow stripe on the collision prevention wall. There are effects realised with lights, including the traffic markings and the illumination, making the tunnel look really cool all over.

摄影:杨慧丽

微观杭州
HANGZHOU: TRADITION AND MODERN TIMES

斑马线前车让人

Yielding at the Crosswalk

在其他城市过马路，先要看看两边是不是有车，没车就快速通过人行横道，通过时还要随时避让汽车。而在杭州过马路，车里的驾驶员却挥手让行人先过。杭州车让人的风气起于2009年，而早在2005年，"人行横道前礼让行人"就被列入了杭州公交集团规章。有数据统计，杭州汽车礼让率已达94%，公交车礼让率更是高达99%。

In other cities when you cross the road it's important to look left and look right, and then cross as quickly as possible when the road is clear while still watching out for cars. In Hangzhou, drivers will wave you along and ask you to cross first. This really took hold in 2009, but started as early as 2005 when "letting people cross at the intersection" was added to the list of traffic rules for Hangzhou. Statistics show that 94% of drivers let people cross before them, and for buses, that figure is 99%.

摄影：许敬

时尚·潮涌
Fashion and Waves

摄影：赵翠阳

公园中的夕阳乐
Setting Sun in the Park

家附近有个公园，是周围小区大爷和大妈们娱乐的地方。白天，一帮戏曲歌唱爱好者组成了好几个小乐队，在凉亭里、阴凉地里吹拉弹唱。一到夜晚，公园就成了广场舞的天下，有六七个队伍分散在公园的各个地方。不同的曲风、不同的舞姿，但大妈们都跳得非常尽兴、专注，有时，还能发现几个老大爷。

There's a park near my place that's a playground for old people. During the day, you see people who are there to sing or play music, organising little groups so that they can make their music in the little pavillions, and at night you will see the place transformed into a dancing venue, with six or seven separate groups in various places at the park dancing different dances to different songs. They're mostly women, but if you look long and hard you'll find some old men in the mix too.

下沙大学城
Xiasha University City

二十年前，在杭州本地人眼中，下沙是不折不扣的乡下。稻花飘香，芦苇摇曳，江色怡人，仍改变不了老杭州们对它的不屑。如今，高校林立，车水马龙，公交畅通，地铁飞驰，下沙瞬间融入现代生活。大量高校教师入住下沙，也从实质上提高了下沙的居住品质。瞧，不少老杭州也把新家安到了下沙。

Twenty years ago, in the eyes of Hangzhou locals, Xiasha was through-and-through countryside. The fragrance of rice flowers, reeds rustling in the wind, nice scenery – all these things can't change Hangzhou people's view of the place. Today, there are universities and schools everywhere, people going to and fro, replete transportation infrastructure, a quick underground line – Xiasha's in the modern era now. Many college teachers have selected to live here, raising the cultural bar. Even people from other parts of Hangzhou have chosen to move here.

微观杭州
HANGZHOU: TRADITION AND MODERN TIMES

摄影：孙宏茂

G20 峰会在杭州
G20 Summit in Hangzhou

继北京之后，杭州成为中国第二个举办 G20 峰会的城市，这是杭州的荣誉。瞧，杭州已经为迎接这一盛会忙碌起来了：餐饮业"大比武"，将为峰会准备 20 道"峰菜"；交通运输业召开誓师大会，全力推进 56 个交通项目建设；就连青少年也不甘落后，踊跃参加"迎 G20 峰会平安杭州"墙绘大赛，为杭州增光添彩。

After Beijing, Hangzhou had the honour of becoming the second Chinese city to host a G20 summit. Lots of preparation went into the welcoming procedures: the culinary industry brought its game with 20 "summit dishes", the transport sector stepped up with mass activities that included 56 new transit construction projects, and the youth turned out too, participating in a "Welcome G20" wall-painting competition that added a bit of colour to the city.

龙井夜骑族
Night Rider

夜晚来临，喜欢自行车运动的年轻人就会聚集到龙井路上，开始他们的"飞车狂飙"。他们全副武装，以车会友，每聚集到一定人数就一起出发。没错，如果你晚上不经意间经过这里，就会看到一辆辆闪着红色夜骑信号灯的自行车飞驰呼啸而过。他们到达翁家山顶，摘下头盔，共同的爱好使他们瞬时成为好友。

At night, youths who like cycling gather at Longjing Road for their wild ride. Dressed in full gear, these enthusiasts gather critical mass and then head out. If you happen to pass by them at night you'll see bikes with red signal lights whooshing past. When they arrive at the peak of Mount Wengjia, they take off their helmets and make friends.

时尚·潮涌
Fashion and Waves

跑在风景里的马拉松
Scenic Marathon

每年秋天，杭州都会举办西湖马拉松。比赛分10公里、半程和全程马拉松，还有家庭跑和情侣跑等，参赛者近两万人。比赛从黄龙体育中心出发，一路跑过西湖，跨过钱塘江，沿着滨江大道与奔流的潮水同行，被大家赞为"跑在风景里的马拉松"。每年都吸引众多高手前来参赛，已然成为杭州走向世界的一张名片。

Every autumn, Hangzhou has the West Lake Marathon. There is a 10k, half-marathon, and full marathon race, as well as a family race and couple's race. Almost 20,000 people participate. The activities start at Huanglong Athletic Centre, and the route takes runners past the West Lake, the Qiantang River, and along the Beijing-Hangzhou Grand Canal. It's been called a "scenic marathon". Every year many pros participate, widening the fame of Hangzhou.

滚叔街拍
Uncle Roll

"你好，我是滚叔。你今天穿得很漂亮，能给你拍张照片吗？"每天下午，街拍摄影师滚叔都会操着这句开场白，出现在杭州的时尚地带。滚叔的镜头里拍的都是穿搭时尚的潮男潮女。有的人经常精心装扮去滚叔蹲点的地方与他偶遇，然后乐滋滋地等待自己的照片出现在滚叔的微博上。如果你遇到他，记得摆好Pose。

"Yo, it's Uncle Roll. You're looking fine today; are you down to get your photo taken?" Every afternoon, Uncle Roll is up in the hizzy, visiting fashionable places in Hangzhou. He captures fashionable males and females with his lens, and is well known enough that people will dress up and go to places he is known to appear in the hopes of having their picture taken and then later seeing it on his microblog. If you go to Hangzhou, you better make sure your pose game is on fleek in case you run into this guy.

摄影：滚叔

微观杭州
HANGZHOU: TRADITION AND MODERN TIMES

时尚女装街
Fashion Street

每有外来女性朋友抱怨自己着装赶不上潮流，我就建议她去武林时尚女装街逛逛。这条"中国时尚女装第一街"拥有几十个杭州著名女装品牌，包括杭州十大女装品牌和杭州十佳设计师品牌。除了女装外，还有数不清的饰品店、化妆品店、发型设计店……令人应接不暇。不过进入了电商时代，这条街也面临着转型的挑战。

Every time I have a female friend visit from somewhere else, and she complains her clothes aren't fashionable enough, I tell her to go to the Wulin Fashion Street. This is said to be one of the best places for fashion in China, where there are dozens of Hangzhou-based brands for girls' clothing, including the 10 top female brands of Hangzhou and the 10 best designers of Hangzhou. Aside from women's clothing, there are also accessory shops, make-up shops, hair salons, and more… It's a lot to take in. We'll see how the place fares in the age of e-commerce, though.

临安登山
Climbing in Lin'an

古城临安四季如画，而一年之中最美的季节还是秋天。深秋的杭徽高速，车行其中，两边是山林多彩的视觉冲击；骑一辆单车穿行在02省道上，更是看不尽的层林尽染，赏不够的金秋美景；喜欢登山的驴友"走三尖"，"穿古道"，会遇见各种肤色、各种口音的背包客。在自然中找寻自我，在登高中体悟自然。

The old city area of Lin'an is picturesque all year round, and most beautiful in autumn. Deep in the fall on the Hangzhou-Anhui expressway you'll be flanked on either side by colourful trees, and when you're on the 02 inter-provincial highway, you'll see awesome scenes. You'll find all kinds of people from all kinds of places climbing the mountains around here. If you're looking to find yourself, this is a good place.

千岛湖边的马拉松
Thousand Island Lake Marathon

2015千岛湖秀水节九月就拉开帷幕，各种新潮好戏轮番上演。而它的最后一站迎来了一场超酷的马拉松。2015首届千岛湖马拉松11月29日于千岛湖所在地淳安县鸣枪起跑，这条沿着湖边的超美赛道让我兴奋不已。线路是沿着千岛湖最经典的亲水线路，从秀水广场出发，途经旅游码头，折返回秀水广场，比赛总里程42.195公里。

The Beautiful Water Cultural Festival kicked off in September of 2015, with all kinds of exciting and fashionable performances. Its last stop was a super-cool marathon – the Thousand Island Lake Marathon was held on the 29th of November, and I was so pumped, man. I ran along the lake; the scenes were awesome. The route took us past the nicest scenes on the lake, from Xiushui Square to the wharf, and then back to the square – 42.195 kilometres in total.

时尚·潮涌
Fashion and Waves

摄影：俞燕君

最美杭州人
Beautiful Hangzhou People

"最美妈妈"吴菊萍，"最美司机"吴斌，"最美爸爸"黄小荣……"用山清水秀出最美"来形容杭州人的美一点也不为过。杭州人的温婉有理，杭州人的乐于助人，杭州人的向善向美，使杭州成为一座有着大爱、流淌着道德血液的城市。在杭州，崇尚道德已经成为越来越多人的生活方式。生活在杭州，真幸福。

The "most beautiful mother" Wu Juping, the "most beautiful driver" Wu Bin, the "most beautiful father" Huang Xiaorong – everything is beautiful in Hangzhou. The people of Hangzhou are gentle and like to help others. They are virtuous, and the city is full of love and virtue. In Hangzhou, more and more people are leading virtuous lives. It's a great place to live in.

木马电影复古市集
Rocking Horse Cinema

现在我们看电影都是在舒适华丽、视听效果绝佳的电影院里，可有时还会回想起小时候整个村子的人聚在一起看露天电影的日子。前不久，杭州的木马电影复古市集就举办了这样一场活动。我们不仅可以重温儿时看露天电影的暖心记忆，还可以装扮成喜欢的电影人物，更深刻地体验看电影的乐趣。

When we go to the cinema now, we're used to having awesome audio and images pumped into a nice, clean room with all the latest technology. Sometimes, though, I think about my childhood, when everyone in the village would gather and watch a film together outside. The Hangzhou Rocking Horse Market is having an activity this time. Not only can we relive the nice memories of our past, we can also dress up as film characters, and really get into the fun of enjoying a movie.

微观杭州
HANGZHOU: TRADITION AND MODERN TIMES

万人过后不留一片垃圾
The Big March

2015年杭州迎来了第五次毅行,喜迎G20是这次的主题。4.2万人参加了这次大会,包括新老杭州人和国际友人,他们用行动为我们丈量美丽杭州。这次大会的亮点是动漫元素的加入,真正实现了"动漫我城市"的理念。让人感动的是,参赛者们人手一个环保袋,践行了万人过后不留一片垃圾的环保理念。

2015 saw the fifth International Trailwalk Conference, and this time it had the theme of welcoming the G20 summit. 42,000 people participated, including new and old locals and visitors from abroad, pacing out the beautiful city of Hangzhou as they walked together. There were manga and anime elements added this time in line with the theme of "My City of Cartoon and Animation". What's nice is all the participants had reusable shopping bags, and after everyone passed by there was no litter on the street.

茶香丽舍
Tea and Xianglishe

香丽舍,非香艳之地,而是个青年旅社。在四眼井众多民宿中,这里以茶香引人。住是在花簇藤绕的精心营造的小园内,除了你住的屋子,你还可以去主家为住客专置的宽敞茶屋:印度风的装饰,贴心的靠椅沙发,别致的茶器,香形俱佳的茶叶。自沏一壶,轻啜着,看看窗外的繁花、绿树,就算浪掷了浮生又何妨。

Xianglishe is a youth hostel. Near the Four Hole Well, it attracts people with the fragrance of tea. Staying in a courtyard that is covered with flowers and vines, besides your room, you can also go to the tea room. This place has it turned up, with Indian-style decoration and cool sofas, nice tea ware and some really good tea. Make a pot of tea, take a sip, look out the window. Resplendence, trees. Why not take a break from the mundane world?

主编供稿

时尚·潮涌
Fashion and Waves

摄影：俞燕君

没有橹的刚朵拉

A Gondola without an Oar

坐在东河小公交船上，从三两个空空无人的桥洞下缓缓穿过，行在一边白墙黑檐、一边翁郁河岸的水流里。这颇似威尼斯的"刚朵拉"，只是没橹，也没摇橹人。白墙上总有幽窗寂寞开着，间或人影一闪。每行过几个桥洞，船便悠悠靠岸，三两人徐徐走上船。你好像回到了前朝，但隐约的汽车声又提醒你，不是前朝。

Riding a boat on the Donghe River, you will see lush greenery and traditional buildings with white walls and black eaves upon the shores as you pass under empty bridges. It's a bit like the gondolas of Venice, except without oars or oarsmen. The white buildings always have their little windows open, and occasionally you will catch a glimpse of a person inside. As you approach the shore, maybe two or three people board the boat. You feel like you've gone back to a previous dynasty, but the sound of cars reminds you that you're in the present.

毅行

International Trailwalk Conference

有一种壮观只能在一年一度的国际（杭州）毅行大会上才能感受到。15000多人浩浩荡荡徒步在城市行走50公里，从白天走到黑夜，只为一个共同的终点前进。我问一位参加毅行的女大学生为什么能坚持走那么久，她说："我也不知道自己的极限，但没试过怎么知道做不到呢？"

Every year there is a very large march in Hangzhou – the International Trailwalk Conference. More than 15,000 people take a 50 kilometre walk in the city from day into night as they progress towards a common destination. I asked a girl in university how she could go on for so long, and she reminded me that you will never know your limits until you try to push yourself to them.

微观杭州
HANGZHOU: TRADITION AND MODERN TIMES

车与人，礼相揖
Cars and People

看完西湖喷泉，散场的时候，人流走到旁边不宽的马路边。杭州的道路大部分是窄窄的，但机动车不会抢行，自觉停下来让行人先过。当然，行人也会尽量快步地通过道路。衡量一个城市是否发达，高楼大厦不是主要标准。市民守秩序，公共场所文明礼让，人与人互相尊重……这些软实力的提升或许才是大众认可的标准。

After seeing the fountain light show at the West Lake, when people are leaving, people walk down the narrow streets. Even though most of the streets in Hangzhou aren't very wide, motor vehicles don't try to cut in front of everyone else. Instead, they stop to let pedestrians pass, who do so quickly as to not delay the cars. To gauge the development of a city, you don't have to look at the number of tall buildings. The degree to which people follow rules and respect each other is a truer measure of how far a city has developed.

微型市集
Micro Market

来杭州这么久，第一次去朋友家拜访。一路爬山，不累，反倒欣喜得不得了。这山不高也不陡，偶尔会看到三三两两的人从山下过来，大概是刚锻炼完吧！从东和宿舍过来约半小时路程，灯火通明的西和校区一点儿不比东和冷清呀！来往的人群、车辆很多，小商贩的叫卖声更是不绝于耳，俨然一个微型市集！

I'd been in Hangzhou for a while, but this was my first time visiting a friend's house. It was a mountain climb, but it wasn't tiring. In fact, it was quite nice. The mountain wasn't high or steep, and I saw groups of two or three people coming down as I went up. I thought they probably had just finished exercising. It was about a 30 minute walk from the Donghe Dormitory, and the lamps in the Xihe Campus made the place feel nice. There were many cars coming and going, and the calls of merchants hawking their wares were everywhere. It was like a tiny market!

家庭医生
Family Doctor

数年前在国外工作时最怕就是生病了，只因外国多实行家庭医生制，人们在看病前会先找家庭医生，再由其安排专科医生或住院事宜。而作为过客的我自是没有这个待遇的，唯有祈求健康，那时就想着能有一个自己的家庭医生。这一心愿如今有了实现的可能，2014年杭州大力推动家庭医生项目，目前已有50余万人签约。

When I was working abroad a few years ago, the thing I was most afraid of was getting sick. As family doctors are common in foreign nations, people usually first visit one who later arranges for them to meet with a specialist or stay at a hospital. I didn't have this, and could just pray to stay healthy. At that time, I wished I had a family doctor. This wish is now a possibility as Hangzhou rolled out a family doctor scheme in 2014, for which more than 500,000 people have signed up for.

时尚·潮涌
Fashion and Waves

摄影：王建华

西溪湿地的慢生活
Slow Life in the West Creek Wetlands

在西溪湿地里面有一条慢生活街区，街区里面有着独具特色的小店。找一处心怡地方，点一杯咖啡或者一壶清茶，静静地享受时光悠走，突然发现，这就是品味生活。当夜幕降临，华灯初上，脑海中不禁浮现一句话："有些事不用一次做完，我们又不赶时间。"

There is a slow living area in the West Creek Wetlands. Within there are many stores and shops. You can find a place to relax and have a cup of coffee or a pot of tea and quietly enjoy the leisurely passage of time. You'll discover that it's a nice way to do things. As the curtain of night falls, lanterns illuminate, you think in your mind that you don't have to shotgun everything you can do – you can take your time to finish things.

悦览树书店
Yuelan Tree Bookstore

"当城市进入午夜，书店就是灯火"，悦览树是一个二十四小时不打烊、文艺又时尚的书店。此书店毗邻西湖，又靠近市中心，就在青年路和解放路交界，是一个闹中取静的场所。试想，某夜夜归，褪去白天的铅华，在灯火与书香之间小坐，沏一杯茶，拿一本书。这便是杭州的夜生活，除了酒吧、咖啡馆，还有书店的灯光。

"When midnight arrives in the city, the lights are shining bright in the bookstore." The Yuelan Tree Bookstore is a 24-hour bookstore which is both artistic and fashionable. Located next to the West Lake and the city centre, it stands at the intersection of Qingnian Road and Jiefang Road, and is a place to get some quiet in the middle of the noisy city. Think about it, on some night, you can forget the worries of the day and just chill out in the bookstore, accompanied by soft lighting, the smell of incense, a cup of tea, and a book. This is Hangzhou nightlife – not just bars and cafés, but bookstores too.

微观杭州
HANGZHOU: TRADITION AND MODERN TIMES

主编供稿

懒墅庭院
Lazy Garden Villa

这是西湖边的一家民宿，注意到它，是因为其名引起的遐想。"懒"是贬义的，但这里的风格确是一副"我是懒人，我自豪"的做派。在这里时间不再是宝贵的，闲坐、发呆、放空都是可以的，大有一种远离城市喧嚣、体验懒人生活的意味。所以，"懒"也未必不可，与其忙忙碌碌，不如走走停停，或许会有另一番景象。

This is B&B on the West Lake which is notable for its name. Lazy is a word with negative connotations, but the vibe here is "I'm lazy, and I'm proud of that". Here, time isn't precious. You can just sit down and do nothing. It feels like you're far away from the noise of the city, experiencing lazy life. It's a different way of doing things, apart from all that business and stopping and going.

武林路
皇后公园
Wulin Road Empress Park

名曰"公园"，实则是缩小版的"新天地"，这里有创意集市、复古服装、黑胶唱片、原创手工作品……这里的明星店和很多自主品牌，绝对经得起你犀利的眼光和对品牌的考验。还有来自韩国的"漫咖啡"，给你足够的文艺感。周末的时候不妨来到这里，淘点独一无二的玩意儿。

This "park" is actually more like a miniature Xintiandi, with creative markets, shops selling traditional clothing, vinyl records, and original creations… Among the famous shops and some stores that carry their own original clothing – you're sure to find something you like if you look. There's also the Korean Maan Coffee. You should take the chance if you've got time on the weekend, and shop for some unique stuff.

时尚・潮涌
Fashion and Waves

浙江卫视中国蓝
Zhejiang Satellite: China Blue

日出江花红胜火，春来江水绿如蓝。蓝色代表海阔天空，生生不息，波澜壮阔，是江南文化品质的象征。浙江卫视近年来凭借着综艺节目和卫视独播剧场的火爆收视率，在地方卫视百花争艳的环境中异军突起，已然成为江南卫视频道中的佼佼者。"中国蓝，蓝无界，境自远！"

The sun rises and the flowers along the river are in bloom, The water of the river is so deep green it's almost blue. Blue is the symbol of Jiangnan Culture, and represents the waters, wide blue sky, life, and strong waves. Zhejiang Satellite has built itself up with variety shows and original dramas in recent history, making it a strong competitor in the tough TV market. "China blue, endless blue, near and far!"

杭州国际设计周
Hangzhou International Design Week

这是一个看脸的时代，不仅人要颜值，万物都要颜值。杭州国际设计周的设计师们就是用艺术和创意，让你身边看似普通的物品变成高颜值、高价值的创造。这是一场美的盛宴，它让艺术设计不再是少数设计师的专利，而越来越公开化、大众化。来杭州，聆听艺术的声音，遇见城市的美丽。

Appearances are important – not just for people, but for things, too. The designers of Hangzhou International Design Week use art and innovation to make everyday objects look nicer. It's a banquet of beauty, making art no longer the domain of only the privileged few, giving everyone access. Come to Hangzhou to hear the sounds and see the sights of this beautiful city.

摄影：徐征难

微观杭州
HANGZHOU: TRADITION AND MODERN TIMES

摄影：俞洋

老厂房也有春天
Spring Comes to the Old Factory

如果评判一家餐馆的颜值，东信和创园31幢绝对排得上号，这是一个餐厅、展厅的集合空间。复古主题的怀旧设计搭配现代化的法式装修，你一定想不到这是一间老厂房的改造成果。设计师为老厂房重新赋予了新的生命，在保留原有斑驳气质的外表下赋予它时代感，让这个近乎销声匿迹的老厂房迎来了春天。

If you wanted to make a ranking of nice-looking restaurants, the Dongxin-Hechuang Innovation Park #31 is a restaurant, and a gallery all in one. It's decorated in a classical style that imitates French architecture – you'd never think this is an old factory. In order to give a new life to this old factory, the designer retained some of the original elements for a patchwork effect that makes the structure look like it's from a different era. Spring has come again to this old factory.

时尚·潮涌
Fashion and Waves

最美司机 吴斌
Wu Bin

当一大块铁片突然从天而降,击碎挡风玻璃直接砸向他的腹部和手臂,他只是本能地用右手捂了一下腹部,没有紧急刹车或猛打方向盘,然后强忍着腹部剧痛缓缓减速,拉起手刹,开启双跳灯并打开车门。车上 24 位乘客得救了,而最美司机吴斌,却用他生命中最后的 76 秒诠释了什么是职业道德,什么是"最美"。

When a steel plate suddenly fell from the sky, crashing through the windscreen and straight into his chest and hands, he instinctively used his right hand to hold his abdomen, and didn't slam on the brakes or steer wildly. Instead, he gradually slowed the bus, turned on the emergency lights and opened the doors. The lives of the 24 passengers were saved, and he used the last 76 seconds of his life to show what true dedication to one's job is.

最美学子 徐建龙
Xu Jianlong

他做完家教返校途中在中北桥上遇到轻生女子跳河,他没有片刻犹豫,而是奋不顾身、果断勇敢地跳入冰冷的河中将落水女子救起。徐建龙,这位当时浙江科技学院大四的最美学子,用自己主动关爱他人、关爱社会的实际行动,响亮地宣告:"我们 90 后也是有担当、有理想的一代,我们已经接过了雷锋的接力棒。"

When he saw a girl fall off the Zhongbei Bridge on his way home from tutoring, he didn't hesitate, but instead jumped into the river and bravely swam through the ice-cold water to save the girl. Xu Jianlong, a 4th-year student at the Zhejiang University of Science and Technology stepped up to the plate, and inspired others too. He said: "For those born in the '90s, we have ideals. We have carried the baton for people like Lei Feng."

寄往 G20 的明信片
Postcards for G20

为了迎接 G20 峰会,杭州九堡街道特意向辖区居民派发了 1 万张特制明信片,准备把所有寄语拼接做成一面"我在钱塘智慧城,寄语 G20"展示墙向峰会献礼。"数字时代,已经好多年没写过明信片了,如今为杭州办峰会提笔写寄语,心情特别激动,杭州越来越开放和国际化了。"亲自把明信片送到街道的汪老开心地说。

For the G20 summit, the sub-district Office of Jiubao Street area sent 10,000 postcards to the area residents so that they could write their wishes upon them and put them together to form a giant wall display. "In the digital age, I hadn't written a postcard for many years. I was moved as I wrote my wishes for the summit held in Hangzhou, thinking about Hangzhou is becoming more open and international." Mr. Wang said this as he delivered his card personally.

微观杭州
HANGZHOU: TRADITION AND MODERN TIMES

最美妈妈 吴菊萍
Wu Juping

当两岁的妞妞从10楼高空坠下时,她以妈妈的本能甩掉高跟鞋,奋不顾身地冲上去用双手接住了孩子,以自己左手臂的粉碎性骨折换回了孩子的生命。当网友称她为"英雄妈妈""最美妈妈"时,她低调地说:"我不是英雄,只是恰好碰到了。"吴菊萍,带着爱的温度,使杭城的最美由她而始如同涟漪般不断扩散。

When a two-year-old girl fell from the 10th floor, she threw off her high heels and rushed over to catch the child in her arms, breaking bones of her left arms but saving the child's life. She was called a hero online, but responded by saying that she is no hero, but simply did what she had to. They story of her love spread throughout the city.

白马湖生态创意城
White Horse Lake Ecological Creative City

位于钱塘江南岸的杭州滨江区白马湖的农居和山水田园风光,将会成为杭州的一个"童话王国"。一边是产业基础雄厚的高新技术聚集地,一边是曾经宁静而异常美丽的朴实村庄。两种截然不同的气质将因为创意与休闲元素的融合而进入彼此的灵魂。凭借着动漫元素结合旅游生态的创意,为杭州带来源源不断的惊喜。

Located in White Horse Lake District on the south bank of the Qiantang River in Hangzhou, it has a rural, agricultural feeling, and looks like a scene from a fairy tale. To one side there is a technological development centre, and to the other side is a quiet and especially beautiful little village. These two contrasting elements with their different characters blend innovation and relaxation, incorporating anime elements and ecological innovation, bringing a new source of surprises to Hangzhou.

摄影:俞洋

时尚·潮涌
Fashion and Waves

"轮到我了"
My Turn

"0389号请到49号窗口办理，"广播呼声未落，一人嘟囔着"轮到我了"，走到49号前。这是杭州办证中心的一个小片段。除了法定节假日，这里永远是此起彼落的呼叫号码声和不时有些小骚动的等待人群。小到公交卡充值、水电交款，大到护照、房产办证，都可在这两个楼层内搞定。方便了市民，政府效率也高。

"Number 0389, please come to window number 49." Before the announcement ended, someone stood up and said "that's me" as he walked to window 49. This is a scene from the document centre in Hangzhou. Except for national holidays, numbers are always being called here left and right as people wait. All kinds of things get done here: public transit cards, water and electricity bills, passports, property deeds and more can all be settled here. It's convenient for the people and represents the efficiency of the government.

楼友会
Louyouhui

杭州有个地方叫楼友会，这里是创客们的平台，有创业咖啡、众创空间、创业投资、创业服务、创业公寓等，带上你的头脑就可以开启创业之路。为项目找资金，为资金找项目，为项目找团队……这些看起来繁琐的事情，楼友会都会给你搭建一个平台。这样的空间还有很多，梦想小镇、迭代空间、西湖创客会等。

There is a place in Hangzhou called Louyouhui. Within there is a platform for creators: creators of a café, a group-working space, investment, services, apartments, and so on. Bring your brain and make something happen. Finding investment for projects, or projects for investments, or a team. These things look complicated from the outside, but Louyouhui's got it covered. There's a lot of spaces like this: Dream Town, Iteration Space, the West Lake Maker Space, etc.

浙江第一码头
Zhejiang's First Pier

浙江第一码头在钱塘江四桥（复兴大桥）北岸，没造桥前，过江的货车都在这里摆渡。现在的码头，只留下几只小船和两个游轮，一个是"丽星号"，还有一个是"玉皇号"。现在只有丽星号游轮在运营，也不对游客开放，只经营包租业务。这使得人们无法欣赏钱塘江夜景了，真是一件遗憾的事情。有谁来投资开发吗？

Zhejiang's first pier is located on the north bank of the Qiantang River, next to Fuxing Bridge. Before the bridge was built, trucks carrying cargo all had to cross here by ferry. Only several small boats and two cruisers remain at the pier now: "Beautiful Star" and "Jade Emperor". Right now only Beautiful Star is in service, and isn't open for general use – it can only be rented out. People can't enjoy the scenes of the Qiantang River anymore, which really is a shame. Someone should come along with investment and get things up and running again.

微观杭州
HANGZHOU: TRADITION AND MODERN TIMES

拾荒情
Bits and Pieces

2015年末，一为拾荒老人塑雕像的微信刷爆杭州朋友圈。去杭图看书要先洗手的退休教师、拾荒老人韦思浩再次进入人们的视野。这位杭大中文系毕业的老人，本可安心养老，却省吃俭用资助失学儿童，留下丰满的爱，高贵的精神。心存崇敬之心，杭州人在心底里先为老人"塑"了一座雕像。

At the end of 2015, the image of an old man who collects rubbish was all over social media in Hangzhou. A retired teacher who washed his hand before entering the library, Wei Sihao entered into the public view. A teacher graduated from the Department of Chinese Language at Hangzhou University, in his old age he lives modestly and contributes financially to young children who would otherwise be unable to attend school. He's left a lasting impression of love and spirit. His respect for other people has earned him the respect of people in Hangzhou.

图书馆排队
Library Queue

博尔赫斯说："如果有天堂，天堂应该是图书馆的模样。"每个周末，距离开馆尚有二三十分钟，天堂的图书馆，无论是杭图还是浙图，门口都已有不少读者在等待。若是九点多点儿到馆，稍好点的座位基本无望。这就是杭州的图书馆的吸引力。此外，还有上天竺的佛学分馆，林木掩映间，放空养神，书入心，景静心。

Jorges Luis Borges said: "I have always imagined that Paradise will be a king of library." Every weekend, twenty or thirty minutes, the heavenly Hangzhou and Zhejiang libraries have people waiting in front of the door. When it opens just after 9, you'll quickly find yourself without hope of finding a seat – this is the attractive power the libraries have. You can also go to the Tianzhu branch which focuses on Buddhism, where you can relax among the trees, let your spirt be nourished, and take the words of a book into your heart as you're calmed by the still scenery.

摄影：许雪梅

索 引 | Index |

（按照正文顺序排序，第二栏为文字作者姓名）

都市·乐活 City and Leisure

今日西湖	沈贻伟	The West Lake Today	2
西溪湿地	俞燕君	The West Creek Wetlands	3
娟娟饭馆	张 娜	Juanjuan Restaurant	3
办张公园年卡	施麟麒	A Yearly Park Pass	4
爱情之都	沈贻伟	The City of Love	4
西湖龙井	刘天捷	Longjing Tea	5
让洞于民	施麟麒	Into the Caves	5
问路	夏利亚	Asking For Direction	6
小吃街夫妻档	孙宏茂	Husband-and-Wife Snack Street	6
开茶节	胡云晚	The Tea Festival	6
翻丝棉大妈	程永艳	The Women Who Process Silk Floss	7
红树醉西泠	余优留	Red Leaves at Xiling Bridge	7
王奶奶的西湖绸伞情缘	程永艳	The Love Story of Granny Wang and the Silk Umbrella	8
交芦田庄	杨新红	Jiaolutian Village	8
创意民宿	俞燕君	Innovative B&B's	9
排长队的李记酥鱼	孙宏茂	A Fish Shop with a Long Queue	9
"三无"餐厅	施麟麒	The Restaurant Lacking Three Things	10
吴山庙会	程永艳	The Wushan Temple Fair	10
热衷游泳	明 艺	Passion for Swimming	10
赏桂花	王晨露	Appreciating Osmanthus Flowers	11
运河水上巴士	杨慧丽	Travelling on the Canal Bus	11
心之向往	陆 洋	The Heart's Direction	12
时尚的广场舞	江 坤	Fashionable Dance	12
千变杭州	陆 洋	Ever-Changing Hangzhou	13
浣纱溪的遗憾	程永艳	The Sad Story of Huansha Creek	13
放心	陆 洋	Relax	14
安宁的模样	季 洁	Models of Calm	14
服装第一街	周 毅	The Street for Clothing	15
夏天到，蝈蝈儿叫	程永艳	Crickets in the Summer	15

223

小酒吧老板	俞燕君	The Boss of a Small Bar	16
美丽校园	俞燕君	A Beautiful Campus	16
小区绿化	杨 瑞	Greenery in Compounds	17
学院路夜市	杨 瑞	Xueyuan Road Night Market	17
堵城的交通	俞燕君	A Congested City	18
喜"闲"的杭州人	程永艳	Leisure-Loving Hangzhou	18
适宜散步的城市	俞燕君	A Good City for Walking	19
杭城小弄堂	王晨露	Alleyways in Hangzhou	19
火柿映西溪	余优留	Fiery Persimmons at the West Creek	20
热心红娘伍大姐	程永艳	Lady Wu, a Matchmaker	20
爱心凉茶摊	程永艳	Friendly with Cold Tea	21
林荫隧道	陈 杰	The Shady Tunnel	21
钢镚儿找零	俞 洋	Coins	22
孝道文化	王 贵	A Culture of Filial Piety	22
现代化城市建设	陈海芳	Modernising Urban Construction	23
虎跑泉趣事	俞燕君	The Story of Running Tiger Spring	23
免费凉茶	明 艺	Free Cold Tea	24
城区	赵翠阳	The City Area	24

轶史・钩沉 History and Reflections

宋城抛绣球	崔赛凤	Throwing an Embroidered Ball	26
月老和月老祠	施麟麒	The Matchmaker and Matchmaker's Temple	26
相亲圣地	施麟麒	A Place for Meeting One's Love	27
秦始皇和杭州	俞燕君	Emperor Qin Shihuang and Hangzhou	27
此为胜处	施麟麒	A Nice Place	28
荷花与美酒	施麟麒	Lotus Blossoms and Fine Wine	28
杭州通司徒雷登	程永艳	John Leighton Stuart	29
小热昏的第六代传人	程永艳	A Sixth-Generation Xiaorehun Singer	29
传说中的才女	崔赛凤	A Talented Woman of Legend	29
不应忘却的范市长	施麟麒	A Mayor that Should Not Be Forgotten	30
为何西溪鳞塘多	夏利亚	Lakes around the West Creek	30
胡适的烟霞洞	周 毅	Hu Shi's Cave of Smoky Red Clouds	30
东、西穆坞的方向为什么是反的	夏利亚	Why West and East Muwu are Reversed	31
苏东坡的红颜知己	沈贻伟	Su Dongpo's Red-faced Companion	31

望仙桥上盼仙归	夏利亚	Waiting for the Return of a Sage on Wangxian Bridge		32
斗富不成成"豆腐"	夏利亚	The Unprosperous "Tofu"		33
油条的起源	徐征难	The Origin of Youtiao		33
杭城故事	赵翠阳	A Hangzhou Story		34
风雨茅庐	施麟麒	Wind and Rain over the Thatched Cottage		34
梅妻鹤子的传说	徐征难	The Legend of the Plum Wife and Crane Children		35
西溪且留下	徐征难	Let the West Creek Remain		36
岳王庙里忆岳飞	俞燕君	Remembering Yue Fei		37
"受降镇"小史	施麟麒	The History of Shouxiang Village		38
李渔操办文化产业	沈贻伟	Li Yu's Involvement in Cultural Industry		38
昌化石缘	程永艳	The Stones of Changhua		39
钱塘第一井	程永艳	The First Well at Qiantang		39
立马回头	胡云晚	Limahuitou		40
广济桥	施麟麒	The Guangji Bridge		40
外婆的同学录	潘益青	Grandmother's Yearbook		41
宋江路	夏利亚	Songjiang Road		41
桃花错	程永艳	The Missed Peach Blossom		42
未央村	胡云晚	Weiyang Village		42
知味之余,知音不断	陈海芳	Zhiweiguan Restaurant		42
杭城雅号	赵翠阳	Nicknames for Hangzhou		43
子久草堂	周毅	Zijiu Thatched Cottage		43
杭州话里的"爹爹"	刘天捷	"Diedie" in Hangzhou Dialect		44
碑林	周毅	Forest of Steles		44
十门城谣	程永艳	A City of Ten Gates		45
浣纱路	孙宏茂	Huansha Road		45
凤凰展翅越千年	程永艳	The Phoenix Spreads its Wings to Cross Milennia		45
八卦田	徐征难	Field of the Eight Diagrams		46
古韵书香文澜阁	程永艳	Ancient Books in the Wenlan Pavillion		46

地域・物产 Areas and Products

王星记"杭扇"	王嫱	Wangxingji's "Hangzhou Fans"		48
快似风走的张小泉剪刀	王杰于	Zhangxiaoquan Scissors		48

轻车熟驾	江　坤	Sightseeing by Bike	49
地铁站纳凉	施麟麒	Cooling off in the Subway Station	49
塘栖的枇杷	王杰于	Loquats at Tangqi	50
湖滨"呆萌"小松鼠	程永艳	Lakeside Squirrels	51
酱一酱再吃	俞燕君	Sauce it up	51
市井纳凉	杨慧丽	Cooling off at the Alleyways	52
吴山夜市	胡云晚	Night Market at Mount Wu	52
美景美食的西溪	冯　芹	Nice Scenery and Food at West Creek	53
书吧	施麟麒	Book Bar	53
炒新茶	俞燕君	New Tea	54
龙井白露私房茶	程永艳	Dragon Well, White Dew	54
蒸谷米	程永艳	Parboiled Rice	55
天空之镜——千岛湖	俞　洋	The Mirror of the Sky – the Thousand Island Lake	55
小朋友的小天堂	陈海芳	Heaven for Little Kids	56
塘栖"土灶月饼"香	程永艳	The Fragrance of Mooncakes Baked in Tangqi	56
餐厨垃圾处理的"杭州模式"	潘益青	Kitchen Waste in the "Hangzhou Model"	57
杭州最美骑行道	俞　洋	The Nicest Bike Ride in Hangzhou	57
里西湖的划艇	潘益青	Rowboats in the Inner West Lake	58
孔凤春	施麟麒	Kong Fengchun	58
民间绝技"翻九楼"	程永艳	Fanjiulou, a Unique Skill	59
城市文化墙	程永艳	Cultural Wall	59
市树	夏利亚	City Trees	60
蒋村船拳	程永艳	Jiang Village Boat Boxing	60
民间圣音"楼塔细十番"	程永艳	Ten Pieces of Instruments at the Tower	61
萧山萝卜干	施麟麒	Dried Carrots of Xiaoshan	61
虎跑的铁杆粉	潘益青	Running Tiger	62
玉兰花	杨　瑞	Magnolia Flowers	62
江南铜屋	胡云晚	Copper House	63
杭州天堂伞	刘天捷	Heavenly Umbrellas of Hangzhou	64
"小阿六头"	张　娜	Little Liu Tou	64
杭州竹篮	杨同用	Hangzhou's Bamboo Baskets	64
江南雨伞	刘天捷	Jiangnan Umbrellas	66

大井巷	杨同用	Dajing Lane		66
杭帮菜	俞燕君	Hangzhou Cuisine		66

西湖·印象 West Lake and Impressions

夜西湖	周 毅	The West Lake at Night		68
浴鹄湾	周 毅	Yuhu Bay		68
雪湖热游	周 毅	Snowy Lake, Hot Trip		69
十里荷花	周 毅	Lotus Flower		69
西湖记忆	赵翠阳	Memories of the West Lake		70
桥未断,为何叫断桥?	徐征难	The Unbroken Broken Bridge		70
孤山,孤还是不孤?	徐征难	Is the Lonely Mountain Lonely?		71
杨公堤	夏利亚	Yang Gong Causeway		71
西湖的水,我的泪	江 坤	My Tears Are the Water of the West Lake		72
北山路秋梧桐的震撼	程永艳	Parasol Trees along Beishan Road in Autumn		72
白娘子的雷峰塔	程永艳	Leifeng Pagoda and Lady Bai		73
西湖船娘	王晨露	The Girl's Boat of the West Lake		73
长桥不长,为何叫长桥?	徐征难	The Not-long Long Bridge		74
西湖的山	赵翠阳	The Mountains of the West Lake		74
花港红鲤	夏利亚	Red Carp in the Flower Harbour		75
一树桃花一树柳	徐征难	Peach Blossoms and Willows		75
风月无边	夏利亚	Gentle Breeze and Bright Moonlight		76
西湖又叫什么湖?	徐征难	Other Names of the West Lake		76
丰子恺与西湖杨柳	施麟麒	Feng Zikai and the Willows of the West Lake		77
南宋御街	周 珊	Southern Song Imperial Street		77
莲滩鹭影	杨新红	Herons on the Lotus Beach		78
十里银铛	孙宏茂	Ten-Li Chain		78
夜探宝石	陈海芳	Searching for Gems in the Night		79
秋芦飞雪	杨新红	Rushes in the Autumn, Flying Snow		79
曲水寻梅	杨新红	Looking for Plums among the Water		80
回归富春山居的恬静	俞 洋	Tranquility on Mount Fuchun		80
一座山的守望	俞 洋	Mountain View		81
西湖的观法	施麟麒	Viewing the West Lake		81
音乐喷泉	马思敏	Musical Fountains		82

纳凉圣地紫来洞	程永艳	The Best Place to Cool off	82
西湖猫	朱玉芬	The Cats of the West Lake	83
坐画舫和看画舫	周 毅	Painted Pleasure Boats	84
白堤	赵翠阳	White Causeway	84
扬帆西湖	程永艳	Setting Sail on the West Lake	85
夜骑西湖"六吊桥"	程永艳	Six Drawbridges	85
临安大明山赏枫叶红	俞 洋	Red Maple Leaves	86
雨纷纷	夏利亚	Abundant Rain	86
灵峰探梅	周 毅	Searching for Plums among the Sacred Peaks	87
西泠印社	王 津	Xiling Society of Seal Arts	87
徐志摩的丑西湖	施麟麒	Xu Zhimo's Ugly West Lake	88
泛舟湖上	张 娜	Boating upon the Lake	88
傍晚江南	张 娜	Jiangnan at Dusk	89
雨巷觅浪漫	周 珊	Looking for Romance in a Rainy Lane	89
王澍的世外桃源	潘益青	Wang Shu's Paradise	90
高庄之秋	张 娜	Autumn Scenes in Gaozhuang	90
满陇桂雨	孙宏茂	Sweet Osmanthus Rain at Manjuelong Village	91
冬日西湖美妙的音符	程永艳	Musical Notes upon the West Lake on Winter Days	91

互联·创新 Internet and Innovation

智慧城市	施麟麒	A Smart City	94
鲁冠球与万向集团	施麟麒	Lu Guanqiu and the Wanxiang Group	94
"农夫山泉有点甜"	施麟麒	"Nongfu Spring Water is a Bit Sweet"	95
自来水管将放出"农夫山泉"	施麟麒	Purified Water from the Tap	95
诺贝尔奖背后的华立集团	施麟麒	Nobel Prize and Huali Group	96
微公交	夏利亚	Microtransit	96
阿里巴巴	赵翠阳	Alibaba	97
"互联网+"和老店采芝斋	程永艳	Internet+ and Caizhizhai	97
城市阳台	周 毅	Hangzhou Balconies	97
智慧医疗	陈海芳	Smart Medicine	98
G20平安志愿者	张 娜	G20 Peace Volunteers	98
动漫	侯晓岚	Cartoon and Animation	98

移动革命	施麟麒	Mobile Revolution	99
到处支付宝	潘益青	Alipay Everywhere	99
刷微信坐地铁	陈海芳	Checking WeChat in the Subway	100
最富的区	夏利亚	The Richest District	100
地铁也卖萌	俞洋	Cute Stuff on the Underground	100
云栖小镇	潘益青	Cloud Town	101
出门不带钱	王嫱	No Need to Carry Cash	101
大四的 CEO	潘益青	A Student CEO	102
可以出售的好空气	刘兴宇	Air You Can Sell	102
创客的野心	潘益青	Maker's Ambition	103
e+ 时代的"萝卜车"	王杰于	"Radish Cars"	103
支付宝的老家	明艺	Alipay's Hometown	104
旧厂房的昨日今朝	潘益青	Now and Then at the Old Factory	104
古仓新生	潘益青	New Life for an Old Storehouse	105
"西湖发布"微矩阵	程永艳	"West Lake Announcements" Micromatrix	105
小镇实现大梦想	潘益青	Small Town, Big Dream	106
双创小镇	潘益青	Little Town Combo	107
电博会	潘益青	Electric Expo	107
"土"产品也来赶时髦	潘益青	Products of the Times	107
西溪谷	潘益青	West Creek Valley	108
跨境电商生鲜产品	俞洋	Cross-Border Electronic Trade of Fresh Goods	108
传感谷	俞洋	Sensing Valley	109
网购的不平等条约	俞洋	The Unequal Treaty of Online Shopping	109
淘宝卖茶具,却讲出了人生	俞洋	Learning Life Lessons While Shopping	109
创意良渚基地	侯晓岚	Creative Liangzhu Base	110
"潘多拉"盒子	侯晓岚	Pandora's Box	110
创意者的先驱	杨同用	A Creative Pioneer	110
淘宝孕育出的"网红经济"	俞洋	Taobao's "Web Celebrity Economy"	111
浙大科技园	俞洋	Zhejiang University Technology Park	111
让汉服走向世界	赵海涛	Han Chinese Clothing: from China to the World	112
公交全员 WiFi	陈海芳	WiFi on the Bus	112

西溪创意产业园	侯晓岚	West Creek Creative Industry Park	113
I-hangzhou	陈海芳	I-hangzhou	114
杭州国际动漫节	崔赛凤	CICAF	114

古城·寻踪 Ancient City and Traces

胡雪岩故居——破败后的辉煌	俞 洋	Hu Xueyan's Old Residence	116
最后一片消失的绿野	俞燕君	The Last Green Area	117
余杭双塔	施麟麒	Yuhang Twin Towers	117
夜游河坊街	樊 华	Hefang Street at Night	118
西溪别韵	杨新红	Rhythm of the West Creek	118
钱塘江为何又叫"之江"	俞燕君	The Name of Qiantang River	119
飞来峰	侯晓岚	Feilai Peak	119
青芝坞	周 毅	Qingzhiwu	120
西山游步	施麟麒	Walking about the West Mountains	120
枫林咽泉	施麟麒	Fenglinyan Spring	121
满陇桂无语	周 毅	Manjuelong Osmanthus	121
三台山	杨 瑞	Santai Mountain	121
徒步林径幽	潘益青	Walking a Quiet Path	122
信义坊	杨 瑞	Xinyifang	123
小河直街	杨 瑞	Xiaohezhi Street	123
秋意	赵翠阳	Autumn Feelings	124
"小西湖"华家池	夏利亚	Huajia Pond	124
宋江村的来历	夏利亚	The History of Songjiang Village	125
吴山广场	夏利亚	Mount Wu Square	125
赏雨好去处	夏利亚	Rain View	126
古杭州城门	赵翠阳	The City Gates of Old Hangzhou	126
吴山天风	俞燕君	Wind on Mount Wu	127
西湘记	俞燕君	Twin Lakes	127
桥的故事	俞燕君	Story of the Bridges	128
秋雪庵	周 毅	The Hut of Autumn Snow	128
三墩	赵翠阳	San Dun Town	129
越剧首演地	夏利亚	Site of the First Yue Opera	129
"塘栖"的由来	夏利亚	The Origin of "Tangqi"	130
夏日避暑地	顾永芳	A Place to Avoid the Summer Heat	130

盛夏的老宅子	俞 洋	An Old House in Midsummer	130
御街	李雨霖	Imperial Street	131
半山的来历	徐征难	History of the Banshan Mountain	132
一块朝内挂的匾	潘益青	An Inward-facing Sign	132
贴沙河	沈贻伟	Tiesha River	133
人家尽枕河	侯晓岚	Living Near the River	133
历史的杭州	孙宏茂	Historical Hangzhou	134
方回春堂的金字招牌	程永艳	Fang Huichun Tang's Golden Sign	134
江南私家名园郭庄	程永艳	Guo's Villa	134
坚守只为那份信念	程永艳	Holding to Faith	135
有"腔调"的富义仓	程永艳	Fuyi Granary	135
江墅铁路遗址公园	程永艳	Jiangshu Railway Park	136
一所大学一座城	程永艳	University and City	136
"头顶天，脚踏边"	程永艳	Tianzhang Hat and Bianfumao Shoes	137
寂寞的"饾版"技艺	程永艳	A Lonely Printing Technology	137
"欧Ⅲ公园"背后的城市记忆	程永艳	Memories of the City	137
良渚博物院	张 娜	Liangzhu Museum	138
杭州话"儿"字童谣	张 娜	Children's Rhymes	138
南宋官窑博物馆	张 娜	Southern Song Official Kiln Museum	139
朝晖枫叶	陈海芳	Maples at Dawn	139
宋城	夏利亚	Song City	140
胡庆余堂老师傅	潘益青	The Old Man at Hu Qingyu Tang	140

舌尖·记忆 Taste and Memories

奎元馆的两碗面	施麟麒	Two Kinds of Noodles at the Kuiyuan Hall	142
乌米饭非黑米饭	施麟麒	Crow Rice, Not Black Rice	142
胖子烧饼	杨 瑞	Fatty's Baked Cakes	143
咸豆浆怎么了	施麟麒	Salty Soy Milk	144
猫耳朵	陈海芳	Cat Ears	144
龙井虾仁	俞燕君	Longjing Shrimp	145
青梅滋味	沈贻伟	The Taste of Green Plum	145
小笼包	杨 瑞	Small Steamed Buns	146
小钵头甜酒酿	程永艳	Jars of Sweet Liquor	146
金黄脆嫩油墩儿	程永艳	Golden, Crispy, Oily Cakes	147

宝宝的荷花糕	程永艳	Lotus Cake for Baby		147
吴山酥油饼	程永艳	Crispy Oil Cakes on Mount Wu		148
一品南乳肉	程永艳	Top-tier Southern Roasted Pork		148
灵隐寺的腊八粥	傅佳玲	Laba Congee at Lingyin Temple		148
"甘其食"包子	程永艳	"Ganqishi" Steamed Buns		149
葱包烩儿香	程永艳	Fragrant Onion Rolls		149
独当一面的片儿川	俞燕君	Pian Er Chuan Noodle		150
西湖莼菜汤	程永艳	Water-shield Soup of the West Lake		150
东坡肉	徐征难	Dongpo Meat		151
湖畔居喝茶	周 毅	Drinking Tea in a Lakeside House		151
吃馆子和懒得烧	周 毅	Eating Out, Too Lazy		152
撤不去的茶食	周 毅	Chinese Pastry		152
知味观点心	茹彦龙	Zhiweiguan Dim Sum		153
东坞山豆腐皮	茹彦龙	Mount Dongwu Bean Curd Skin		153
红糖麻花	孙宏茂	Brown Sugar and Dough-Twists		153
芡实糕	胡云晚	Foxnut Cake		154
老头儿油爆虾	胡云晚	Old Man Fried Shrimp		154
康康饭店	孙宏茂	Kangkang Restaurant		154
楼外楼	茹彦龙	Louwailou		155
城东美食小街	葛瑾萍	East Town Food Street		155
蛋黄南瓜	陈海芳	Egg-yolk Pumpkin		156
幸福双	张 娜	Double Happiness		156
西湖醋鱼	胡云晚	West Lake Fish		156

吴越·包融 Wu-Yue and Inclusiveness

古荡蚕桑	程永艳	Sericulture in Gudang		158
细十番	施麟麒	Xishifan		158
越剧	赵翠阳	Shaoxing Opera		159
滚灯	施麟麒	Rolling Lamps		159
不能买饭的饭馆	孙宏茂	A Restaurant that Doesn't Sell Rice		160
孤山名人	潘益青	Famous Personages at Mount Gu		160
"别墅型"的民居	孙宏茂	"Villa-style" Residences		160
水上人家	俞燕君	Life on the Water		162
最后的绿皮火车	施麟麒	The Last Green Train		162

民间艺人节	王 津	Folk Arts Day		163
城标起航	施麟麒	Sign of the City		164
邻居节	程永艳	Neighbours' Festival		164
"62"骂人?	赵翠阳	Hey "62"		165
西湖绸伞	王 嫱	Silk Umbrellas of the West Lake		165
用音乐为逝者送行	俞燕君	Seeing the Deceased off with Music		166
演奏会	潘益青	Concert		166
垃圾与文化博物馆	潘益青	Museum of Rubbish and Culture		166
鬼节	夏利亚	Spirit's Day		167
茶道之源	施麟麒	The Origin of the Tea Ceremony		167
书法新闻	潘益青	Calligraphy News		168
金属球	夏利亚	Metal Balls		169
天竺筷	茹彦龙	Tianzhu Chopsticks		169
舒羽的情思	王 嫱	Feelings of Shu Yu		169
大学校园里的小茶园	周 毅	A Small Tea Garden on Campus		170
水乡婚礼	茹彦龙	Wedding in a Water Town		170
"到门"何解	胡云晚	"To the Door"		171
浙派古琴	茹彦龙	Zhejiang-Style Zither		171
当苏轼遇见"苹果"	潘益青	When Su Shi Met "the Apple"		172
耶稣弄堂	孙宏茂	Jesus Alley		173
杭州话"跑单帮"	胡云晚	"Bill Runners" in Hangzhou		173
"煨灶猫"到"灰灶猫"	侯晓岚	Cooked Cat to Ashy Cat		174
南北相融的酒球会	程永艳	A Mixture of North and South		174
杭州人不会说杭州话	程永艳	Hangzhou People and Dialect		174
湖蟹坐飞机——"悬空八只脚"	侯晓岚	"Eight Legs in the Air"		175
工大向日葵	崔赛凤	Sunflowers		175
杭州话里的"虾"	胡云晚	"Shrimp" in Hangzhou Dialect		175
中国扇博物馆	周 珊	China Fan Museum		176
晓风书屋	周 珊	Xiaofeng Bookstore		176
晕车也值得	张 娜	Bus of Love		177
腊八粥	谢 媚	Laba Rice Porridge		177
中国伞博物馆	周 珊	China Umbrella Museum		177
杭剧	茹彦龙	Hangzhou Opera		178

印世界	张 娜	Seal Arts	178
用"闹"发嗲	张 娜	You Must Be Joking	179
商人重利亦重情	江 坤	Money and Emotion	179
数数童谣	孙宏茂	Counting Rhymes	179

佛国·诗话 Buddhas and Stories

深山静寺	江 坤	Quiet Temple Deep in the Mountains	182
扫叶人	崔赛凤	Leafraker	182
佛都	周 珊	Buddhist Capital	183
幽谷之中寻法华	周 珊	Searching for Fahua Temple in the Quiet Valleys	183
江南名石"绉云峰"	程永艳	The Peak of Creased Clouds	184
活佛济公	夏利亚	Living Buddha Ji Gong	185
禅意图书馆	施麟麒	Zen Library	185
阿弥陀佛的生日	施麟麒	The Birthday of the Amitabha	186
灵隐寺	孙宏茂	Lingyin Temple	186
弘一与叔同	明 艺	Master Hongyi	187
三生石	夏利亚	Sansheng Stone	187
飞来峰下弥勒佛	徐征难	Maitreya beneath Feilai Peak	187
月下白云庵	王 嫱	White Cloud Pagoda under the Moonlight	188
来一场身体的修行	俞 洋	Physical Self-Cultivation	188
杭州寺庙	刘天捷	The Temples of Hangzhou	188
山门在寺外的仙林寺	夏利亚	A Separate Temple and Gate	190
伊斯兰教的杭州圣地	王杰于	Hangzhou as an Islamic Site	190
天竺三寺	杨同用	The Three Temples of Tianzhu	190
灵隐寺里寻佛缘	周 珊	Looking for the Buddha at Lingyin Temple	191
灵隐之隐	崔赛凤	The Retreat of Lingyin Temple	192
上天竺的斋饭	周 毅	Eating at Upper Tianzhu	192
腊八节	夏利亚	Laba Porridge Festival	193
灵隐寺里韦陀像	夏利亚	Vedda at Lingyin Temple	193
菩萨过生	江 坤	Bodhisattvha's Birthday	193
呼猿洞的来历	夏利亚	The Origins of Calling Monkey Cave	194
观音道场上天竺	夏利亚	Avalokitesvara at Upper Tianzhu	194
校园里的寺庙	夏利亚	Temple on Campus	194

东南佛国	夏利亚	The Buddhism Kingdom of Southeast China		195
吴越寺塔	韩晓芬	Temples and Towers of Wuyue		195

时尚·潮涌 Fashion and Waves

文史书店	王庆铃	Wenshi Bookshop		198
找不到教室的大学	俞 洋	A University with Hard-to-Find Classrooms		198
人情味	李雨霖	A Human Touch		199
星级公厕	夏利亚	Star-Rated Toilet		200
此地免费	杨慧丽	This Place Is Free		200
新式环卫工	夏利亚	New-Style Sanitation Workers		201
防空洞的华丽变身	程永艳	A Beautiful Transformation		201
爱心熊猫	夏利亚	Loving Panda		202
流动书柜	俞燕君	Mobile Bookcase		203
YHA 国际青年旅舍	潘益青	Youth Hostels		203
自行车，城市新风景线	王 嫱	Bikes and Scenery		204
浪漫公交	施麟麒	Romantic Bus		204
杭州姑娘的旗袍	陆 磊	Qipao of Hangzhou Girls		205
"彩虹"隧道	杨慧丽	"Rainbow" Tunnel		205
斑马线前车让人	杨同用	Yielding at the Crosswalk		206
公园中的夕阳乐	赵翠阳	Setting Sun in the Park		207
下沙大学城	杨 瑞	Xiasha University City		207
G20 峰会在杭州	刘天捷	G20 Summit in Hangzhou		208
龙井夜骑族	程永艳	Night Rider		208
跑在风景里的马拉松	俞燕君	Scenic Marathon		209
滚叔街拍	俞 洋	Uncle Roll		209
时尚女装街	施麟麒	Fashion Street		210
临安登山	江 坤	Climbing in Lin'an		210
千岛湖边的马拉松	江 坤	Thousand Island Lake Marathon		210
最美杭州人	程永艳	Beautiful Hangzhou People		211
木马电影复古市集	崔赛凤	Rocking Horse Cinema		211
万人过后不留一片垃圾	明 艺	The Big March		212
茶香丽舍	周 毅	Tea and Xianglishe		212
没有橹的刚朵拉	周 毅	A Gondola without an Oar		213

毅行	王 津	International Trailwalk Conference	213
车与人，礼相揖	潘益青	Cars and People	214
微型市集	胡云晓	Micro Market	214
家庭医生	陈海芳	Family Doctor	214
西溪湿地的慢生活	俞 洋	Slow Life in the West Creek Wetlands	215
悦览树书店	王晨露	Yuelan Tree Bookstore	215
懒墅庭院	杨同用	Lazy Garden Villa	216
武林路皇后公园	杨同用	Wulin Road Empress Park	216
浙江卫视中国蓝	王 津	Zhejiang Satellite: China Blue	217
杭州国际设计周	王 津	Hangzhou International Design Week	217
老厂房也有春天	俞 洋	Spring Comes to the Old Factory	218
最美司机吴斌	程永艳	Wu Bin	219
最美学子徐建龙	程永艳	Xu Jianlong	219
寄往G20的明信片	程永艳	Postcards for G20	219
最美妈妈吴菊萍	程永艳	Wu Juping	220
白马湖生态创意城	侯晓岚	White Horse Lake Ecological Creative City	220
"轮到我了"	周 毅	My Turn	221
楼友会	韩晓芬	Louyouhui	221
浙江第一码头	徐征难	Zhejiang's First Pier	221
拾荒情	冯 芹	Bits and Pieces	222
图书馆排队	周 毅	Library Queue	222

折得荷花浑忘却，空将荷叶盖头归。——丰子恺

图书在版编目(CIP)数据

微观杭州:汉英对照/王建华主编.—北京:商务印书馆,2016
(微观中国)
ISBN 978-7-100-12453-9

Ⅰ.①微… Ⅱ.①王… Ⅲ.①杭州市—概况—汉、英 Ⅳ.①K925.51

中国版本图书馆 CIP 数据核字(2016)第 182632 号

所有权利保留。
未经许可,不得以任何方式使用。

微观杭州
(汉英版)
HANGZHOU:TRADITION AND MODERN TIMES
王建华 主编

商 务 印 书 馆 出 版
(北京王府井大街36号 邮政编码100710)
商 务 印 书 馆 发 行
北京新华印刷有限公司印刷
ISBN 978-7-100-12453-9

2016年8月第1版　　开本 787×1092　1/16
2016年8月北京第1次印刷　印张 15½
定价:68.00元